The Making of the
Tudor Dynasty

The Making of the
Tudor Dynasty

Ralph A. Griffiths and Roger S. Thomas

ST. MARTIN'S PRESS   New York

ISBN 0-312-50745-3

In memory of
Stanley Bertram Chrimes
Biographer of Henry VII

... this kingdom is at present so situated as has not been seen for the last five hundred years till now, as those say who know best, and as appears by the chronicles; because there were always brambles and thorns of such a kind that the English had occasion not to remain peacefully in obedience to their king, there being divers heirs of the kingdom and of such a quality that the matter could be disputed between the two sides. Now it has pleased God that all should be thoroughly and duly purged and cleansed, so that not a doubtful drop of royal blood remains in this kingdom, except the true blood of the king and queen, ...

(The Spanish ambassador, Roderigo Gonsalez de Puebla, reporting to King Ferdinand and Queen Isabella of Spain on the state of England in January 1500)

PREFACE

The genesis of this book is not altogether conventional. A few years ago, Dr. Colin Richmond and I spent an informative afternoon tramping the alleged site of the Battle of Bosworth. At the 'Battlefield Centre', large and splendid reproductions of the famous sixteenth-century portrait of King Richard III were on sale. A request for a large and splendid reproduction of Michiel Sittow's equally famous (and contemporary) portrait of King Henry VII produced a copy that was a fraction of the size of the Ricardian portrait, and an expression of genuine regret that no one ever asked for Henry's picture at Bosworth. Dr. Richmond seemed less worried about this state of affairs than I was. Round about the same time new investigations into several aspects of the early history of the Tudor family made it possible to contemplate an authoritative, coherent account of the earliest Tudors, including the Bosworth campaign itself. Already in 1971 my former pupil, Dr. Roger S. Thomas, had completed a distinguished doctoral thesis on Jasper Tudor which revealed the central role of Henry VII's uncle. Several of the following chapters (especially Chapters 4–7) are so heavily indebted to sections of Dr. Thomas's work that it is right that his name should appear as this book's co-author. Other aspects of the Tudor saga – notably, Henry Tudor's years in France, the events of 1485, and the impact of Henry's antecedents on his rule as king – needed fresh examination.

In the course of constructing from these various strands an account that is both popular and scholarly, I have incurred a substantial number of debts which it is a pleasure to record. My special thanks go to several of my colleagues, Stuart Clark, George Evans, John Hall and Prys Morgan; to Ian Arthurson, Michael Jones (Bristol) and M.C.E. Jones (Nottingham); to Terry James (Dyfed Archaeological Trust); to I. Llwyd Williams (Bangor); to K.H. Rogers (County Archivist of Wiltshire) and John Reeves (Royal Commission on Historical Monuments, Salisbury); to Ann Rhydderch (Gwynedd Archives Service), M.J. Moore (Leicestershire Museum Services), and the Curators of Chichester District Museum; to the Directeurs des Services d'Archives du Morbihan (Vannes) et d'Ille-et-Vilaine (Rennes); to Mary Lewis (Wales Tourist Board), Lisa Markwell (Country Life) and the Archdeacon of St. David's; and to the Earl Cawdor. I am especially grateful to Roger Davies for his indispensable help with most of the illustrations; to David Robinson, who generously produced the maps; to the Secretaries of the Department of History of the University College of Swansea for typing the manuscript with their customary expedition; and, once again, to the staff of the College's Library whose good-humoured co-operation is to be valued more highly than the infernal technology with which they have to work. Finally, my appreciation goes to Alan Sutton, Peter Clifford and their colleagues, whose loyalties to Richard III and the Yorkists have not prevented them from publishing in record time.

Dr. Thomas and I have jointly seen this book through the Press.

R.A.G.

St. David's Day, 1985

CONTENTS

LIST OF ILLUSTRATIONS

Nos. 14 and 26 appear by gracious permission of Her Majesty the Queen. Thanks are also due to the following: Bargello Museum, Florence (60); British Museum (20, 27, 76); Cadw: Welsh Historic Monuments (25, 28, 29); Dean and Chapter of Canterbury (17, 44, 48); Michael Chevis (81); President and Fellows of Corpus Christi College, Oxford (73); Country Life (41, 42); French Government Tourist Office (39); Photographie Giraudon (12, 13, 37, 56, 58, 61); Terry James (21, 63); Master and Fellows of King's College, Cambridge (62); Vicar of Ludham Church, Suffolk (79); Badminton Estate Office and National Library of Wales (74); National Museum of Wales (10); National Portrait Gallery (33, 50, 71); Pitkin Pictorials Ltd. (75); Public Record Office (Crown Copyright) (59); Master and Fellows of Queen's College, Cambridge (46); Royal Commission on Ancient and Historical Monuments (Wales) (9, 11, 31, 36); Royal Commission on Historical Monuments (England) (18, 32, 34, 47, 49, 82); Dean and Chapter of St. David's Cathedral (23); Master and Fellows of St. John's College, Cambridge (45); Shrewsbury Borough Museum Service (67); Society of Antiquaries of London (69, 70); Tenby Museum (35); Roger S. Thomas (3, 19, 80); Victoria and Albert Museum (72); Wales Tourist Board (1, 2, 22); Warburg Institute (83, 84); Dean and Chapter of Westminster (8, 15, 77, 78, 85).

The photographs in No. 65 are from T. Dineley, *The Official Progress of the First Duke of Beaufort* (London), and S.R. Meyrick, *Heraldic Visitations of Wales*, Vol. I (Llandovery). No. 66 is from *Miscellanea Genealogica et Heraldica*, 4th Series, V.

Jacket: detail from *The Plucking of the Red and White Rose in the Old Temple Gardens* by Henry Payne, House of Commons. Based on the fictitious scene in Shakespeare's *Henry VI, Part I*, in which Richard, duke of York (the white rose) challenges John Beaufort, duke of Somerset (the red rose). Henry Tudor ended the Wars of the Roses and symbolically united the roses by marrying Elizabeth of York. Photograph: The Fotomas Index, London. The border incorporates the symbolic representation of Henry's Welsh dragon triumphing over Richard's boar, from an engraving by George Vertue. Jacket concept: Geoffrey Wheeler. Design: Martin Latham.

Prologue

Since the Battle of Bosworth 500 years ago, the royal dynasty of the Tudors has consistently attracted more popular and scholarly interest and admiration than any other dynasty in English history. And on the European stage, only the Bourbons and the Habsburgs have rivalled it. The resplendent figures of King Henry VIII and Queen Elizabeth I dominated their own age and still fire the imagination of novelists, film and television producers, historians and popular writers, while 'England under the Tudors' continues to have an extraordinary fascination for countless school children and their history teachers.

The peculiar origins of the Tudors and the improbable saga of their rise and fall and rise again during the 250 years before Bosworth have attracted far, far less attention. It is true that patriotic writers and biographers of an earlier age and romantic novelists of our own day have presented some of the earliest Tudors to the public. Certain episodes in the Tudor story caught their interest above all others. The victory in battle of Henry Tudor, a penniless outcast, in 1485 and his seizure of the English crown against all the odds make for stirring reading as both history and romance. The wanderings of Henry's uncle, Jasper, after his defeat at Mortimer's Cross in 1461, his steadfast loyalty to his young nephew, and the risks he ran in upholding the royal house of Lancaster – all this is inspiring as fact and as the basis for fiction. The courtship and marriage of Jasper's father, Owen Tudor, and Katherine, princess of France and queen of England, exemplifies the love-story of the queen and the pauper that has long been a central theme of European romantic literature. And the valiant support which earlier Tudors gave to the ambitious Welsh prince, Owain Glyndŵr (Shakespeare's *Glendower*), in his vain struggle to create an independent Welsh state has excited several writers, particularly in Wales. But there has been no coherent and authoritative account written of the saga as a whole, uncluttered by invention and wishful thinking. Little in history is inexplicable if the evidence survives, and the fortunes of the earliest Tudors provide an instructive as well as fascinating backdrop to their entrance on to the European stage in 1485.

As we shall see later, it was probably Henry Tudor himself who, after 1485, brought together and publicised some of the information that was then available about his ancestors. He did so partly for his own interest and partly to demonstrate that his family – particularly his grandfather, Owen Tudor – was not as lowly or disreputable as his enemies maintained. His court historian, the

Italian Polydore Vergil, wrote an account of Henry's early life and adventures in Brittany and at the French court which has not been bettered since it was published in the mid-sixteenth century. Vergil's pages became a quarry from which other Tudor writers took their information, including information about Henry's early exploits, in order to flatter and extol the Tudor monarchs.

The first book to be devoted solely to the heroic exile of the first Tudor king was based squarely on these early writers. *The First Booke of the Preservation of King Henry VII*, though unfinished, was published in 1599 and dedicated to Henry's aged grand-daughter, Queen Elizabeth, the last of the dynasty. Whereas some writers had been using the events of the fifteenth century to criticise the authoritarian régime of the old queen, this anonymous author chose to emphasise the illustrious quality of the dynasty by recording Henry's fortitude in exile prior to his great victory over Richard III. Retelling this story in 1599 may have been connected with the anticipated accession of James VI of Scotland, who was impatiently waiting in the wings for Elizabeth to die. James was the great-grandson of Margaret, the eldest daughter of King Henry VII. When he inherited the Tudor crown in 1603, several writers harked back to the beginnings of Tudor rule, by way of comparison, instruction or contrast.

An interest in the Tudor genealogy would underpin James's claim to Elizabeth's throne, and in 1604 a Welsh antiquary-clergyman, G.O. Harry, published *The genealogy of King James I, king of Great Brittayn, where is also handled the worthy descent of his Majesty's ancestor Owen Tudyr*. The British associations of the Tudors' Welsh antecedents helped to celebrate a monarchy that now embraced the British Isles. Henry Tudor's own name was called into the service of the new dynasty in 1610 with the appearance of *The vision and discourse of Henry the 7th concerning the Unitie of Great Brittaine*. In this period, too, the romantic imagination of the English renaissance flowered alongside the professional writing of analytical history. Michael Drayton's elegant version of imaginary letters exchanged by Owen Tudor and Queen Katherine was the basis of Hugh Holland's extravagant poem, *Pancharis: the first Booke. Containing the Preparation of the Love between Owen Tudyr and the Queene*. Holland was a poet-scholar from Denbigh who intended presenting his work to Queen Elizabeth; but in 1603 he had to rest content with offering it instead to James I. More sober and scholarly was Francis Bacon's famous *History of the Reign of King Henry the Seventh*, which first appeared in 1622. This had little to say about Henry's early life and even less about his ancestors, but its assessment of Henry's character and the nature of his rule – an assessment that has been remarkably influential ever since – did at least explain his parsimony by alluding to the poverty of his youth. As to the Battle of Bosworth, Sir John Beaumont tried to reconstruct the action of 22 August 1485 and to identify the participants, but how much invention and tradition are mingled with reliable information in his account, and in what proportions, cannot now be known.

After the first generation of Stuart rule, the interest subsided and disillusion with the Stuarts and their kingship set in. When fascination with Tudor forebears revived, it did so especially in France, after Charles II and James II had forged strong links with Louis XIV and the French court. Bacon's work was translated into French in 1673, but it was Owen Tudor's dalliance with

Henry Tudor in heroic pose at Bosworth Field. Sculpted by E.G. Gillick and unveiled in 1916 in the new City Hall, Cardiff, this statue is one of a series commemorating great figures from the Welsh past in the romantic vein of the Victorian Age.

Katherine of Valois that the French literary public savoured most. This love-story inspired a romantic historical novel, *Tideric, Prince de Galles*, which was published in Paris in 1677; it was quickly translated into English and published the following year in a London that was enjoying the cultural freedom of the Restoration. Another highly fictionalised account of their relationship appeared in Paris in 1696. At the same time, after James II had been forced from his throne and fled to Paris, his Tudor ancestors attracted a certain amount of political interest abroad. J. Marsollier's *Histoire de Henri VII, Roi d'Angleterre*, 'surnamed the wise and the Solomon of England ' (Paris, 1697), was dedicated to the duke of Maine and Aumale. This book stressed the ex-king's Tudor descent from Katherine of Valois, his steadfast religion and his principles, and how, as the representative of an illustrious dynasty, he merited the aid of France to help him recover his throne.

The Enlightenment and the accession of the Hanoverian dynasty led to a lengthy neglect of the romantic and political potential of the Tudor story, although several travellers in Wales and some Welsh antiquarians teased out of the countryside nuggets of fact and tradition about the earliest Tudors. It was not until the Victorian age that interest really revived. The stimulus was Agnes Strickland's biographies – based on fact and fiction – of the queens of England, among them Katherine of Valois and Henry VII's consort, Elizabeth of York. First published at the beginning of Victoria's reign, these studies retained their popularity for long after and provided ample material for the Victorian novelist to use. The story of Owen Tudor, the poor untutored Welshman, and the ardent young widowed queen, Katherine of Valois, attracted most attention. By contrast, the reputation for coldness, reticence, even dullness, which Henry VII was gradually acquiring at the hands of modern historians deterred the novelists, and the reputation of the fifteenth century as an age of political decadence and civil war diverted scholarly attention away from Jasper and Henry Tudor. After two world wars, the romantic strain has returned with vigour, exploiting the story of Owen and Katherine in particular. Since 1954 several plays and novels have appeared regularly from the pen of English and Welsh authors. In the 1970s alone at least five large books on this theme were published, with the promise of more to come. Few works of authentic historical scholarship have concentrated on the fortunes of the Tudors before 1485, although the authoritative biography of Henry VII by S.B. Chrimes (1972) gives due regard to the value of Polydore Vergil's account of Henry's early years.

It might be expected that the passion for the Tudors would have been greatest in Wales, especially among patriotic and nationalist writers. And so it was until the present century. But Henry VIII's Act of Union, marking the incorporation of Wales in an English state and accelerating the Anglicisation of Welsh life, has also proved an embarrassment, even a betrayal. To the doyen of political nationalism in contemporary Wales, Gwynfor Evans, in his *Aros Mae* (1971), translated into English as *The Land of My Fathers*, the accession of a part-Welsh dynasty in 1485 was a wrong-turning for Wales and for Welshmen.

From whatever perspective they are viewed, the earliest Tudors and the part they played in the making of England's royal dynasty hold a fascination that requires explanation.

1 Servants of Welsh Princes

The first Tudor monarch, Henry VII, was one-quarter Welsh, one-quarter French, and half English. Yet it is his Welsh blood that identified him to contemporaries and to posterity. And it is by his great-great-grandfather's Welsh Christian name of Tudur (Anglicised as Tudor) that he and his descendants are known. Not that these Welsh ancestors of his had any royal or princely blood in their veins, but their family first sprang to prominence in the service of the most ambitious and constructive of Welsh princely houses.

During the first three-quarters of the thirteenth century, the Welsh rulers of Gwynedd, whose principality included the rugged fastnesses of Snowdonia as well as the fertile lowlands of Anglesey, strove to create a powerful and organised fledgling state. Changes that were taking place in the monarchies of Western Europe – in their forms of government, their methods of administration and their rulers' powers – were well known in Wales, not least through the English example. Under Llywelyn ab Iorwerth (1202–40), known as Llywelyn the Great, a capable, determined and ruthless prince, Gwynedd became (for Wales) a comparatively strong principality. Indeed, it claimed the allegiance of all other Welsh princes and its ruler later adopted the style and dignity of Prince of Wales. Llywelyn controlled almost all of Gwynedd by 1202 and when, ten years later, in 1212, he negotiated a treaty with the king of France, he claimed to speak for other Welsh rulers too. He was instrumental in forcing King John to submit to the demands of the English barons at Runnymede, and Welsh demands were included in the *Magna Carta* sealed there in 1215. Llywelyn the Great was able to maintain his and his principality's strength and independence until his death twenty-five years later in 1240.

It was in these decades of vigorous political development in North Wales that the Welsh ancestors of King Henry VII achieved a prominence that made them one of the most influential and respected of Welsh families in the thirteenth century. They hitched their star to the prince of Gwynedd, making themselves indispensable as councillors, servants, diplomats and soldiers in a polity which, like that of other European rulers, came to rely on an 'aristocracy of service'. The earliest Tudors were a family of such aristocrats. They augmented and consolidated the family fortunes along the way.

Despite their vital importance to the prince of Gwynedd, none of Henry Tudor's forebears married into the princely line. Rather were they trusted

Stone Coffin allegedly of Prince Llywelyn the Great. It dates from the fourteenth century and so was not his burial coffin. Now in the Gwydir Chapel of Llanrwst Church, Gwynedd, it may have been brought from Aberconway Abbey, where Llywelyn was buried, at the Dissolution of the Monasteries. The companion coffin of Llywelyn's wife, Joan, is in Beaumaris Church, Anglesey.

lieutenants of Llywelyn the Great and his successors. In England such distinguished servants of the king could have expected an earldom. In North Wales, repute, property and power were their anticipated reward. Not that it was a record of uninterrupted progress towards position, wealth and power, for the rise of Gwynedd was frequently beset with enemies and obstacles: other Welsh princes were jealous and resented the rulers of Gwynedd; English kings were suspicious and opposed their claims; and English barons with lordships in the march (or borderland) of Wales were hostile. An ambitious Welsh family in the service of the prince of Gwynedd would be well advised to keep one eye on Gwynedd's rivals and opponents, and perhaps even be prepared to engage in political manoeuvre, in order to preserve what it had gained from good service in North Wales. All this the ancestors of the Tudor monarchs achieved, often with conspicuous success and rarely with serious lapses. When the principality of Gwynedd was destroyed by King Edward I in 1282–3, this family managed to re-emerge with much of its influence, if not its reputation, intact.

The earliest Tudors of all lived near Abergele, in the district (or commote) of

Rhos in the region east of the River Conwy known as the Four Cantrefs (or, in Welsh, the Perfeddwlad), much of which later became the lordship of Denbigh. In their origins they were modest landowners in the countryside east of the Conwy and not far from the coast. When this region was brought under the control of Gwynedd by Llywelyn the Great himself, some of the family entered the personal service of their new lord. It is even possible that one or two members of the family were employed by Llywelyn's predecessor at the end of the twelfth century. Cynfrig ab Iorwerth is the first of their stock who is known to have found a niche in the primitive administration of Gwynedd. His sons and grandsons followed in his footsteps with astonishing regularity. We can only speculate about the abilities and intelligence of Cynfrig's descendants, but whatever their qualities they were constantly employed by the thirteenth-century rulers of Gwynedd. Indeed, Cynfrig and his relatives formed the largest single family group of servants used by the princes in their various enterprises. If Cynfrig had made the initial and crucial mark, it was his son Ednyfed Fychan (Ednyfed the Younger) who acquired the greatest reputation of all his family and who ensured that his sons and grandsons had a place in the government and society of North Wales that was second only to that of the princely house itself.

Ednyfed Fychan was in Llywelyn the Great's service by 1215 and he never left it before Llywelyn's death in 1240. He was often in the prince's company; he witnessed Llywelyn's charters, and for a long time he was seneschal or steward (or, in Welsh, *distain*), the most important administrative, political and judicial official the prince had. He was in this exalted position by about 1216, if not earlier. As such he represented Llywelyn in negotiations with the English king, Henry III, certain English marcher lords, and other Welsh princes, bishops and ecclesiastics. He was the prince's *alter ego*, answerable only to Llywelyn himself but exercising a very considerable authority on his behalf. Ednyfed was no less highly valued in war. In the sixteenth century there was a tradition that he had once (perhaps in 1210) led the prince's forces to battle against the earl of Chester and other supporters of King John; he was said to have presented three bloody English heads to Llywelyn after the victory – heads which supposedly were represented on the arms of Ednyfed Fychan and his family thereafter. The qualities which Ednyfed displayed in exploits like these enabled him to aim high in his search for a wife. He married Gwenllian, a daughter of the famed Lord Rhys (who died in 1197). Rhys not only created a personal dominion for himself in South-West Wales (or Deheubarth), but he was regarded elsewhere as the leading Welsh prince of his day. To be linked with such a reputable lineage enhanced Ednyfed Fychan's own standing. Even King Henry III acknowledged him to be an outstanding Welshman, and when Ednyfed passed through London in June 1235, apparently en route to the Holy Land and the crusade, the king arranged to send a silver cup to his lodgings as a token of respect.

Llywelyn the Great died in 1240. As the elder statesman of Gwynedd, Ednyfed Fychan played a key roll in arranging the succession of the prince's son, David (1240–6). And in an age when the authority of rulers depended on personal ability and good advisers, no one was better qualified than this experienced and loyal servant to play a guiding role at the new prince's court. When Ednyfed himself died in 1246, ten years after his wife, the annals that

Effigy allegedly of the Lord Rhys ap Gruffydd (d. 1197), Ednyfed Fychan's father-in-law. It is in the south choir aisle of St. David's Cathedral, where Rhys was buried. The effigy itself is of fourteenth-century date.

were then being compiled at St. Werburgh's Abbey in Chester recorded the event as if it were a turning-point in the history of Gwynedd and North Wales more generally. Ednyfed was remembered as the justiciar of Wales, a title which ranked him with those great justiciars or royal lieutenants who were employed by English monarchs to act in their stead when they were out of the kingdom or otherwise unavailable. It was a fitting tribute to the great servant of Llywelyn the Great and David ap Llywelyn.

Cynfrig ab Iorwerth had had two other sons besides Ednyfed Fychan: Heilyn and Goronwy. They too appear to have served Prince Llywelyn and Prince David, though not with the brilliance of their brother. Their public actions seem to have been concentrated in the eastern part of Gwynedd, in the countryside of their ancestors, east of the Conwy. They and their descendants never won the prominence, repute or affection felt in North Wales for Ednyfed's brood (*Wyrion Eden*).

Ednyfed Fychan had at least six – more probably seven – sons. The fact that every one of them followed their father in serving Gwynedd's princes, often attaining positions that he had filled, is in part testimony to the high regard in which Ednyfed himself was held and the skill with which he advanced the careers of his relatives. We must recognise, too, that it may reflect their own capabilities. Goronwy and Gruffydd ab Ednyfed were old enough to join their father at Prince Llywelyn's court, and to support Ednyfed in negotiations with the earl of Chester round about 1222. Gruffydd, however, perhaps through youthful indiscretion, deeply offended Llywelyn by making slanderous remarks about the prince's wife, an illegitimate daughter of King John whom Llywelyn had married in 1204. Gruffydd was thereupon forced to flee to Ireland. In fact, he was the first member of the family known to have quarrelled with his prince. Despite Gruffydd's disgrace, Ednyfed's position was unchallenged, and his other sons reaped handsome rewards. Several of them reached manhood during the short reign of Prince David (1240–6). The young prince may have welcomed the opportunity to draw younger people close to him as well as to rely on his father's old minister. Indeed, in negotiations with several marcher lords in 1241, Tudur ab Ednyfed was acknowledged to be the prince's steward even during Ednyfed's lifetime, though it may only have been a temporary promotion to strengthen his role as a negotiator. Ednyfed's son Rhys was also in Prince David's service by 1241.

The second breach in the loyalty of Ednyfed Fychan's family to the princes of

Dolwyddelan Castle, Gwynedd. One of Prince Llywelyn the Great's new fortresses dominating Snowdonia, it was originally a two-storey building. Prince Llywelyn the Last extended it, and the castle served as a residence for all three princes of North Wales and their entourages.

Gwynedd occurred ironically as a result of their service to the princes. In November 1245 Tudur ab Ednyfed was captured by Henry III in North Wales and he was sent as a hostage to the Tower of London, possibly as a guarantee of Prince David's submission to the king. David's own brother, Gruffydd, had also been a hostage in the Tower, but in 1244 he was killed while trying to escape. In the following year, Tudur was conveyed by stages to London, first by the Anglophile lord of Southern Powys, Gruffydd ap Gwenwynwyn, and then by John Lestrange, a Shropshire baron who had been the king's justiciar of Chester until shortly before. He was then handed over to the sheriff of Oxfordshire's men for the final stage of the journey under escort to the Tower, where he was placed in one of the inner buildings. When he was released in September 1246, the year in which both Prince David and Ednyfed Fychan died, he had to leave two of his sons as hostages in the Tower, though they do not seem to have suffered the worst rigours of imprisonment. As a further price of his release, Tudur was forced to swear fealty to Henry III, and he did homage to the king for his lands in North Wales which were now confirmed to him. He also received from the king gifts and more land, including the township of Maenan in the Perfeddwlad. Tudur ab Ednyfed had declared himself to be a loyal subject of King Henry III, an act which was bound to damage his relationship with the ruler of Gwynedd. Henry and his advisers were evidently eager to attract influential Welshmen to their side and in the years that followed Tudur received yet more property from the beneficent king. Indeed, Tudur was used as an envoy by King Henry in the truce negotiations in 1259–60 with Prince David's nephew and successor, Llywelyn ap Gruffydd; and eventually Tudur's son, Heilyn, was released from the Tower of London in February 1263.

This change of allegiance by Tudur ab Ednyfed meant that he broke the tradition of service in Gwynedd which his father and grandfather had begun half a century earlier. It may not have been conviction that induced Tudur to throw in his lot with the English king. Royal gifts and land grants were doubtless enticing, but the continued confinement of his sons in London was the most powerful factor. In any case, with the death of both Prince David and Ednyfed Fychan in 1246, an internal power struggle had begun for control of Gwynedd. This may have made the future of Ednyfed's family seem less certain and a closer relationship with King Henry a sensible precaution. However that may be, after 1263, by which time Llywelyn ap Gruffydd had emerged as the undisputed master of North Wales (and Heilyn ap Tudur had been released from prison), Tudur ab Ednyfed felt able to resume his career in Gwynedd.

When Llywelyn ap Gruffydd (known as Llywelyn the Last after his death) established his personal ascendancy in Gwynedd in 1255, all of Ednyfed Fychan's sons were old enough to enter his service and eventually they all did so. They became the agents of a régime which re-established a large Welsh principality extending from the Llŷn peninsula in the far west to the River Dee in the east, with client Welsh lordships to the south in Powys, Cardiganshire and Carmarthenshire, and conquests as far as Montgomery in the south-east and the borders of Glamorgan in the south. Territorially, Llywelyn exceeded even his grandfather's achievement. He re-asserted Gwynedd's claim to lordship over all other Welsh princes and by 1258 he was confidently styling himself Prince of

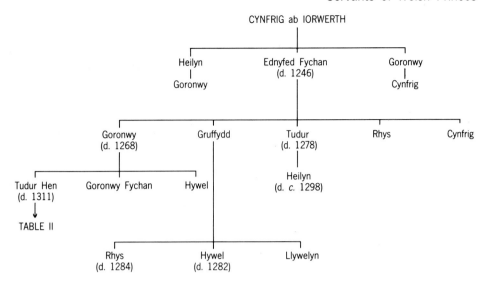

Table I: Ednyfed Fychan and his sons.

Wales. In the Anglo-Welsh treaty concluded at Montgomery in September 1267, Henry III himself recognised and accepted Llywelyn's position. The sons of Ednyfed Fychan had played a central part in it all. The eldest, Goronwy, had stepped into his father's shoes as steward by 1258. He continued to fill this crucial office for another ten years, dispensing justice at the highest level, negotiating with the English king and with the marcher lords, the bishop of Bangor and other Welsh princes. Like his father before him, he led the armies of Gwynedd on campaign, and in February 1263 took them as far as Gwent against the great marcher lords of the south. When Goronwy died on 17 October 1268, one Welsh chronicler recalled his courage and distinction in arms, as well as his wisdom and integrity. Goronwy was a true son of his father and the grief which the chronicler felt at his passing was ill-concealed.

Ednyfed Fychan's second son, Gruffydd, eventually returned from Ireland and disgrace. By 1247 he could be found in Prince Llywelyn ap Gruffydd's company; he witnessed his charters, negotiated with Henry III in 1256, and perhaps he initially acted as steward to the new prince in preference to his elder brother Goronwy. As for Tudur ab Ednyfed, he resumed his career in North Wales, despite his enforced association with Henry III. After 1263, he not only witnessed Prince Llywelyn ap Gruffydd's charters and assisted Llywelyn in disputes with the bishop of Bangor, with other Welsh princes and certain marcher lords; but after Goronwy's death in 1268, he succeeded to the stewardship and for a further decade monopolised what was indisputably one of the most powerful positions in Llywelyn's principality.

The two youngest of Ednyfed Fychan's sons, Rhys and Cynfrig, followed divergent careers. Cynfrig, who had his paternal grandfather's name, was also in

Prince Llywelyn's service by 1256, engaged in the same diplomatic and judicial work as his brothers. But Rhys, whose name recalls his maternal grandfather, seems to have fallen out with Prince Llywelyn. Although it is not possible to say that the descendants of Cynfrig ab Iorwerth monopolised the chief office of the princes of Gwynedd, the stewardship, without a break from at least 1216 to 1278, Ednyfed Fychan and several of his sons certainly controlled it for long stretches of that time. Their family steadfastly served Llywelyn ab Iorwerth and his two successors with distinction. Even the occasional rupture in relations with one prince or another hardly detracts from a record that was second to none among the dominant families of North Wales in the thirteenth century.

Outstanding service of this order merited rich rewards, and patronage was the surest way to attract and retain such loyalty. Our knowledge of the extensive grants of land which were made to members of Cynfrig ab Iorwerth's progeny comes almost entirely from the fourteenth century, when townships and properties were still being identified by local administrators as once belonging to Ednyfed Fychan and held by him on the most generous of terms. His family's homeland lay east of the River Conwy in modern Denbighshire. Most of the land granted to Ednyfed by the princes of Gwynedd was situated in Anglesey (especially at Penmynydd and Trecastell) and in Caernarfonshire west of the Conwy. These properties, which were granted to him and his heirs, had special rights and privileges attached to them, in place of traditional kinship obligations and customary services to the prince. It is likely that these lands were granted to Ednyfed Fychan before 1240 by Llywelyn the Great. In addition, Ednyfed bought other land in the Perfeddwlad (notably Rhos Fyneich), and he was also granted an estate in Cardiganshire. Ednyfed's sons added to the family possessions in more modest ways; for example, at the time of his allegiance to Henry III, Tudur acquired estates in Flint and Dyffryn Clwyd. These scattered lands, akin to the estates of a nobleman in England, placed the family of Ednyfed Fychan among the wealthiest landowners of North Wales, with all that that implied in terms of local significance and influence.

As elsewhere in medieval Europe, the link between the Church and the State in North Wales was a direct one. The bishoprics of Bangor and St. Asaph lay entirely within the principality of Gwynedd at its widest extent, and therefore to some degree they were under the princes' control. Moreover, those who served the princes in secular matters often had relatives who did so in the religious sphere. Yet another of Ednyfed Fychan's sons can probably be identified with Hywel, bishop of St. Asaph from about 1240 until his death in 1247. If so, the bishop's nephew, Llywelyn, Gruffydd ab Ednyfed's son, was most likely prior of Bangor some years later. And the family seems to have been among the early benefactors of the Dominican Friary that was founded near Bangor by 1251; Goronwy ab Ednyfed may have donated land to the friars in the vicinity of what is now Penrhyn Park. Indeed, Goronwy, who is known to have been buried somewhere in Bangor, may have been laid to rest in the new friary – just as, in the next century, several of Ednyfed's descendants regarded it as their mausoleum.

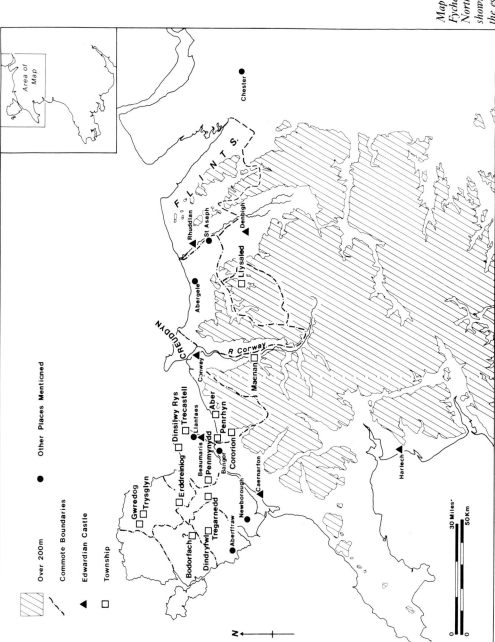

Map A: Estates of Ednyfed Fychan and his sons in North Wales. The commotes shown are those in which the estates were situated.

The place of this family among North Wales society is reflected in the poems which several thirteenth-century poets wrote in their honour and the eulogies that marked their death. Ednyfed Fychan's passing in 1246 was recorded with deep sorrow, and Elidir Sais, one of the leading poets of the first half of the thirteenth century, affected to have mourned at the graveside:

> Above the fresh grave of Ednyfed have I been,
> My tears streaming.

Ednyfed's daughter was fêted in verse by Einion ap Gwalchmai, while on the death of her brother Gruffydd, Dafydd Benfras expressed a more public regret. Goronwy ab Ednyfed was the subject of odes of praise by both Bleddyn Fardd and Prydydd Bychan. To them he was 'the rampart of Gwynedd' and 'the wall of the city', an heroic figure whose martial exploits in the defence of Gwynedd were matched by a wise and noble character – qualities which were echoed on his death by the chronicler of the Welsh princes.

This remarkable family enjoyed the trust and gratitude of three princes of Gwynedd. Ednyfed and his sons were given power, wealth and pre-eminence that spread their fame beyond the borders of Gwynedd to the marcher lordships, the Welsh principalities of the south, even to the English court. They survived political troubles in Gwynedd itself as well as the severe tensions that arose from time to time between Gwynedd, the king of England and other lords in Wales.

2 A Question of Allegiance

The Conquest of Edward I

There had been times – admittedly few of them – in the thirteenth century when some members of Ednyfed Fychan's family had wavered in their devotion to the princes of Gwynedd and threw in their lot with the English king. These were occasions when personal and family interests took precedence over loyalty to their princely masters. The principality of Gwynedd was a very recent creation and its frontiers were still liable to shift. The homeland of Ednyfed Fychan's family in the Perfeddwlad periodically fell into English hands, and so it was natural that those with roots in the countryside east of the Conwy should find their loyalties tested and torn. After Edward I ascended the English throne in 1272, their instinct for survival became sharper and Ednyfed Fychan's offspring eventually deserted the Welsh cause.

After the resounding success of King Edward in his first war against Prince Llywelyn in 1276–7, common prudence suggested that the family at least establish a channel of communication with the great Edward in case further misfortune befell Llywelyn in the future. As early as the 1240s, Ednyfed Fychan's son Tudur had emerged the wealthier from his enforced association with Henry III. Now, several of Ednyfed's descendants made their peace with King Edward and benefited accordingly. During the recent conflict, Ednyfed's grandson, Llywelyn ap Gruffydd, a Dominican friar who was probably prior of Bangor, acted as intermediary between his brother Rhys, who had been one of Prince Llywelyn's servants, and the king. The aim was to reconcile Rhys and two of his kinsmen with the English. These three men may have taken part in a plot to desert the prince and defect to Edward. When Prince Llywelyn was induced to make the treaty of Conway with the king in 1277, he promised to free Rhys from captivity and restore him to his position. Afterwards, Rhys entered the king's service and his relations with Prince Llywelyn became very strained. On one occasion, while he was at Llywelyn's court at Aberffraw in Anglesey, he was fined £100 for disobedience and contempt. Thus, when Edward I launched his second Welsh war in 1282, Rhys and his brother, Hywel ap Gruffydd ab Ednyfed, joined the king on campaign in North Wales. As the English were

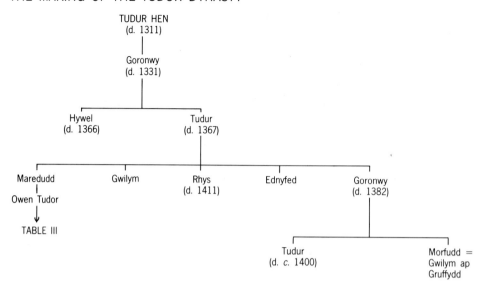

Table II: Ancestors of Owen Tudor

crossing the Menai Strait after landing in Anglesey, they were attacked by Prince Llywelyn's men and Hywel was among those who were slain.

The sons of Gruffydd ab Ednyfed Fychan were not alone in seeking an agreement with King Edward. In September 1278 the king restored certain lands to Tudur, Goronwy Fychan and Hywel, who were very likely the sons of Goronwy ab Ednyfed Fychan. And other kinsmen were serving Edward I in the Perfeddwlad by 1279. The local loyalties and community ties of these Welshmen, together with their instinct to survive in perilous times, weakened their sense of obligation to the ruler of Snowdonia and led them to prefer peace with Edward I. This seemed the surer way of preserving their influence, position and prosperity in the Perfeddwlad. The reputation for inconstancy which Welshmen have acquired down the ages, their supposed ability to turn every situation to advantage, is in part a function of intense local attachments at the expense of wider loyalties. When Prince Llywelyn was killed in 1282 and Edward I conquered his principality of North Wales, the family of Ednyfed Fychan was assured of an influential future.

Although Goronwy ab Ednyfed's three sons reconciled themselves to the English régime after 1282, they did not necessarily do so easily or irrevocably. Indeed, when major rebellion erupted in various parts of Wales in 1294–5, as a reaction against tighter royal control, Tudur (known as Tudur the Elder, or Tudur Hen) and Goronwy (known as Goronwy the Younger or Goronwy Fychan) ap Goronwy joined the rising of the northern rebel leader, Madog ap Llywelyn. It is likely that Tudur Hen was Madog's steward and Goronwy may have been in the rebel's service too. But with the failure of these revolts – the last of the uprisings to spring directly from the Edwardian conquest of Gwynedd – the family quickly made its peace with the English authorities. Tudur Hen was a member of the delegation from North Wales that pledged its loyalty to Edward I in 1296, and when the king's son, Edward of Caernarfon, was proclaimed the first English prince of Wales in 1301, Tudur Hen was there to swear fealty and to do homage for the lands he held in Wales. In the following years, he served as a royal official in the Perfeddwlad, as several of his forebears had done during the thirteenth century. Tudur Hen enjoyed his considerable inherited lands in North Wales and Cardiganshire until his death in 1311, when they passed without a hitch to his son, Goronwy ap Tudur Hen. *

With only one exception, Tudur Hen's descendants proved to be loyal, influential and prosperous landowners in North Wales. Their prominent role in society is reflected in their patronage of local religious houses, in the reputation they enjoyed among the poets who moved from house to house in the region, and in their extensive lands, many of them inherited from Ednyfed Fychan and tenaciously retained through all the political turbulence of Edward I's reign. Goronwy ap Tudur Hen was loyal enough to Edward II, and even in the last crisis of Edward's reign, when the king was hunted down and deposed by his enemies, Goronwy stood by him. He had been one of the leaders of the Welsh troops who joined the king at Newcastle-upon-Tyne in 1314 in readiness for the invasion of Scotland, and a few years later, in 1318–9, as the king's yeoman he was appointed forester of Snowdon. By the time he died in 1331, Goronwy's family had purged all taint of rebellion and was secure in the favour of the new monarch, Edward III.

Conciliation and Co-operation

The fortune and security which the descendants of Ednyfed Fychan achieved after the troublous days of Edward I are well illustrated by the careers of Goronwy ap Tudur Hen's two sons, Hywel the cleric and Tudur the landowner.

From the beginning, their family had a close relationship with some of the most important churches and religious institutions in North Wales. The society in which they moved was Christian in its faith and here as elsewhere the institutions of the church rested squarely on the support and patronage of wealthy laymen. A tradition dating back at least to the eighteenth century claims that Tudur Hen was the founder of the Franciscan Friary at Bangor, though it is now clear that this friary was in existence from about 1250 and that Tudur Hen was rather its rebuilder and benefactor after the devastation of wartime. The friars had sided with Edward I in his two Welsh wars, but round about 1293 Tudur set about renovating the buildings. He arranged his own burial in the south wall of the friary's chapel and his interment there on 11 October 1311 was remembered for long after. The body of his son, Goronwy ap Tudur Hen, was conveyed to the same mausoleum on 11 December 1331.

Of Goronwy's sons, Hywel rose to high office in the church in North Wales. Though he is likely to have been his father's elder son, he was nevertheless educated for the priesthood; he became a canon of Bangor Cathedral and then, in 1357, archdeacon of Anglesey. When he died in 1366, he too was buried in

Portrait of King Richard II (1367–1400), seated in majesty. Said to be the first portrait of an English king from life, it was probably painted when Richard was about 20. It is in the nave of Westminster Abbey, to which Richard was a generous patron.

Bangor's friary, before the high altar as befitted such a high-ranking member of the ecclesiastical hierarchy.

Hywel's brother Tudur followed him to his grave in Bangor Friary on 19 September 1367 – this time the tomb was placed in the south wall of the chancel. Tudur's influential position in lay society complemented that of Hywel in the church. He lived at the ancestral township of Trecastell in Anglesey, and like his father and grandfather before him, he was a royal officer on the island. He married well, into the Cardiganshire family of Thomas ap Llywelyn, whose sister was the mother of the rebel prince, Owain Glyndŵr. Tudur may even have served in the glorious campaigns of Edward III in France after 1337; centuries later it was widely believed that while in Edward's service he assumed the title of knight, though without the king's permission.

In 1345 the careers of both brothers, Hywel and Tudur, were placed in jeopardy. In that year, a plot was hatched to waylay and assassinate William de

Shaldford, the unpopular attorney in North Wales of the king's son, Edward the Black Prince. Hywel and Tudur were two of the main suspects in the conspiracy and the attempt on Shaldford's life seems to have taken place near Hywel's home. The brothers were arrested and spent some time in custody. But the incident – which was less of a general protest against the English régime than an isolated attack on a particularly oppressive official – did not harm the prospects of either brother and they were soon released. The burgesses of Caernarfon ruefully complained of the family that 'no Welsh man dare indict them'. The family poet, Gruffydd ap Maredudd ap Dafydd, took a different perspective and was much more enthusiastic in his comments on the family, but he made the same fundamental point. He compared Tudur, Hywel and their kinsmen to great oak trees, strong, lasting, their branches far-spreading and offering shelter to those beneath.

It was in the second half of the fourteenth century, and especially during the reign of King Richard II, that Ednyfed Fychan's descendants reached heights of influence and responsibility in North Wales that were almost comparable with those scaled by Ednyfed Fychan himself 150 years before. All five of Tudur's sons, Goronwy, Ednyfed, Rhys, Gwilym and Maredudd, were well integrated in the society and government of a North Wales that was part of the king's principality of Wales. Most of them lived in Anglesey, where Rhys and his brother Goronwy virtually monopolised the office of rhaglaw (or bailiff) in the commote of Dindaethwy in the 1370s, '80s and '90s. Their brother Maredudd was rhaglaw of the neighbouring commote of Malltraeth at some point between 1387 and 1395, and he also moved into the small Anglesey borough of Newborough as a burgess. Moreover, for the first time members of the family filled some of the most important offices in North Wales usually reserved for Englishmen. Thus, Rhys became sheriff of Anglesey in 1374–5 and 1381–4. Goronwy was even appointed to the key military post of constable of Beaumaris Castle in 1382, just four days before he died; and Maredudd was escheator of Anglesey between 1388 and 1391. The trust which Richard II reposed in them is obvious, for the brothers were his most loyal servants in North Wales. Rhys and Gwilym were two of the leaders of the Caernarfonshire contingent raised in 1386 as a precaution against a French invasion, and indeed these two were personally retained by Richard for life in 1398, each receiving £10 a year from him. They accompanied the king on his expedition to subdue the chieftains of Ireland in 1398, and doubtless felt betrayed when Richard was captured and deposed after he returned to England in September 1399. The part which Rhys, Gwilym and Maredudd played in the subsequent rebellion against the usurper, King Henry IV, is partly attributable to these experiences.

Two other brothers, Ednyfed and Goronwy, had also entered the king's service, though much earlier and in France. Several of the poets who praised Goronwy may have had his war retinue in mind when they commented on the number of his uniformed retainers and the way in which, according to Iolo Goch, a contemporary poet from the Vale of Clwyd, 'on a feast day [he could] hand out liveries and striking speckled cloth of the finest green available'. But apparently while they were disembarking at one of the Kentish ports in 1382, Ednyfed and Goronwy were drowned. Their bodies were recovered and taken to

Alabaster Effigies of Goronwy ap Tudur (d. 1382) and his wife on their altar tomb. Now in Penmynydd Church, Anglesey, one of the townships of the earliest Tudors, the tomb was probably brought from the dissolved friary church at Llanfaes not far away.

London, and Goronwy's at least was taken back to North Wales and interred in the friary at Llanfaes – or so says a funeral elegy composed by Gruffydd ap Maredudd ap Dafydd. According to Iolo Goch, their death cast a cloud over all Anglesey, though if another poet, Rhisierdyn, is to be believed, he and his fraternity had a special reason to lament Goronwy's death because he had been 'a judge of words and metre' and appreciated better than most the complex technicalities of the poetry sung to him. Goronwy's fine alabaster tomb, carved in the latest style perfected in the Nottingham region, can still be seen in the church at Penmynydd, whence it was transferred after the Dissolution of the Monasteries in the middle of the sixteenth century. Goronwy and his wife, Myfanwy, whose qualities (to take one poet at his word) of pride, courage, nobility and refinement were inherited from her own family of equal respectability in North Wales, lie together in the tomb. Both Goronwy and his brother Ednyfed thereby avoided the dilemma of which allegiance to choose when the great Welsh rebellion began in 1400.

The Glyndŵr Rebellion

Just as Ednyfed Fychan's sons had been faced with a momentous choice when Edward I invaded North Wales, so Tudur's offspring had to take difficult decisions in 1400 when their cousin, Owain Glyndŵr, raised the standard of rebellion against King Henry IV, the usurper who had violently dethroned their patron, Richard II. Their family's past counselled cautious co-operation with the new régime, but in 1400 Tudur's sons openly supported Glyndŵr and responded to the call of kinship and patriotism. When the rebellion collapsed, the surviving sons of Tudur ap Goronwy went down with it. Unlike the Edwardian conquest, the Lancastrian victory spelt disaster for the family. Never again would they dominate North Wales.

The precise reasons why the family joined the rebellion are not easy to comprehend. Resentment at the deposition and death of their former patron, Richard II, may have been a potent factor. So too was their kinship with Owain Glyndŵr. Moreover, the Franciscan friars at Llanfaes and Bangor, with whom Tudur's sons were intimately connected, were partisans of Richard II. More immediately to the point were the financial implications of office-holding, for by 1398 Rhys ap Tudur was in arrears to the tune of £60 from his term as rhaglaw of Dindaethwy; he was summoned before the king's justiciar of North Wales in 1398 to explain himself and perhaps the new king put further pressure on him.

Owain Glyndŵr's initial rising in North-East Wales in 1400 quickly ran out of steam, despite his claim to be Prince of Wales. At the other end of the country, Gwilym and Rhys ap Tudur put themselves at the head of a rising in Anglesey in September 1400. When Henry IV arrived with an army, Rhys and his men set an ambush for them on Rhos Fawr ('the Great Moor'), one of the highest spots in the eastern part of the island. The harrying of Anglesey and its population by the angry king was severe: Llanfaes Friary was set alight, some of the friars were killed, and the countryside roundabout was devastated. But when he encountered Rhys and his men on Rhos Fawr, Henry was forced to turn tail and retire to the safety of Beaumaris. It is hardly surprising that when the king tried to pacify North Wales by issuing a general pardon in March 1401, he excluded Rhys and Gwilym, as well as Owain Glyndŵr, from its terms.

The most spectacular incident involving Tudur's sons occurred in 1401, when the brothers staged one of the most daring raids of the entire rebellion. 'In the annals of insurrection in these islands there is hardly a single exploit to compare with it in sheer audacity and cunning' (K. Williams-Jones). On Good Friday 1401, Gwilym and Rhys ap Tudur, with forty-four men, who had been excluded from the pardons offered to other rebels in 1400–1, took the soldiers in Conway Castle by surprise. That evening, while the castle's garrison was attending divine service in Conway's parish church, Gwilym and Rhys and their men succeeded in infiltrating the great fortress with the help of a carpenter who persuaded the guards that he was arriving for work. They were a very varied gang, with ruffians rubbing shoulders with landowners, local officials and some who were well-to-do. After seizing the castle, the Welshmen demanded a pardon as the price of returning it to its custodians. On 13 April negotiations were authorised to be conducted by the earl of Northumberland's son, Henry (Shakespeare's famous *Hotspur*), and this gave Gwilym ap Tudur an opportunity to publicise in detail the insurgents' demands: a comprehensive and general

Arms of Owain Glyndŵr, as they appear on an enamelled brass martingale of the early fifteenth century. It was discovered at Harlech Castle, Gwynedd, one of the last outposts of Owain's power.

pardon like that offered to other rebels some months earlier; the recovery of lands and possessions that had been confiscated from Welshmen; a safe-conduct enabling the rebels to return to their homes; no hounding by the authorities for at least six months; and no charges to be brought against them for burning the town of Conway (causing £5,000 worth of damage and the loss of official records) and robbing its burgesses and the houses of royal officials. Finally, it was demanded that should there be any trial to consider these or related charges, the jury would consist of an equal number of Welshmen and Englishmen, presumably to ensure fairness.

Most of these demands were conceded during the negotiations that followed, but on 20 April 1401 the tentative arrangements made in North Wales were disowned by the king. Conway Castle therefore remained in Welsh hands. There were further discussions which produced another agreement at the end of May or early in June, but this too fell through. Only on 24 June was a settlement at last reached, after Gwilym ap Tudur had sent a second set of demands to King Henry IV himself. These were more conciliatory in tone than the earlier version, but high on the list was the same demand for a full pardon. Even so, eight or nine of the insurgents were executed before the others were forgiven their treason.

South Front of Conway Castle, Gwynedd. This formidable fortress, built by Edward I in 1283–9, was occupied for several months in 1401 by Rhys and Gwilym ap Tudur, kinsmen of Glyndŵr.

In the years of rebellion that followed, the sons of Tudur ap Goronwy continued to support Glyndŵr, though they played a less dramatic role and rarely caught the attention of contemporary commentators. However, Rhys ap Tudur intrigued with the English noble house of Percy in 1403, prior to the Battle of Shrewsbury, where Henry Hotspur was defeated and killed by Henry IV. In their rebellion against the king, the Percies looked to Glyndŵr and his rebels for help, and it is possible that the negotiations at Conway in 1401 between Hotspur and Tudur's sons – negotiations which the king abruptly terminated – paved the way for their collaboration two years later. Maredudd, the youngest brother, was again at the head of rebels in North-East Wales in January 1405. And Gwilym was still at large in 1408–9. All three brothers were outlawed by the king in 1406.

With the failure of the rebellion and the disappearance of Glyndŵr himself, the brothers found themselves vulnerable and in great danger. According to a chronicler from the southern borderland, Adam of Usk, Rhys and two other rebel leaders were captured by the constable of Welshpool Castle. Rhys was taken to Chester and executed, probably in 1412, though later tradition maintains that he died at his home at Erddreiniog in Anglesey and was buried in Bangor Friary among his ancestors. However that may be, Rhys's death was movingly lamented by Gruffydd Gryg, a notable contemporary poet who was himself an Anglesey man:

> Were not his bright deeds, Môn's [i.e. Anglesey's] praise,
> And his eyes like an eagle's?
> He paid heed to my sorrow,
> Sweet lord, was his fee not fair?

Did he not show, fine vintage,
Wisdom at the court of France?
Was he not merry, modest,
This Elffin, poured wine, brave Rhys?
Is not Gwynedd, grand my style,
Empty for a dark eagle,
For Rhys, lad of grim ruin,
Gold chain, Tudur's line, sword's edge,
True keeper, and it grieves me,
War's victor, of Snowdon's stage?

Execution was the fate of a number of prominent rebel leaders. Others emerged from the rebellion with their lives and managed to rehabilitate themselves and repair their fortunes: Gwilym ap Tudur was one of these, for in 1413 he secured a pardon for his treason. Yet other Welshmen prospered during the rebellion and even attained wealth and greatness on the backs of their fellow countrymen – even of their own relatives. Gwilym ap Gruffydd, a kinsman of the sons of Tudur, falls into this category.

Gwilym ap Gruffydd's rise was closely connected with the fall of Tudur ap Goronwy's sons. He acquired a good deal of their property after their treason against the king. Most of his lands in Anglesey and Caernarfonshire, which were worth more than £112 a year by the end of his life, once belonged to Tudur's sons. Gwilym's wife was Morfudd, the daughter of Goronwy ap Tudur (died 1382), and probably through her he got his hands on Penmynydd and Penrhyn. He obtained other properties in Anglesey and Caernarfonshire which were forfeited by Rhys and Gwilym ap Tudur at the outset of the rebellion. Gwilym ap Gruffydd even lived at Penmynydd before moving his family seat to Penrhyn in Caernarfonshire in about 1420.

Only the estates of Maredudd ap Tudur did not pass to Gwilym ap Gruffydd, though they had been confiscated (by 1407) like the rest. Maredudd's fate is unclear. He may well have been the youngest brother of all – perhaps even the son of a second wife of Tudur ap Goronwy. He is traditionally said to have gone into exile after committing murder, which perhaps reflects his activities during the rebellion. In 1405 he was an esquire in the service of the bishop of Bangor, who was himself an enthusiastic supporter of Glyndŵr. But thereafter he disappears from view. Owen, the son of Maredudd and his Anglesey-born wife Marged (or Margaret), was born at this time of greatest crisis in the annals of the family. He alone of Ednyfed Fychan's descendants was to explore new avenues with even brighter prospects ahead.

3 From the Country to the Court

The Tudors of North Wales emerged from the Glyndŵr rebellion defeated and dispossessed. Like other Welshmen, they were debarred by recent statutes from holding office, carrying arms and living in towns. Their place in the community was taken by those who had remained loyal to the English cause and were therefore exempt from the penalties imposed by the king. Yet one of the youngest of the family, Owen, the son of Maredudd ap Tudur, was to embark on an entirely different course in the decades that followed the rebellion. It was a course which, by pure chance, raised his family to a position of unique significance in the annals of the British monarchy. Owen attracted the attention of the dowager-queen of England, Katherine of Valois, princess of France, and their children were the half-brothers of the third Lancastrian king of England, Henry VI. Thenceforward, the fortunes of the house of Tudor rose and fell on a far wider stage and were entwined with the fortunes of the royal houses of Lancaster and York.

Katherine of Valois

King Charles VI of France (1368–1422), though insane for much of the last thirty years of his life, managed to sire at least twelve children. His wife, Isabelle of Bavaria, whilst performing this first duty of a queen in exemplary fashion, was notorious for her promiscuity and the range of lovers she took. Katherine was the youngest daughter of this unpromising pair. She was born at the royal palace in Paris known as the Hôtel of St. Pôl on 27 October 1401. There is some uncertainty as to whether she was neglected as a child by her wayward mother. As a royal princess, she was certainly the subject of diplomatic discussions from time to time. As early as 1413 the possibility was canvassed that more peaceful relations could be established between England and France if she were to marry King Henry IV's heir, Henry (Shakespeare's *Prince Hal*). Nothing came of this proposal because Henry IV died soon afterwards. When his successor, Henry V, revived the idea a year later, he coupled it with such exorbitant demands for a dowry and an acknowledgement of his right to the French throne that a war, rather than a wedding, was the result. After the outbreak of fighting in 1415, the English victory at Agincourt, and the large-scale invasion of Normandy, the wonder is that plans for such a marriage survived at all. But they did. Reports

Effigy of King Charles VI of France (d. 1422), father of Katherine of Valois. From 1392 until his death he suffered increasingly severe attacks of insanity. His tomb, with its effigy by Pierre de Thoiry, is in the abbey church of St. Denis, Paris.

Effigy of Isabelle of Bavaria, queen of France and mother of Katherine of Valois, from her tomb effigy at St. Denis, Paris. The effigy seems to have been sculpted from life. Isabelle's personal reputation was not of the sweetest.

were sent to Henry about Katherine's beauty and her attractive figure, and portraits were painted of her to impress the hero-king. Eventually, by the end of 1419, Henry's conquests had made the French more ready to discuss peace and a marriage, and when Henry and Katherine met for the first time at Meulan the great king was completely captivated by her charm and her beauty; Katherine blushed winningly when Henry kissed her and took her hand. At the city of Troyes in May 1420 the Anglo-French treaty was sealed, Henry was acknowledged to be King Charles's heir, and the marriage with Katherine was arranged. The wedding took place, not in Troyes Cathedral, but in the humbler parish church of St. John, whose fourteenth-century nave is all that remains today of the church in which Henry V and Katherine of Valois took their marriage vows before the archbishop of Sens. The king was thirty-three, his bride eighteen.

Katherine did not have long with her new husband. After a splendid ceremonial entry into Paris in December 1420, they sailed for England where, at Dover, they were carried triumphantly ashore by enthusiastic barons of the Cinque Ports. Katherine's coronation in Westminster Abbey in February 1421 was a glittering affair, and she followed it by joining the king on his public progress through the midland and northern shires of England. But in June 1421, almost a year to the day since his marriage, Henry returned to France for further campaigning. He left knowing that his queen was pregnant, and on 6 December

Portrait of King Henry V (1387–1422), first husband of Katherine of Valois. The portrait is one of a series painted early in the sixteenth century, though probably based on a contemporary likeness.

1421 she gave birth at Windsor Castle to a baby son, Henry, whom his father would never see. Katherine herself travelled to France, without her baby, in the following May. Henry met her and they spent a few weeks together before the king went off to besiege Meaux and Katherine took up residence with her parents at Senlis, some twenty-five miles north of Paris. She never saw her husband again. During the siege, Henry contracted some sort of wasting disease akin to dysentery, from which he never recovered. At the château of Vincennes, outside Paris, he died on 31 August 1422, two weeks short of his thirty-fifth birthday. Katherine of Valois, who was not quite twenty-one years of age, was now a widow and queen dowager of England.

After this shattering experience, Katherine was much occupied with the upbringing of her baby son, who succeeded not only to the English throne but also, in accordance with the treaty of Troyes, to the throne of France after Charles VI's death on 21 October 1422. Katherine spent a good deal of her time with her son and accompanied him when he made public, ceremonial appearances in London and the South-East in the 1420s. When he was taken to Parliament, she was always there to hold his hand and sit with him. On more private occasions, she took him to her manor of Waltham or her castle at

Hertford as often as she resided with the court at Windsor. So much was to be expected of a mother.

Katherine's position as a dowager-queen was a matter of concern to the royal Council and the protector of the realm, Humphrey, duke of Gloucester, the baby king's uncle. She was young and of such a lively and vivacious character that one chronicler asserted that she was 'unable fully to curb her carnal passions'. Moreover, she continued to live in England and might well wish to marry again. This was a novel situation. Neither of the two queens of England who had outlived their royal husbands and married a second time – King John's consort and Richard II's – had stayed in England. So the possibility of Queen Katherine remarrying was of great significance after 1422. The two most powerful men in the kingdom were the protector himself, Duke Humphrey, and his uncle, Henry Beaufort, bishop of Winchester. They rarely saw eye to eye on political issues and the question of the queen's remarriage seems to have been a further cause of friction between them. One contemporary claimed that Katherine formed a strong attachment with the bishop's nephew, Edmund Beaufort, count of Mortain; sometime in the 1420s there were rumours that the couple would marry.

Such a match would be bound to cause considerable fluttering in the political dovecotes. No dowager-queen of England since the Norman Conquest had married one of her late husband's subjects, and Duke Humphrey was especially hostile to the plan. It is this association between Queen Katherine and Edmund Beaufort which was probably in the forefront of the Council's mind when a bill governing the remarriage of dowager-queens was introduced in the Parliament of 1427–8, while Beaufort was campaigning in France. Those who drew up the bill were clear about the problems such a marriage would create. A new husband whose social status was inferior to that of the queen would prejudice the honour of the queen and therefore of the crown itself, and such disparagement would shock contemporaries. Parliament ordained that if such a marriage took place without the king's permission, the queen's new husband should suffer forfeiture of his lands and other possessions during his lifetime, though it was implicitly recognised that the children of such a match would be members of the royal family and should not themselves be punished. Behind the statute, too, was a fear that a new husband might seek to play a part in English politics. Consequently, it was provided that permission to marry the queen could be given by the king only when he reached years of discretion. This clause, it was hoped, would effectively delay Queen Katherine's remarriage for some years, for at the end of 1427 Henry VI was only six years old; for the time being, there would be no step-father to influence the upbringing of an impressionable boy-king.

Apart from the statute, from the autumn of 1427 more practical constraints were placed on Queen Katherine's activities. During the next three years (perhaps even longer) she and her entourage lived in the king's own household, where councillors and royal servants could keep an eye on her; she may even have travelled with her son to France in April 1430 for his coronation as king of France. But these precautions failed to prevent or discourage her extraordinary liaison with the Welshman, Owen ap Maredudd ap Tudur.

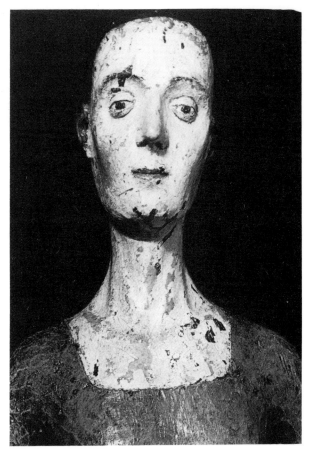

The painted wooden funeral effigy of Katherine of Valois (1400–37), daughter of Charles VI of France and Queen Isabelle. After Henry V's death (1422), Katherine married Owen Tudor. Her body now rests in Henry V's Chantry Chapel in Westminster Abbey and the effigy is in the Abbey Museum.

Owen Tudor

We do not know the date of Owen's marriage to Queen Katherine, largely because, for obvious reasons, it took place in secret and did not become common knowledge until the queen's death at the beginning of 1437. However, they may have married about 1431–2, after the queen ceased to live in her son's household; and the fact that they had four children tends to support this suggestion. Moreover, in the Parliament which began in May 1432, Owen was given the rights of an Englishman, thereby releasing him from the embarrassing provisions of Henry IV's statutes against Welshmen.

We can be no more sure of how and where the queen and the Welshman met. Later stories – such as that Owen fought at Agincourt, or on crusade in Greece, or was advanced at court by Welshmen reconciled after Glyndŵr's rebellion – cannot be substantiated and are likely to be romantic conjectures. If, as seems likely, he was born about 1400, he may have been the 'Owen Meredith' who was in the retinue of Sir Walter Hungerford, steward of Henry V's household, that went to France in May 1421. If so, this was probably his first taste of warfare and the connection with Hungerford could have provided him with an entrée to the king's household.

From the late fifteenth century onwards, a number of writers described Owen's station in life at the time of his marriage to the queen. Some of these were intent on belittling the origins of the Tudor dynasty: witness the story that he was the queen's tailor, or Richard III's statement that his father was an innkeeper of Conway. Others seem more credible: they assert that Owen was keeper of the queen's household or keeper of her wardrobe or her sewer, and the earliest reference of all, dating from Richard III's reign, places Owen as a servant in Queen Katherine's chamber. A man of Owen's modest Welsh background could hardly have aspired to much more than a post in the queen's household after her marriage in 1420.

More than that: they were attracted to one another. The pot-pourri of myth, romanticism, tradition and anti-Tudor propaganda surrounding this match is rarely borne out by historical fact. However, one of the strongest traditions is that Owen first caught Katherine's attention at a ball when he was so unsteady on his feet that he fell into her lap. A hint of some such story first appears in a poem written by Robin Ddu of Anglesey at the time of Owen's death in 1461: 'though he once on a holiday, clapped his ardent humble affection on the daughter of the king of the land of wine'. This tale was elaborated by more inventive writers at the end of Elizabeth I's reign.

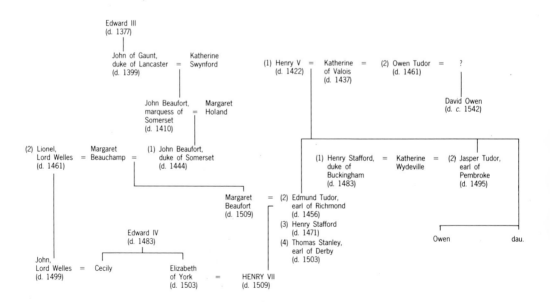

Table III: Family of King Henry VII

The mid-sixteenth century chronicler from Flintshire, Elis Gruffydd, has a different story. He relates how the queen first saw Owen one summer's day when he and his friends were swimming in a river near the court. Attracted by his good looks, she decided to play the part of a 'peeping Tom'; she secretly changed roles with her maid and arranged to meet Owen in disguise. But the young man was too ardent and when he attempted to kiss her, she struggled and received a slight wound on the cheek. The following day, as Owen was serving the queen at dinner, he realised her true identity and was ashamed of what he had done. He was forgiven and the couple fell in love and were married.

It is not easy to distinguish any fragments of fact among these flights of fancy, and it may be that Owen had a more prosaic role in managing the dowager-queen's estates in Wales. Yet despite the mystery, no one doubted that the couple were actually married, not even Richard III. And no one claimed that the children of the marriage were illegitimate.

Katherine's desire to marry was stronger than her respect for English statute. However, according to one chronicler, she did take care to choose an obscure commoner so that the king's Council 'might not reasonably take vengeance on his life'. And to counter the charge that she had degraded herself by choosing a modest Welshman, Katherine may have produced her husband's pedigree to demonstrate that his ancestors were of no ordinary lineage. The Tudor antiquary, John Leland, said that he had seen such a pedigree which Queen Katherine showed to the lords in Parliament. It is easy to imagine the queen being curious about her husband's forebears and Sir John Wynn of Gwydir later noted that

> Queen Katherine being a French woman born, knew no difference between the English and Welsh nation until her marriage being published, Owen Tudor's kindred and country were objected, to disgrace him, as most vile and barbarous.

These remarks

> made her desirous to see some of his kinsmen, whereupon he brought to her presence John ap Maredudd and Hywel ap Llywelyn ap Hywel, his near cousins, men of goodly stature and personage, but wholly destitute of bringing up and nurture, for when the queen had spoken to them in divers languages and they were not able to answer her, she said they were the goodliest dumb creatures that ever she saw.

Katherine and Owen lived together quietly for several years. In 1432 he was naturalized and in March 1434 she granted him custody of the lands and marriage of the heir of John Conway, one of Flintshire's prominent landowners. In an English environment, the Welsh patronymic form of Owen ap Maredudd ap Tudur doubtless seemed cumbersome and eccentric, perhaps even embarrassing in a queen's consort. Although occasionally called Owen fitz Maredudd, the English fashion for surnames led Owen eventually to be known – inaccurately – as Owen Tudor.

As many as four children seem to have been born to the couple, three sons and one daughter, though the daughter died young. Neither Edmund nor Jasper was born in London, but in Hertfordshire away from the eyes of the court and the Council and in houses that were not even the queen's: Edmund at Much Hadham, a manor belonging to the bishop of London, and Jasper at Hatfield, one of the bishop of Ely's estates. Of the other son, Owen, we know nothing at this early stage of his life, but it is worth noting that the names chosen for the three boys reflected the English, French and Welsh connections of their parents.

Some little while before her death, Katherine entered Bermondsey Abbey, perhaps to secure better medical treatment for the illness which, in her will, she described as a 'long, grievous malady, in the which I have been long, and yet am, troubled and vexed by the visitation of God'. This illness proved fatal and before the end came she may have become deranged. Katherine made her will on 1 January 1437 and two days later she died.

Owen now found himself in trouble with the king's Council. His and his late wife's enemies could at last proceed against him for violating the statute of 1427–8. Owen was safe only so long as Queen Katherine was alive to protect him. Soon after her death, Humphrey, duke of Gloucester began to harrass him. He was eventually persuaded to come to London but immediately sought sanctuary in Westminster Abbey. He resisted his friends' pleas that he come out and face his attackers because he believed that the king's mind had been poisoned against him. At last Owen appeared before the Council and acquitted himself of all the charges, which presumably related to his marriage. He was accordingly released, but while on his way to Wales he was arrested. His possessions were seized, including gold and silver vessels worth in all more than £137. Owen was committed to Newgate jail along with his chaplain and a servant. After contriving to escape in January or early February 1438, they were recaptured and returned to prison, Owen ultimately ending up at Windsor Castle in July 1438.

The King's Kinsmen

After Katherine's death and Owen's flight, their two elder sons, Edmund and Jasper, were placed in the honourable care of the earl of Suffolk's sister, Katherine de la Pole, who was abbess of Barking. They were at the abbey by July 1437 and were still there in March 1442. The abbess kept them in food and clothing and they had their servants with them as befitted young gentlemen. Sometime after 1442, their half-brother, King Henry VI, began to take a personal interest in their welfare and upbringing as they entered their 'teens. According to his biographer and chaplain, John Blacman, who wrote in or shortly before 1485, Henry

> before he was married, being as a youth a pupil of chastity . . . would keep careful watch through hidden windows of his chamber, lest any foolish impertinence of women coming into the house should grow to a head, and cause the fall of any of his household. And like pains did he apply in the case of his two half-brothers, the Lords Jasper and Edmund, in their boyhood and youth; providing for them most strict and safe guardianship, putting them under the care of virtuous and worthy priests, both for

teaching and for right living and conversation, lest the untamed practices of youth should grow rank if they lacked any to prune them.

Their father remained in Windsor Castle for a year until his release in July 1439 on a very substantial bail of £2,000 and on condition that he appear before the king whenever summoned to do so. He was pardoned all his offences in November 1439 and the bail was cancelled on New Year's Day 1440. Thereafter, Owen led the life of an English gentleman generously treated by his step-son, Henry VI, and taken into his household until at least the mid-1450s.

His two sons, Edmund and Jasper, were in the king's entourage but not yet formally part of the royal family. But in 1452, partly for political reasons and partly because of the king's affection for them, it was decided that they should be ennobled. Their younger brother, Owen, had probably already become a monk: he entered the Benedictine Order and spent his life among the brethren of Westminster Abbey. As far as we know, no thought was given to creating him a nobleman or to making him a bishop. Edmund and Jasper were quite another case. They were about to become the premier earls of England and be recognised as the king's half-brothers, with precedence over all other laymen in the realm apart from dukes. They would be endowed with a handsome patrimony and introduced to English political life. The Tudors were about to become standard-bearers of the house of Lancaster.

Henry VI and his ministers cannot have been wholly unaware of the advantages which the ennoblement of these two young men might offer. Although the king had been married to Margaret of Anjou for seven years by 1452, he still had no children, and the death of Humphrey, duke of Gloucester in 1447 removed his last surviving uncle from the scene. There was no question of the Tudor brothers being considered possible heirs to the throne, for although they had French royal blood in their veins, they had none of English kings. Nevertheless, their ennoblement and formal recognition as the king's half-brothers would buttress the depleted royal family. The alternative would be to reject or ignore them and their father, which might lead to damaging gossip about their legitimacy and cast a slur on the memory of Queen Katherine. In any case, such a course might further weaken the standing of the house of Lancaster; it might even result in the two men becoming a focus for political discontent.

Even though these political implications were apparent to the king, Henry also felt a close personal attachment to his half-brothers. He had in effect already recognised them as his kinsmen by making special provision for their upbringing and education, and the step he was about to take was consistent with that attitude. On 23 November 1452 Edmund and Jasper Tudor were created earls: earl of Richmond in Edmund's case and earl of Pembroke in Jasper's.

The titles are significant. They were titles held by the two uncles whom King Henry could remember, John, duke of Bedford and Humphrey, duke of Gloucester. And Edmund and Jasper were given a special position among the English nobility, with precedence over all other noblemen below the rank of duke. In addition to their new style and title, Earl Edmund and his male heirs were given the estates of the honour of Richmond, though Jasper had to rest content for the moment with a £20 annuity because the honour of Pembroke was not yet available.

The ceremony of investiture with the king's sword was held over until the end of the Christmas holiday, and in preparation for it Edmund and Jasper were provided with a sumptuous wardrobe of velvets, cloth of gold and furs, as well as saddles and other trappings for their horses. When Henry and Queen Margaret returned to the capital after celebrating Christmas at Greenwich, the investiture took place in the Tower of London on Friday, 5 January 1453. Next day Henry formally created them earls with great solemnity. Their elevation was given maximum publicity when the two brothers were summoned to Parliament on 20 January. On the day Parliament opened, 6 March, they took their seats as the premier earls of England and the Commons formally presented a petition to Henry VI begging him to recognise them as his legitimate brothers born of the same mother (that is, his 'uterine' brothers). They also asked him to release them from any statutory disabilities arising from the fact that their father was not English. This Henry graciously did, and at the same time the estates of the earldom of Pembroke were granted to Jasper in the same way as the earldom of Richmond had earlier been given to Edmund.

From almost complete obscurity, Edmund and Jasper Tudor had been brought to the steps of the throne itself. No earl could sustain his high position without a substantial income; and penniless half-brothers of a king had to be endowed with profitable estates. Between November 1452 and July 1453 the two new earls received large and regular grants, though they tailed off when Henry became seriously ill in August. The lands associated with their titles represented the biggest concentration of territorial wealth and power which each enjoyed. Those of the honour of Richmond lay in a broad arc down the fertile eastern side of England, between Yorkshire and Norfolk. The other major properties which Edmund received were some lordships in the fell country across the Pennines, in Westmorland and Lancashire. All the signs are that the honour of Richmond was efficiently run and prosperous, and aside from the rural manors of the countryside, Edmund had a commercial interest in the famous wool-exporting port of Boston. His estates in the north-west were less well managed and less productive agriculturally.

Earl Jasper's honour of Pembroke was based on Pembroke itself and the adjacent lordships of Cilgerran and Llanstephan in South-West Wales. Apart from the rolling acres of Dyfed, trade and coal-mining played a significant part in the economy of his estates grouped about the great inland waterway of Milford Haven. Most noblemen had their town-houses or 'inns' in London: Edmund was given the large fortified house of Baynard's Castle beside the Thames, while Jasper and one of his councillors, Thomas Vaughan, acquired a house in Brook Street, Stepney. Taking all their resources into account, it looks as if each of the Tudors had a clear annual income of at least £925. Compared with a duke of Buckingham or a Richard of York, they had modest fortunes. But when it is remembered that Edmund and Jasper had been endowed by the king alone in a very short space of time, the extent of Henry VI's generosity appears remarkable. Edmund's early death meant that Jasper became even richer because they had held a number of properties jointly. Thus, after 1456, the

Alabaster Tomb Effigies of John Beaufort (d. 1410), earl of Somerset, his wife, Margaret Holand (d. 1437), and her second husband, Thomas, Duke of Clarence (d. 1421). John and Margaret were the grandparents of Lady Margaret Beaufort. The effigies of the earl and the duke have the Lancastrian collar of SS round their neck. The tomb is in Canterbury Cathedral.

income of the earl of Pembroke may have soared as high as £1,500 a year and he owed it all to Henry VI, with a reasonable expectation of more to come.

A Beaufort Wife

Once the king's half-brothers had been ennobled and endowed, they had to be found suitable brides. As a step in this direction, on 24 March 1453 Edmund and Jasper were jointly given custody of one of England's richest and most eligible heiresses: Margaret Beaufort, only daughter and heiress of John Beaufort, duke of Somerset. She was also the king's kinswoman.

Margaret was the grand-daughter of John Beaufort (died 1410), the eldest of the bastard sons of John of Gaunt, duke of Lancaster, whose eldest legitimate son was the first Lancastrian king of England. These Beauforts took their name from Beaufort Castle in Champagne, where John was born to Gaunt's mistress (later his third wife). They had been declared legitimate by Parliament (1397) in

Alabaster Tomb Effigies of John Beaufort (d. 1444), duke of Somerset, and his wife, Margaret Beauchamp, the parents of Lady Margaret Beaufort. The duke, who may have committed suicide, and the duchess wear the Lancastrian collar of SS. The table tomb of Purbeck marble is in Wimborne Minster, Dorset.

Richard II's reign, but when their kinsman, Henry IV, came to the throne and confirmed this act (1407), he added a rider to the effect that the Beauforts should never succeed to the English throne. It is unclear whether a royal declaration like this could determine English custom relating to the succession and, of course, no number of public statements could alter the fact that the Beauforts were born bastards. These two question-marks were to hang over the Beaufort family and their relationship with the house of Lancaster for long after.

The rise of the Beauforts was strikingly similar to that of the Tudors fifty years later. They were of the royal blood but not fully so. They relied for their wealth and position on royal patronage, rather than on inherited estates. And both families shared the political misfortunes of their royal kinsmen, to whom they gave loyal service. John Beaufort was created earl of Somerset and marquess of Dorset by Richard II in 1397, two titles which the family held for the next seventy-five years. After 1399 he served his half-brother, Henry IV, in personal, diplomatic, military and advisory capacities, as did John's younger brothers, Henry, bishop of Winchester, and Thomas, later duke of Exeter. John's lands were situated mainly in the West Country, though he had a palace at Woking (Surrey) as well as a residence at Corfe Castle on the Dorset coast. John's second son, also called John, succeeded to the earldom of Somerset in 1418 and had a life of military misfortune. He was captured at the battle of

Baugé in 1421 and spent the next seventeen years in prison in France. Only after his release did he marry; in 1442 his bride was a lady of relatively modest rank, Margaret, the daughter of Sir John Beauchamp of Bletsoe in Bedfordshire. John was thirty-eight years old, and in the following year he was created duke of Somerset. On 31 May 1443 their only child, who was given her mother's name of Margaret, was born at Bletsoe. She never really knew her father who, after leading a disastrous expedition to France in 1443, died in disgrace at Wimborne in Dorset on 27 May 1444, some say by his own hand. His wife survived him by thirty-eight years and was married again, to Lionel, Lord Welles. Both of Margaret Beaufort's parents lie buried in Wimborne Minster.

When Somerset died, his daughter was less than a year old. Her vast inheritance was the reason why she was married a few years later to John de la Pole, the son and heir of Henry VI's chief minister, the marquess of Suffolk. The significance of Margaret, the senior Beaufort heir, as a direct descendant of John of Gaunt is shown by the charge that Suffolk was planning to place Margaret and his son on the throne of England should Henry VI fail to father an heir of his own. Suffolk was murdered in May 1450 and in February or March 1453 his son's marriage to Margaret Beaufort was annulled. The reason for this may have been the king's wish to marry her to his half-brother, Edmund Tudor. By 1455 Edmund and Margaret were married. If their only child, Henry Tudor, had any royal English blood in his veins, it came, with all its imperfections, from Margaret Beaufort.

As for Jasper Tudor, it took him more than thirty years to find a bride. There may, of course, have been a shortage of suitable heiresses in England, certainly of the quality of Margaret Beaufort. Moreover, the increasing divisions among the nobility of England may have reduced the choice, while between 1461 and 1485 Jasper was a fugitive and hardly an attractive prospect for any English lady. It is also possible that the young man's religious education and the influence of his pious and prudish half-brother inclined him to the life of a bachelor.

Bachelor or not, after the death of his brother in November 1456, Jasper was one of Henry VI's closest and most dependable advisers. He protected his widowed sister-in-law until she remarried, and even after that he seems to have taken the young Henry Tudor under his wing. It was Henry, even more than Jasper, who embodied the extraordinary revolution in the fortunes of the Tudors of North Wales. These Tudors were related to the royal family by the marriage of Owen and Queen Katherine; but it was the marriage of Edmund and Margaret Beaufort that gave their son sufficient Plantagenet blood to secure him the crown in 1485.

4 The King's Brothers and the Civil War, 1452–61

The ennoblement and endowment of the Tudor brothers in 1452–3 gave Edmund and Jasper an exalted status, a royal dignity and extensive estates. Henceforward, they filled a number of significant roles in English society and politics. They gave personal support to the king, their half-brother; they joined his Council and circle of advisers; they strove to maintain his authority in South and West Wales; and they rekindled in several parts of Wales that affection for their family which had grown cold since Glyndŵr's time. Edmund and Jasper, therefore, played an influential – though not decisive – part in the years prior to the outbreak of the civil war known as the Wars of the Roses. By their defence of the Lancastrian monarchy against the attacks of the duke of York and his supporters, they extended the dynastic and political divisions to Wales. From it all sprouted an affection for the two earls, their father Owen Tudor, and for Edmund's baby son, Henry, which was to be sustained in the hearts of some Welshmen long after 1485.

In 1452 the new earls of Richmond and Pembroke joined a small and exclusive group of influential English noblemen who included the king's relatives and his closest advisers. Henry VI was sadly bereft of close blood relations in the 1450s. He had no brothers or sisters, and his uncles, the dukes of Bedford, Clarence and Gloucester, were long dead and had left no legitimate children. The king's Tudor half-brothers therefore filled an emotional and a dynastic gap at court. At the same time, Henry VI's choice of ministers – especially the dukes of Suffolk and Somerset – had aroused bitter criticism and had even helped to cause the popular uprising in the South-East of England in 1450, known as Cade's Rebellion. And there was mounting opposition to the king's government for its military defeats in France and its increasing taxation at home. On top of that, many were uneasy about the very survival of the dynasty, because Henry and his queen, Margaret of Anjou, had produced no children after almost eight years of marriage. This atmosphere of criticism, uncertainty and despondency focussed time and again on the king's cousin, Richard, duke of York, who seemed to many to be the most likely source of stability, reform and salvation. In these circumstances, King Henry looked to his small group of relatives – the Beauforts, the Holands, the Staffords and the Tudors – with a view to broadening the aristocratic basis of his rule and buttressing his dynasty.

Table Tomb of Edmund Tudor, Earl of Richmond (d. 1456). It has stood in St. David's Cathedral since the sixteenth century, when it was removed from Edmund's burial place in the Franciscan Friary, Carmarthen. The shields of arms, and the brass and legend on top are nineteenth-century replacements of the originals.

The Tudors and English Politics, 1452–6

At first, Edmund and Jasper Tudor did not make a great impression on English politics. At their age, it would be rather strange if they did. In any case, any promise that Edmund might have shown was snuffed out by his early death on 1 November 1456. As for Jasper, his public role down to 1461 seems somewhat obscure to us now, but to begin with his contribution was peripheral to the mainstream of English government and politics. Certainly there is no sign that either brother had a political or military role to play before becoming an earl, unlike the sons of most English magnates. And if their education was indeed provided within the walls of Barking Abbey and then by priests under Henry VI's supervision, then their training as future noblemen was woefully inadequate and not at all comparable with that given to other young aristocrats.

Moreover, when the two young men were at last involved in affairs of state, they were charged with consolidating the royal authority in South and West Wales, beyond the frontiers of the realm. Their father's Welsh blood was presumably part of the explanation for this assignment during the later 1450s.

In the long run, however, the activities in Wales of Earl Jasper especially proved of crucial value to the house of Lancaster, and helped to create the circumstances in which Edmund's son, Henry Tudor, landed in Pembrokeshire in 1485.

Despite their personal relationship with Henry VI and their creation as earls, it would be a mistake to identify Edmund and Jasper Tudor solely with the unpopular and discredited advisers of the king. In fact, they spent some of their time in the company of the duke of York and his friends. This was because in the summer of 1453 King Henry suffered a severe mental and physical collapse which lasted more than seventeen months and during which he recognised nobody, understood nothing and had to be carried from place to place. This illness could not have come at a worse time. In France, King Charles VII and his armies scored one success after another in the English duchy of Aquitaine, while at home there were fierce feuds among the nobility in Yorkshire, Devon and elsewhere. It was imperative that steps be taken as quickly as possible to ensure effective royal government throughout the kingdom, and in view of Henry's incapacity the choice of leader lay between the queen and the duke of York. Throughout the winter of 1453–4, each strove to persuade the English nobility and Parliament to place the king's powers in his or her hands. It is possible that Queen Margaret's uncompromising demand that she be declared regent of England drove a wedge between her and the Tudor brothers. Equally, Richard, duke of York needed allies to support his bid for power and it is reasonably clear that Earl Jasper was prepared to side with him; Edmund's attitude is less easy to gauge but it was probably identical with that of his younger brother.

Jasper took a prominent role in discussing these contentious matters, and on more than one occasion he was present at meetings with other nobles who were York's kinsmen or supporters. By the end of January 1454, the liaison which the Tudor brothers had formed with the duke and his friends was demonstrated in public when it was reported that 'the Earls of Warwick, Richmond and Pembroke come with the Duke of York, as it is said, each of them with a goodly fellowship ... the King's brothers be like to be arrested at their coming to London if they come'. Jasper, though not Edmund, attended the Parliament which, on 3 April 1454, eventually agreed that the duke of York should be protector and defender of England during Henry VI's continuing illness.

It is likely that the brothers remained on amicable terms with York while his régime lasted. Jasper attended Parliament and meetings of the royal Council during the remainder of 1454; and although Edmund was not so much in evidence (perhaps he was ill or else visiting his estates), when he was able to do so he too joined the other nobles. The brothers even attended a Council meeting in November 1454 which drew up ordinances designed to reform and reduce the size of King Henry's household. This directly affected them because they normally stayed with the king and had their own establishment in his household; now each brother was allowed a chaplain, two esquires, two yeomen and two chamberlains, an entourage that was matched only by that of the king's spiritual confessor. The Tudors' role in the reform of the royal household highlights both their concern for sounder and more economical government and their sympathy for York's attempts to achieve it. This position was not as yet

Great Seal of Jasper Tudor, Earl of Pembroke, for his lordship of Pembroke. The obverse shows an armed, mounted knight with a shield carrying Jasper's arms. The reverse shows his arms of France and England quarterly, with a border of martlets (indicating newly won nobility). The supporters are two wolves.

incompatible with their close attachment to the king and the Lancastrian dynasty.

Quite suddenly, at Christmastide 1454, Henry VI recovered his mental faculties. The duke of York was therefore no longer needed as protector and defender of the realm and by the middle of March the king's friends and former advisers had been restored to power; at their head was Edmund Beaufort, duke of Somerset and the uncle of Edmund Tudor's young wife. York and his associates withdrew from London in some disgust. This posed Edmund and Jasper Tudor with a dilemma. On the one hand, although they doubtless rejoiced at the recovery of their half-brother, he had restored the discredited favourites to influence and power. On the other hand, the duke of York, with whom the Tudors had co-operated, had been dismissed from office and was regarded with hostility by the queen and the court. A violent clash between the two rival factions seemed likely. How should the Tudors react?

On Wednesday, 1 May 1455 King Henry left London on his way to Leicester; with him rode a large company of noblemen, including Jasper Tudor (but not Edmund). They spent the night at Watford. The next morning, they travelled on to St. Albans where, however, a force led by York, Warwick and Salisbury was encamped. There, after fruitless parleys, the first blood was shed in the Wars of the Roses, some of it the king's. We do not know what part Jasper Tudor played in the confused events of that day, but we may imagine him shocked and profoundly disturbed by what he saw: street fighting between the king's and York's men, the slaying of some of the king's servants, the death of Somerset, and the wounding of Henry himself in the neck. As far as we know, Jasper had had no military training or experience to prepare him for this skirmish, but he emerged physically unscathed.

After the 'Battle' of St. Albans, the king was escorted back to London by the duke of York and the other victors, and when, on 26 May, a Parliament was summoned to meet at Westminster six weeks later, the Tudor brothers were required to attend. Surprisingly, Jasper's sympathy for York does not seem to have entirely evaporated after the violence at St. Albans, though he may well have regretted the resort to arms. Like other noblemen – the duke of Buckingham and the earl of Shrewsbury especially – he seems to have appreciated the dangers for England and its king that lay in the stark polarisation of political attitudes and ambitions. In the coming months, he was one of those who tried to bring the two factions together.

Even before the Parliament began, Jasper was in the capital discussing with York and other nobles how best the business of government should be managed. When the Parliament opened in Henry VI's presence, Jasper and his brother were prominent and influential. The main measure that was taken to shore up the king's finances, the cancellation of most of the grants which Henry had made since the beginning of his reign, carried a special exemption – one of a small number – in favour of Edmund and Jasper and the estates which they had been granted since 1452. Such exemptions were regarded by York and the Commons in Parliament as seriously weakening this Act of Resumption, but after all the Tudors were members of the royal family as well as potential allies of the duke of York. The brothers' loyalty to Henry VI was beyond question, and in Jasper's case it was recorded publicly and formally when he and the other lords present in the Parliament swore allegiance to Henry in the Great Council Chamber at Westminster.

Edmund cut less of a figure in these proceedings in the capital and, indeed, he seems to have attended fewer meetings of the king's Council than his younger brother in the years following their elevation to the peerage. He may have been a sick man, though there is no evidence to indicate this. He may have spent much of his time outside the capital on official business, perhaps in Wales, but there is no sure evidence of that either. However, his association with the duke of York seems to have been as close as Jasper's. Like his brother (and Buckingham and Shrewsbury), Edmund probably sympathised with the duke's efforts to change the personnel and improve the quality of Henry VI's government, but the deeper the rift between York and the court faction, the more difficult it was for the Tudors to keep a foot in both camps. When the second session of the 1455 Parliament began on 12 November, Edmund and Jasper were absent, probably in Wales. It was this commitment to uphold the king's authority in their father's homeland that not only took them out of the orbit of the duke of York and the king's critics, but also drew them decisively to the Lancastrian court.

The Welsh Connection, 1455–61

Disorder in several parts of Wales was a recurring problem for Henry VI's government. Since the end of the Glyndŵr rebellion forty years before, there had been an uneasy calm, with periodic outbursts of localised violence which proved difficult to curb. The great noblemen who owned lordships in Southern and Eastern Wales, and filled the most senior offices in the royal shires of the North and West, were mostly absentees, handing real power and opportunities for political, social and economic advancement over to their local agents. Many of these more minor local landowners exploited their position and abused their power, and as a result the quality of royal and noble government in Wales steadily declined. In South-East Wales the most prominent Welshmen to take advantage of these circumstances were William Herbert of Raglan, one of the duke of York's tenants in his lordship of Usk, and the Vaughans of Tretower in the duke of Buckingham's lordship of Brecon. In the South-West, the Wogan and Perrot families dominated South Pembrokeshire. But above all, it was Gruffydd ap Nicholas who acquired greatest influence and manipulated the king's authority to most effect, especially in Carmarthenshire. Gruffydd's sons, Thomas and Owain ap Gruffydd, acted as his lieutenants and as such took his influence southwards into Pembrokeshire and northwards into Cardiganshire, so that by the time that Edmund Tudor was made earl of Richmond and Jasper Tudor earl of Pembroke in 1452, Gruffydd ap Nicholas's position in South-West Wales was unchallenged and almost unchallengeable.

In 1455 Edmund, earl of Richmond was sent to Wales as King Henry's representative. Although he had no lands in Wales and no official position there, Edmund was the senior of the king's Welsh half-brothers. He may have been assigned the task by the duke of York after the Battle of St. Albans. In November 1455, when Edmund's presence in South Wales is first noticed, the duke was ruling England as protector and defender for the second time. Moreover, York had his own interests in the region: not only had he replaced the duke of Somerset as constable of Carmarthen and Aberystwyth Castles, but he deeply resented the way in which Gruffydd ap Nicholas had recently tried to elbow his way into lordships near the English border that belonged to York and the duke of Buckingham. Thus, from the autumn of 1455, Earl Edmund intervened personally in South Wales in order to revitalise the royal authority there. On 30 November he was staying at Lamphey in Pembrokeshire, the bishop of St. David's secluded palace situated no more than two miles east of Jasper's castle at Pembroke. The bishop, John de la Bere, was one of King Henry's chaplains, and so he and Edmund may have known one another quite well; indeed, the earl was at Lamphey again in the spring of 1456 and evidently regarded its attractive precinct as his Pembrokeshire headquarters.

Gruffydd ap Nicholas was not the sort of person to relinquish overnight a personal ascendancy it had taken years to achieve. Edmund's presence was resented by the older man and by June 1456 they were 'at war greatly in Wales'. Gruffydd and his sons had taken control of the royal castles at Aberystwyth and Carmarthen and the impregnable fortress in the uplands of Carmarthenshire, Carreg Cennen, which Gruffydd garrisoned with his own men. He occupied

Pembroke Castle, from the south with Milford Sound to the west. The town stretches eastward from the right foreground. The central keep, 5 storeys high, was built about 1210 but the tower in which Henry Tudor was born is thought to be that situated to the left of the great gatehouse in the foreground. The antiquary John Leland reported seeing a new chimney there in the 1530s, with Henry's arms and badges commemorating the event.

also the stoutly fortified castle of Kidwelly on the Carmarthenshire coast. From his trial of strength with Gruffydd, Edmund Tudor emerged at least partly victorious, for by August 1456 he was in possession of Carmarthen Castle. But the countryside around Kidwelly was still disturbed a couple of months later.

By this stage, the duke of York was no longer protector and defender of the realm. Edmund Tudor's campaign in Wales therefore enhanced the authority of the king and his court faction. Indeed, his very success in taking control of Carmarthen may now have been regarded as threatening the duke who was still its constable. By August 1456 some of York's most prominent retainers in Eastern Wales had decided to re-assert their master's authority in the region. On 10 August about 2,000 men from Herefordshire and the neighbouring Welsh lordships set out for West Wales, under the command of Sir William Herbert, his brother-in-law Sir Walter Devereux, and members of the Vaughan family. They made straight for Carmarthen, seized its castle and imprisoned Edmund Tudor. Then, they pressed on to Aberystwyth, where the seaside fortress built by King Edward I was also taken. This campaign re-established York's authority in West Wales after he had lost it at Westminster, though it meant offending a rival source of power in Edmund Tudor. Edmund was

Gatehouse of Carmarthen Castle. This is the most substantial part of the fortress still standing. Edmund Tudor, earl of Richmond, is presumed to have died here on 1 November 1456.

released from prison soon afterwards, but at Carmarthen on 1 November 1456 he died, apparently of some epidemic disease. He was buried nearby in the large Greyfriars Church, before the main altar dedicated to St. Francis. His fine tomb, surmounted by a brass image of the earl, was transferred to St. David's Cathedral after the Dissolution of the Monasteries almost a century later. Coming so soon after the violent events of the summer of 1456 and when Edmund was still in his twenties, his sudden death arouses suspicion of foul play or severe wounds, though no contemporary placed the blame on Herbert, Devereux or the Vaughans at their trial several months later. Alternatively, Edmund may not have enjoyed robust health at any time during his short life.

While his elder brother was wrestling with these problems of law, order and authority in South and West Wales, Jasper Tudor stayed with the king. In June 1456, for example, he was with Henry at the royal manor house of Sheen on the Thames, 'and no more lords' were with them. But after Edmund's death, he travelled to Wales to take his place, and thereafter played a lesser role at court and at the centre of government. Jasper's long association with Wales in the service of the house of Lancaster and then the house of Tudor was to continue uninterruptedly until his death almost forty years later.

Edmund's death focussed popular attention and affection in Wales on the Tudor family for the first time since the end of the Glyndŵr Rebellion. Edmund and Jasper were not only the sons of a Welshman who had achieved the extraordinary by marrying the dowager-queen of England, but they were the first Welshmen to enter the ranks of the English peerage. Edmund's exploits in South and West Wales and those of his brother after him were guaranteed to catch the eye and stir the imagination of several Welsh poets and their patrons. In Southern Caernarfonshire, Dafydd Nanmor was one of the first to lavish praise on Edmund and Jasper as distinguished Welshmen of their generation, with a lineage that stretched back to the legendary foundation of Britain: 'Two noblemen, from Troy and Greece, the root is good'. In a moving elegy composed soon after Edmund's death, he pictured the distraught Jasper offering his protection to Edmund's baby son, a young deer who would grow up into a proud stag; and he commended Jasper for healing, by his own efforts, the emotional wounds inflicted by the tragic death at Carmarthen. In South Wales, Lewis Glyn Cothi of Carmarthenshire likewise proclaimed in verse his sense of loss and despair on hearing of the death of Edmund, 'brother of King Henry, nephew of the Dauphin [King Charles VII of France], and son of Owen' – in that order. He compared a Wales without Edmund to a land without a ruler, a house without a bed, a town without great houses, a beach without water, a house without feasting, a church without a priest, a castle without soldiers, and a hearth without smoke. The hopes of the family and of the Lancastrian dynasty in Wales now rested with Jasper.

The Role of Jasper Tudor

Recent events had severed whatever links Jasper Tudor had once had with the duke of York, and from the beginning of 1457 he was one of the most tenacious supporters of the house of Lancaster. Nor was he alone in this. The duke of Buckingham formed a close personal relationship with the Tudors at about this time, partly because of the polarisation of political opinion in the country at large and partly because of the activities of York's retainers in the vicinity of the Stafford lordships of Newport and Brecon. This relationship with Buckingham enabled Jasper to provide for his brother's widow and her baby son – which was, after all, his most immediate concern. In the weeks following Edmund's death, Margaret Beaufort, countess of Richmond, was installed in Jasper's castle at Pembroke and there, traditionally in one of the towers of the outer ward overlooking the river, she gave birth to a son. Because Margaret was very young and quite small, it was not an easy birth. Henry Tudor was born on 28 January 1457. He was named after his uncle, the king. There is a tradition, first recorded in the sixteenth century by the Welsh chronicler, Elis Gruffydd, who heard it from some old men, that the baby was baptised Ywain (or Owain) but that his mother immediately insisted that the officiating bishop alter his name to Henry. It is a nice story, and if true it would mean that by a hair's breadth England avoided having not only a dynasty called Maredudd instead of Tudor, but also a king called Owain, not

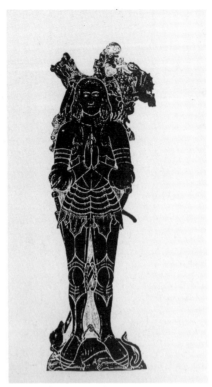

Brass of Edmund Tudor, earl of Richmond, from his tomb in St. David's Cathedral. The present brass was made in 1873 in fifteenth-century style. It occupies the precise dimensions of the original brass which was robbed in the seventeenth century; some details need not be authentic.

Henry VII. But the story almost certainly reflects the conviction among sixteenth-century Welshmen that the accession of Henry Tudor in 1485 fulfilled ancient prophecies that foretold of the reconquest of England by a British prince who was usually identified as Owain.

Margaret must have felt very alone at the time of her son's birth, and both mother and baby were taken by Jasper into his care. He quickly took steps to secure the future of the baby and his mother, who was barely fourteen years old. In March 1457, Jasper visited the duke of Buckingham at his manor of Greenfield, near Newport; present too were Margaret Beaufort and, very likely, her baby. This may have been the occasion when it was arranged that Margaret, who was the wealthiest and best connected widow in England, should marry Buckingham's second son, Henry Stafford; the bishop of Hereford gave his permission for the match on 6 April. Buckingham and Jasper had similar interests, both politically and regionally in South Wales; the marriage helped to bind their two prominent Lancastrian families together and at the same time removed the uncertainty about Margaret Beaufort's future. Moreover, during 1457 the two noblemen kept in touch with one another while Jasper, from his lordship of Pembroke, resumed the task of bringing peace and stability to South Wales which his brother had begun.

'Five Arches' Gateway in Tenby's Town Walls, Dyfed. The walls were much extended and heightened by Jasper Tudor in the late 1450s and made the town a safe haven for the Tudors in 1471.

Meanwhile, attempts were being made to bring the duke of York's lieutenants to justice for their brazen lawlessness in South and West Wales and their humiliation of Edmund Tudor. Despite the efforts of the court, Sir William Herbert remained at liberty during the winter of 1456–7, his men continuing their marauding in South-East Wales. But at the end of March 1457, King Henry, Queen Margaret, the duke of Buckingham, the earl of Shrewsbury, and probably Jasper Tudor too, arrived in Hereford to oversee the trial proceedings against Herbert, Devereux and the rest. The outcome was surprising in view of Edmund's harsh treatment, but in political terms it can be regarded as astute. The tribunal sought to drive a wedge between the various accused by being magnanimous to some and severe towards others. Thus, whereas Sir William Herbert was offered an amnesty and a pardon in June 1457, Sir Walter Devereux was gaoled until February 1458; and while some of Herbert's associates were forgiven, others were not.

In order to consolidate Jasper's authority in the west and south yet further, in April 1457 he was appointed constable of Aberystwyth, Carmarthen and Carreg Cennen Castles in place of the duke of York; and this implicitly meant that he intended to curb the local power of Gruffydd ap Nicholas as well. Personal contact with other magnates of the region, notably with Buckingham, was a great advantage, and Jasper also took military precautions. In December 1457, he encouraged the mayor and burgesses of Tenby to improve the defences of their town. The townsmen proposed that new walls, six feet thick, should be constructed round the town, with a continuous platform running along the top; the town moat should be cleaned and widened throughout to about thirty feet. Jasper undertook to foot half the bill for this major undertaking and the results remain impressive to this day. In addition to the original plan, an extra tower was built along the circuit of the walls, and existing towers and most of the parapets were raised even higher than had been intended.

As far as we know, no other castle or town in Jasper's earldom of Pembroke received such precise attention as did Tenby in the late 1450s. It was evidently regarded as a particularly important citadel of his power in South Wales. It lay close to the fortified palace of the bishop of St. David's at Lamphey, it had a well-defended castle of its own, the town on its rocky site was relatively easy to protect, and its harbour had readier access to the open sea than the various anchorages within Milford Haven.

All the signs are that Jasper Tudor's tour of duty in South Wales was eminently successful. He was reconciled with Gruffydd ap Nicholas and his sons, and he strengthened the garrisons at Kidwelly and Carreg Cennen in the Lancastrian interest. The resentment which Gruffydd and his family had felt towards the Tudors earlier in the decade was now forgotten. Henceforward, Gruffydd (who died in 1460) and his sons proved loyal to King Henry VI and his half-brother in the last months of the Lancastrian monarchy.

Jasper was more highly regarded by the king and the court faction than he had ever been. After Alfonso, king of Aragon and Naples, died in 1458, Jasper was elected to replace him as a knight of the Garter. In May 1459 he was assigned a tower in the palace of Westminster which could serve as his headquarters when he was in the capital.

During the latter part of 1459, the two factions in English politics, the Lancastrian court and the duke of York, prepared for confrontation. In September it came. The duke and his sons were forced into exile and at a Parliament held at Coventry (Jasper attended 'with a good fellowship') the Yorkist lords were victimised and stripped of their estates. All the nobles present, Jasper among them, solemnly swore an oath of loyalty to Henry VI and his son, Prince Edward. Jasper and his father Owen benefited handsomely from the forfeited estates that were now available for redistribution: Owen leased some manors in Kent and Sussex, while Jasper secured the duke of York's castle and estate at Newbury in Berkshire.

The duke had retreated to Ireland, and Jasper therefore repaired to Wales to complete the downfall of the Yorkist faction there and to block any attempt by York to return to England. In January 1460 he was given control for life of the castle and lordship of Denbigh which were York's main channel of communication between England and Ireland; Owen Tudor received some lucrative offices in Denbigh soon afterwards. But in order to make these grants effective and destroy York's power in the lordship, Jasper would first have to besiege Denbigh Castle and bring York's local agents to heel. This was no easy task. A large force was assembled in South-West Wales, where Jasper had the

Gatehouse of Denbigh Castle, as it might have been (according to Alan Sorell) after its completion in the late thirteenth century. It was besieged by Jasper Tudor and captured from the duke of York's forces in 1460.

co-operation of local landowners like the Wogans and the Perrots. He was given authority to pardon and to punish any rebels who fell into his hands; and he was authorised to keep the possessions of those whom he found in Denbigh Castle so that he could reward his own men. More that £650 was provided to meet the cost of reducing Denbigh and other castles in Wales that were held by Yorkist dissidents.

Jasper managed to capture Denbigh, and by May 1460 he was able to return to Pembroke to organise its defences. A Tenby ship, 'The Mary', was commandeered to attack a hostile vessel that had penetrated Milford Sound, and sailors and other men from Tenby were recruited for the operation. The earl's appreciation of the strategic value of Milford's waterway, whose many inlets and harbours offered opportunities for landings from Ireland and the Continent, probably dates from these years and was to prove invaluable in 1485.

Yet the Lancastrian position in England, Wales and elsewhere could never be secure so long as the duke of York and his allies were in exile beyond the king's grasp. By the end of June 1460 the Yorkist nobles, led by the duke's eldest son, Edward, earl of March and the earl of Warwick, were ready to launch an assault on Lancastrian England from Calais. They landed at Sandwich in Kent and reached London on 2 July. After Warwick's crushing victory over the king's forces at Northampton, where Henry VI was captured and the duke of Buckingham and the earl of Shrewsbury killed, Queen Margaret fled to Wales, where Jasper was still undefeated. It was natural that the new Yorkist government should order Jasper and his men to surrender Denbigh Castle and similar orders were sent to the constables of other castles between Conway and Montgomery in North Wales. But it would require a decisive Yorkist victory in the West to make Jasper and the Lancastrians heed these orders and surrender what they held. Lewis Glyn Cothi, the Carmarthenshire poet patronised by Gruffydd ap Nicholas's family and others, pictured Jasper in 1460 recruiting in Wales on behalf of the house of Lancaster and Prince Edward as the hope of the dynasty and the defender of 'the British Isles'.

Queen Margaret had meanwhile reached the safety of Scotland. In order to prevent her from massing an army in the North, the duke of York, who had returned from Ireland in October 1460, led a force northwards to Yorkshire to confront the Lancastrians. At Wakefield on 30 December he was killed in a skirmish with his enemies. The leadership of the Yorkist faction fell to his eldest son, Edward. On hearing the news from Wakefield, Margaret gathered a formidable army of Scots and northern Englishmen and proceeded to march south. She defeated Warwick and the main Yorkist force at St Albans on 17 February 1461.

Jasper Tudor and the earl of Wiltshire had been assembling another army in Wales, and late in January it began to move north-eastwards towards the Herefordshire border. This army included a number of Jasper's Welsh allies, agents and servants on whom he had learned to rely, among them Thomas and Owain, the sons of Gruffydd ap Nicholas, the Perrots of Pembrokeshire, some of Buckingham's men from the borderland, as well as his own father, Owen Tudor. They were supported by a motley collection of Irish, Breton and French soldiers whom Wiltshire had probably recruited and brought to South Wales by sea. For his part, Edward, earl of March raised a larger force in the border shires and in his father's Welsh lordships; they mustered somewhere in the vicinity of Wigmore and Ludlow. With Edward were Sir William Herbert and his brother Richard, Sir Walter Devereux, Roger Vaughan of Tretower, and others who had been responsible for the lawlessness in West Wales in 1456. The battle that ensued had, therefore, something of the air of a forum for the waging of old feuds and the settling of old scores. On 3 February 1461 the two armies met at Mortimer's Cross in Herefordshire, about six miles north-west of Leominster and only four miles from Wigmore, one of York's castles.

Strange omens – particularly three suns – are said to have appeared in the sky which might have sapped the morale of March's men had he not persuaded them that these were a sign of good, not bad, fortune. According to the sixteenth-century chronicler, Edward Hall, this incident was the origin of one of the badges Edward used as king, the sun-burst of York. As for the battle,

> And anon freshly and manly he took the field upon his enemies and put them to flight, and slew 3,000, and some of their captains were taken and beheaded, but Pembroke and Wiltshire stole away privily disguised and fled out of the country.

One of the leading Lancastrians unlucky enough to be captured was Owen Tudor. The earl of March, doubtless bitter at his own father's death a month earlier, ordered that the elderly Welshman be executed a few days later at Hereford. A contemporary chronicler recorded that 'his head [was] set upon the highest step of the market cross, and a mad woman combed his hair and washed away the blood of his face', setting more than a hundred lighted candles about him. Not until the very last moment did he realise that he was about to die, murmuring (it is said) that 'That head shall lie on the stock that was wont to lie on Queen Katherine's lap'. His body was buried in a chapel of the now vanished Greyfriars Church in Hereford, just as his eldest son Edmund had been buried in the same Order's great church at Carmarthen only four years before. Excavations in 1894 and 1933 revealed part of the chancel of the priory church, and three skeletons (one of a man measuring six feet two inches tall) were found, but there is nothing to prove that any of these was the mortal remains of Owen Tudor. The distinction of his sons and the irony of a queen's consort meeting his end in such a fashion were reflected in the elegies that were composed in Wales in or soon after 1461. Poets from Glamorgan, Carmarthenshire, Powys and Anglesey eloquently lamented his death.

Jasper Tudor retreated hastily towards Pembroke, vowing 'with the might of Our Lord, and the assistance of . . . our kinsmen and friends, within short time to avenge' the defeat. He was unaware that his days as a fugitive would last, with only one short interruption, for nearly a quarter of a century.

5 Jasper Tudor: The Lancastrian Champion

Between the spring of 1461 and the summer of 1470, Jasper Tudor led the life of an adventurer. He was a fugitive in Wales and Northern England, and an exile in Scotland and France, whereas the Yorkist earl of March ruled England as Edward IV. Jasper's only nephew, Henry Tudor, spent his childhood in the custody of his family's enemies, the Herberts of Raglan in Gwent, who were loyal supporters of King Edward. Jasper's adventures in these years are remarkable, not only for their drama, but also because of the steadfast loyalty which he showed to his half-brother, the deposed King Henry VI, often in the face of enormous obstacles and against almost impossible odds. Survival was his watchword. Yet Jasper's determination and faith in the Lancastrian cause never faltered, and he was eventually rewarded in 1470 when King Edward was thrust from the throne and King Henry returned for a second reign.

Disaster in Wales

The decisive victory of Edward, earl of March over the Lancastrian forces at Mortimer's Cross in Herefordshire on 3 February 1461 was a devastating blow for Jasper Tudor as well as for Henry VI. Jasper and the earl of Wiltshire, who shared command of the defeated army, were forced to flee in disguise. Three weeks later, Jasper could be found at Tenby in his own lordship of Pembroke, a friendly port which he regarded as a safe haven on more than one occasion. On 25 February he wrote to two of his allies in North Wales – and doubtless to others too – in order to revive Lancastrian spirits and to seek revenge for his recent defeat, his father's execution at Hereford and the setback suffered by Henry VI's forces. Jasper believed that it was not too late to strike at the Yorkists and prevent a complete Lancastrian collapse.

Meanwhile, Henry VI's forceful queen, Margaret of Anjou, and their only son, Prince Edward, were moving down from the north of England with a large army of northerners. They reached St. Albans in Hertfordshire on 17 February, and there the queen's army roundly defeated an ill-prepared Yorkist force under the earl of Warwick. When the battle was over, Margaret recovered her husband, who had been a prisoner in the hands of the Yorkists since the previous summer. She was well placed to crown her success by a march straight on London, followed by the restoration of Henry VI to his throne. Moreover, the

Portrait of King Edward IV (1442–83). This portrait in the Royal Collection is thought to have been painted by a Flemish artist and based on a portrait completed before 1472.

earls of March and Warwick, who quickly joined forces in the Cotswolds – the one after his victory, the other following his defeat – might with speed and a modicum of luck be crushed between the reassembled forces of Jasper Tudor advancing from South Wales and Queen Margaret's northern army in the Home Counties. This was a forlorn hope. Jasper was not able to reconstitute his army in time, and Margaret's men made the cardinal mistake of alienating the countryside through which they marched by their rough northern ways. After winning the Battle of St. Albans, they turned to pillaging the town and terrifying the Londoners, who viewed their advance with growing alarm. The ordinary citizens rose in large numbers and refused to allow her men into the city. She therefore decided to withdraw northwards to Yorkshire. Instead, the gates of London were thrown open to welcome Edward, earl of March and Warwick. On 4 March 1461, Edward was acclaimed king of England. A few weeks later, on 29 March, the new monarch strengthened his hold on the crown by inflicting yet another major defeat on the Lancastrians, this time at Towton, after pursuing them into Northern Yorkshire. Henry VI, Margaret of Anjou, their son Edward and a number of their allies hurried across the border to Scotland and safety, leaving the defeated Jasper Tudor in Wales, unsupported, empty-handed and vulnerable.

As part of the new régime's efforts to crush the Lancastrians in Wales, Sir William Herbert of Raglan was given wide-ranging authority in the south-west. He was given the task of seizing the lordship of Pembroke and all the estates of Jasper Tudor throughout England and Wales. Herbert was evidently being groomed to replace Jasper as the effective ruler of South Wales, this time on behalf of the new Yorkist king. This was made crystal clear on 26 July 1461, when he was raised to the peerage as Lord Herbert of Raglan, Chepstow and Gower. As for Jasper, his humiliation was underlined when Parliament met in the following November. On that occasion, he was counted among those principal supporters of Henry VI who were attainted and deprived of their estates. Most of Jasper's lands were actually given to Herbert early in 1462.

By the end of August 1461, Herbert and his companions were in Wales 'to cleanse the country'. They encountered little or no armed opposition at first, and even Pembroke Castle, Jasper Tudor's main bastion which was well-manned and stocked with provisions to withstand a siege, surrendered on 30 September. For all its imposing fortifications built in the late 1450s, Tenby too capitulated. But Jasper himself eluded capture and continued to raise the Lancastrian banner when and where he could. His escape was one of several bitter disappointments that blighted Edward IV's victory. We do not know exactly where Jasper was in the spring and summer of 1461. He does not appear to have been in Pembroke during its short siege, but we can be certain that he was trying to rally Lancastrian sympathisers in Wales. Later in the year, he appeared in North Wales, where he joined the duke of Exeter, who had escaped from the Battle of Towton. On 16 October 1461, at Twt Hill just outside the north wall of Caernarfon, they menaced the loyal forces within. This was a desperate act of defiance and it availed them nothing. Jasper and Exeter took ship for Scotland, where Henry VI and his queen had also sought refuge after retreating from the field of Towton.

The Whereabouts of Henry Tudor

When he marched into Pembroke Castle, William Herbert may at least have had the satisfaction of discovering inside the four-year-old Henry, earl of Richmond, Jasper Tudor's nephew. The young earl, a member of the Lancastrian royal family, was taken into Herbert's custody, and he later paid a very high price (£1,000) for the wardship of the boy and for control over his marriage. According to the Tudor chronicler, Polydore Vergil, who may have received the information later from Henry's own mouth, the boy was 'kept as prisoner, but honourably brought up with the wife of William Herbert', Anne Devereux, at Raglan Castle. Although he was in custody, this need not have been an altogether unpleasant or restrictive experience for him. Herbert and his wife had a large young family of their own and the earl of Northumberland's son was also in Herbert's care. Henry Tudor, therefore, may well have found the company congenial and the friendships made at Raglan lasting ones; Herbert planned to

William Herbert (d. 1469), earl of Pembroke, and his wife, Anne Devereux. In this miniature from a copy of John Lydgate's Troy Book *(c. 1461–2), they are kneeling before King Edward IV. Henry Tudor was placed in their custody in 1462 and Anne kept Henry's affection even after 1485.*

'Yellow Tower of Gwent' and (left background) the older South Gate of Raglan Castle. These features represent two of the building phases at the hands of Sir William ap Thomas (d. 1445) and his son, William Herbert (d. 1469).

marry him to one of his own daughters, Maud. When he became king in 1485, Henry sent for Anne Devereux to come to London to meet him – and then he allowed her to return home to Raglan with an escort.

At this most sumptuous and beautiful of modern fortresses, Henry was known as the earl of Richmond, even though the Richmond estates of his father had been given to Edward IV's brother, George, duke of Clarence. He was apparently educated with care, in grammar by two Oxford graduates, Edward Haseley and Andrew Scot, who were rewarded years later when Henry became king. More practical instruction – perhaps in the military arts – may have been given him by Sir Hugh Johns. He was a man of some influence and property in Gower, of which Herbert was lord in the 1460s, and his commemorative brass still survives in St. Mary's Church, Swansea. It was presumably through the Herbert connection that Sir Hugh was able to do the young Henry service 'in his tender age' – for which Henry gave him a £10 gift in 1485.

Great Gatehouse and (right) Closet Tower of Raglan Castle, Gwent. Built in the 1460s while Henry Tudor was in residence, Raglan became a veritable palace during William, Lord Herbert's lifetime.

Henry's mother, Margaret Beaufort, had been separated from her son. In the early part of 1457, within months of the death of Edmund Tudor, she married Henry Stafford, with whom she appears to have been happy. Certainly after the fall of Pembroke Castle, Margaret only saw her son intermittently. For one thing, geography separated them, for Margaret lived with Henry Stafford at Bourne in Lincolnshire and then at Woking in Surrey. And although she and Henry Stafford made their peace with Edward IV in 1461, young Henry did not return to her care. Nevertheless, Margaret seems to have been allowed to communicate with her son in the 1460s, and even to visit him at Raglan on at least one occasion.

Plots Galore

If military operations were now forlorn, plots could still be woven and held out some hope of reversing recent events. It was widely rumoured in England that Jasper Tudor and the other Lancastrian lords were planning a major co-ordinated assault on the Yorkist régime. A captured Lancastrian spy revealed that the duke of Exeter and Jasper would land at Beaumaris in Anglesey; the duke of Somerset and others were expected to invade East Anglia with an incredible 60,000 Spaniards; and a third army of Frenchmen and Spaniards would descend on Sandwich in Kent. Then, the kings of Aragon and Portugal, who were related to Henry VI, and the monarchs of France and Denmark, along with

Margaret of Anjou's father, would land in England with almost a quarter of a million men. The lynch-pin of this ambitious operation was said to be John de Vere, earl of Oxford, but in February 1462 he and his son Aubrey were arrested, tried and executed for treason. Exaggerated though these rumours were, Jasper Tudor's role in any Lancastrian offensive was bound to be crucial because he was the half-brother of the Lancastrian king. He was no longer earl of Pembroke and the title technically was in abeyance until – irony of ironies – Lord Herbert was granted the earldom in 1468. No one bothered to victimise Henry Tudor, who continued to use the style and title of earl of Richmond until Richard III finally deprived him of them in 1484.

In preparing for the great descent on England, Jasper Tudor made his way to Brittany, and he was still there in March 1462. The failure of the plot and the earl of Oxford's execution caused him to go to France and the court of King Louis XI, who might still be prepared to assist in an attack on Yorkist England. On 16 April Queen Margaret also arrived in Brittany from Scotland; she was welcomed and she travelled on to Angers to be reunited with her father and to meet King Louis.

In the years of intense Lancastrian lobbying that followed, Jasper Tudor played the part of an international emissary, tirelessly journeying between France, Brittany, Scotland and Wales in attempts to muster support for Henry VI, Queen Margaret and their son. He seems to have paid a brief visit to King Henry VI in Edinburgh, and early in June 1462 he arrived in Flanders and then made his way to Rouen in Normandy, carrying letters from Henry to Louis XI. Jasper went on to the elegant royal palace at Chinon in Touraine where, since 5 June, Queen Margaret and King Louis had been secretly negotiating an alliance between France and the Lancastrians. Jasper arrived to add his weight to these successful talks. On 24 June, therefore, a secret agreement was concluded whereby Louis undertook to lend Queen Margaret 20,000 *livres tournois* on condition that if Henry VI ever recovered Calais from the Yorkists either Jasper or Jean de Foix, who was earl of Kendal and another Lancastrian stalwart, should be made captain of it. The new captain would then swear an oath to hand Calais over to the French within a year or repay the French loan. In return for Calais, Louis promised that he would then pay Henry VI 40,000 crowns. Jasper was thus a party to an expensive agreement whereby, in return for desperately needed funds, the Lancastrians would surrender the colony of Calais which Edward III had won with difficulty in 1347. No wonder the treaty was a secret one!

From Chinon, the English negotiators travelled the short distance to the old city of Tours on the River Loire where, on 28 June 1462, a public treaty was signed, inaugurating a 100-year truce between Henry VI and Louis XI, each promising not to aid the enemies of the other. Jasper Tudor was one of those who signed the treaty of Tours and doubtless was well pleased with the outcome. With this aid, the Lancastrians now appeared to have acquired the full diplomatic support and financial backing of England's largest neighbour and oldest enemy, and a really determined attempt could be made once again to overthrow Edward IV.

From Tours, Margaret of Anjou moved north to Rouen and thence to

Boulogne; late in October, she set sail to join her husband in Scotland. From there, she and the king sailed south and landed in Northumberland, where Bamborough and Alnwick Castles fell into their hands. Jasper followed the queen from France and was one of those installed in Bamborough Castle to hold it for Henry VI. But news of the approach of an army under Edward IV himself caused Queen Margaret, her husband and a large number of their French force to flee back to Scotland. Their ships were battered by fierce winter storms which drove some of them onto the rocks or onto a hostile English coast. Meanwhile, the Lancastrian defenders left in Bamborough, Jasper among them, hoped against hope that the Scots would come to their aid. When they did not materialise, the fortress surrendered on Christmas Eve 1462. The duke of Somerset accepted a pardon and swore fealty to Edward IV; but Jasper and others could get no assurance that their forfeited estates would be restored to them (most of Jasper's had been given to Lord Herbert) and so they withdrew to Scotland. In any case, it is most unlikely that Jasper Tudor, King Henry's half-brother, would have accepted any terms that King Edward might offer.

Although it was rumoured by some that Jasper made his way to Ireland in the winter of 1462–3, to fish in its troubled waters, it is more than likely that he in fact returned to France with Queen Margaret to continue their intrigues there. Their aim was to induce Louis XI to give them yet further aid and to prevent any improvement in his relations with Edward IV. Jasper left Scotland in April 1463 and landed at Sluys in Flanders, where the duke of Burgundy, Philip the Good, allowed them to travel to Lille and Tournai on their way to meet King Louis. At the end of July, Margaret of Anjou and her son followed, and she spent the summer of 1463 trying to prevent Louis from being reconciled with King Edward. She failed, and after the Anglo-French truce of Hesdin in the Pas de Calais on 8 October 1463, only Scotland remained available as a refuge and a source of assistance for the fugitive Lancastrians. Nevertheless, Jasper remained at King Louis's court until December; but then he made plans to return once again to Scotland, with a mere 500 *livres tournois* from King Louis in his pocket. Disconsolate, Queen Margaret stayed in France for the next seven years.

It is difficult not to admire the dogged persistence of the Lancastrian leadership when faced with these crushing military and diplomatic defeats. That they continued to work for Edward IV's overthrow and the rupture of the Anglo-French truce must partly be attributed to Jasper Tudor's unshakeable faith in his half-brother's cause. Not only did he rejoin Henry VI in Scotland, but so also did the duke of Somerset, who had soon deserted King Edward. And at the very end of 1463 there arrived at Bamborough, where Henry VI was then staying, an envoy from Francis II, duke of Brittany, who was still sympathetic to Henry's plight. This envoy, Guillaume de Cousinot, reported to Francis on Henry's popularity in England, the danger he was in, and his need for food, materials and men. These should, Cousinot explained, be sent to Henry himself or to Jasper Tudor in Wales.

Cousinot left Bamborough in February 1464 and Jasper Tudor followed soon afterwards. In March Jasper was in Brittany with letters from Louis XI which urged Francis to give all the aid he could to enable Jasper to return to Wales. Jasper's Welsh homeland was now to be at the centre of his plans in a further

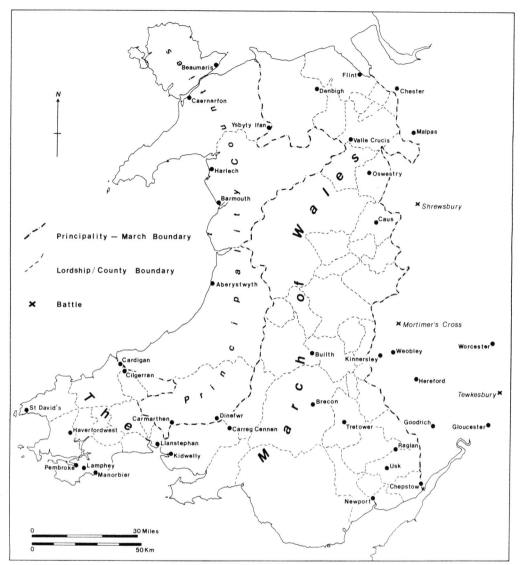

Map B: Wales during the Wars of the Roses.

phase of the struggle against the Yorkists. On 26 March 1464, Duke Francis gave Jasper and his men permission to sail. A fleet of ships from St. Malo and the estuary of the River Rance was placed at their disposal under the command of the vice-admiral of Brittany, Alain de la Motte. Several minor incidents that coincided with Jasper's expedition in the early months of 1464 – disturbances in East Anglia, Gloucestershire, Carmarthenshire, Cheshire, Lancashire and North Wales – had little success and were ruthlessly suppressed. As a result, there is no evidence that Jasper actually landed in Wales in 1464. He may have considered it wiser to remain in Brittany when news of the abortive risings reached him. Moreover, Louis XI, the new ally of Edward IV, was now much less enthusiastic about supporting the exiled Lancastrians, and in June 1464 he urged Francis II to withdraw his aid from Jasper. Francis understandably was puzzled and irritated by the king's change of heart.

Destination Wales

The west and north-west of Wales was the region least amenable to Yorkist rule in the mid-1460s. Although Lord Herbert was able to force most of the castles to surrender in 1461–2, even great Carreg Cennen in the uplands of Carmarthenshire, Harlech stood unsubdued in Lancastrian hands until 1468. And tension continued in counties like Carmarthenshire, Cardiganshire, Merioneth and Caernarfonshire. In 1464–5 the walls of Carmarthen Castle were repaired and the garrisons at Cardigan and Aberystwyth were kept up to strength. Spies were sent by Lord Herbert to glean information about the situation at Harlech, and the north-west generally was not to be trusted 'considering our rebels be daily in the said country' (November 1467).

Several Welsh poets, echoing the sentiments of their patrons among the landowners of North and West Wales, looked on Jasper as an intrepid hero in the 1460s. Until 1461 he was the only Welshman living who had reached the English peerage and he, above all others, bore the banner of the house of Lancaster where there was widespread sympathy for the fallen dynasty. This was the frame of mind in which the poets looked forward in verse to his return to Wales and further adventures against Yorkist authority. Lewis Glyn Cothi from Carmarthenshire even joined Jasper and other insurgents as they raided in North Wales. Tudur Penllyn, a northern poet, wrote romantically about the house at Barmouth from which Jasper sailed to Brittany after one of his forays, and he praised Jasper's ally in the area, Gruffydd Fychan of Corsygedol, who had built the house and was helping to defend Harlech Castle when all other strongholds had fallen to Lord Herbert. A poet from Llangollen, further to the east, wrote admiringly of the agility with which Jasper flitted in and out of North Wales from the Dyfi estuary. And yet another impatiently lamented that Jasper relied too much on men from Northern England – and perhaps spent too much time there – and would do better to come to Wales. These were longings, hopes and expressions of praise for a Welsh nobleman who was a Lancastrian. In no real sense did these poets and their patrons look on Jasper as some kind of freedom-fighter who would cast off English chains, even less seize the English throne for himself or his young nephew Henry. That eventuality was far in the future in the 1460s.

Jasper Tudor, therefore, could still dream of launching a successful invasion of Wales provided he could bring sufficient forces with him and secure practical support from Lancastrian sympathisers in England. Much depended on the tides of European diplomacy, and in 1467–8 these began to flow in favour of Jasper and the Lancastrian cause. In the spring of 1468 Edward IV concluded alliances with the dukes of Burgundy and Brittany which made Louis XI of

* Tÿ Gwyn, the fifteenth-century house at Barmouth, Gwynedd, which Jasper Tudor allegedly used as a headquarters during the 1460s. A first-floor hall built by one of his associates, Gruffydd Fychan of Corsygedol, it was celebrated in verse by the contemporary poet Tudur Penllyn.*

France feel diplomatically vulnerable. Accordingly, Louis began to work to undermine these arrangements, and cast round for any weapon that would embarrass Edward IV. Jasper Tudor was to hand and Louis therefore took him under his wing once more. As early as September 1467, an Italian observer in Paris had heard that Jasper would soon be going to Wales and that Queen Margaret was giving him some of her supporters. However, Louis XI proceeded circumspectly, as always, and only on 1 June 1468 did he authorise his treasurer to provide Jasper with a modest flotilla of three ships and the small sum of 293 *livres tournois* for his journey to Wales.

This was a puny military expedition and as such was doomed to failure. Indeed, King Louis may not have been serious in equipping it: he may only have wished to embarrass Edward IV and not sponsor a full-scale, expensive rebellion against him. Jasper Tudor was the victim of this policy. Shortly after 24 June 1468, Jasper landed once again on Welsh soil, probably in the Dyfi estuary (as the poets record) and near to Harlech, the Lancastrians' last outpost in England and Wales. If Jasper could not give the garrison many fresh supplies or additional men, he could at least fortify their resolve. Indeed, Jasper struck out across North Wales towards Denbigh, and by the time he got there his force is said to have grown to 2,000 men, a figure by no means improbable especially in view of continuing support for the house of Lancaster in Wales. 'The old Lord Jasper and sometime earl of Pembroke . . . rode over the country and held many sessions and assizes in King Harry's name', recorded one English chronicler.

Harlech Castle, Gwynedd. This impregnable fortress, built by Edward I, withstood siege by the Yorkist forces far longer than any other castle. It gave Jasper Tudor a foothold on the Welsh coast before it capitulated in 1468.

This gesture was designed to show, if only momentarily, that Henry VI was still the true king of England and the fount of all justice, and Welsh poets recalled this and other of Jasper's bold adventures with pride and admiration. Having seized Denbigh, a castle and borough with strong personal links with Edward IV and his father, he burned it so that 'the new town . . . was clear defaced with fire by hostility'. According to the sixteenth-century antiquarian, Sir John Wynn of Gwydir, his great-great-grandfather was one of the Lancastrian partisans who served under Jasper at the ravaging of Denbigh. Nor was this the only area to suffer attack from Jasper's men: parts of the neighbouring county of Flintshire were devastated too. So spectacular was this lightning campaign that in July 1468 Milan's ambassador in Paris reported the events to Italy, adding that Margaret of Anjou was planning to meet Louis XI shortly in an attempt to persuade him to give Jasper even more help.

Jasper's *chevauchée* across North Wales from the west coast jolted Edward IV into tackling at long last the outstanding problem of Harlech Castle. On 3 July 1468 Lord Herbert and his brother-in-law, Lord Ferrers, were ordered to raise a substantial army, variously estimated at between seven and ten thousand strong, in the Welsh borderland. Two wings of this army converged on Harlech, one from the east and the other from the south. On 14 August the great fortress, built by Edward I, finally surrendered after only slight resistance.

As for Jasper, he outwitted his enemies yet again. He managed to give Lord Herbert's army the slip and was able to go into hiding. One story, preserved by the sixteenth-century chronicler, Elis Gruffydd, may relate to his activities in 1468. It tells how Jasper was hidden by a gentleman of Mostyn in Flintshire. In order to make good his escape by sea, he supposedly carried a load of peas-straw on his back like a peasant as he made his way to a ship moored not far away at Picton Pool. From there he sailed eventually to Brittany, more by his own skill, it was said, than by that of the sailors who manned the ship. If the journey was broken, this may have been the occasion when he stayed at Gruffydd Fychan's house at Barmouth before escaping by sea and making for a Breton port.

The capture of Harlech, which most contemporary chroniclers felt worth reporting, led to Jasper's greatest humiliation at Edward IV's hands. On 8 September 1468 Lord Herbert was given the earldom of Pembroke as his reward, but the new earl did not enjoy his new dignity for long. The king had gradually been alienating his most powerful supporter, the earl of Warwick, 'the Kingmaker'. By the spring of 1469, the rupture between the two men was complete and Warwick set about gathering an army to overawe King Edward. On 26 July 1469 Warwick decisively defeated at Edgecote a royal force composed mainly of Welshmen led by the new earl of Pembroke. Herbert was summarily executed after the battle, and so was his brother, Sir Richard Herbert. Jasper's earldom was vacant once more.

More significant, however, was the opportunity which this split in the ranks of the Yorkist establishment offered to the exiled Lancastrians, among them Jasper Tudor. From October 1469 until September 1470, Jasper was in France in the company and service of Louis XI, who paid him a monthly pension of 100 *livres tournois*. At this juncture, Louis's chief aim in his relations with England was to inconvenience Edward IV as much as he could and to prevent an Anglo-Burgundian alliance that would threaten France. When, therefore, Warwick and Edward IV's unstable brother, George, duke of Clarence, rebelled and crossed to France at the beginning of May 1470, Louis was glad to receive them. Warwick realised that he would never regain his dominance in England so long as Edward was king, nor could he rely on the feckless duke of Clarence as an alternative. Hence, Warwick and Louis XI began to work for the restoration of King Henry VI (who had been a captive in Edward's hands since 1465) and a marriage between Warwick's daughter and Henry's son, who was with his mother in France.

These astonishing proposals were coldly received initially by Margaret of Anjou. Warwick, after all, had played the major role in deposing her husband in 1460–1. But Louis was a persistent and persuasive mediator, and eventually the strong-willed queen relented. At Angers in the Loire Valley, on 25 July 1470, Edward, prince of Wales was betrothed to Anne Neville, and five days after that an agreement was reached about how to restore Henry VI to the English throne. Warwick and Jasper Tudor would proceed to England, to be followed after a suitable interval by the queen, her son and his Neville bride. Jasper was to be one of the principal architects of the restoration of his half-brother to the English throne.

Wales was Jasper's destination, not least because of the continuing loyalty to Henry VI of many of its inhabitants and Jasper's recent demonstration that he could attract considerable support in the north. However, after sailing from La Hogue in Normandy on 9 September in a large French fleet of sixty ships under the command of the admiral of France, no less, the invading army disembarked after nightfall four days later at Dartmouth and Plymouth in Devon. Jasper immediately set off for Wales to raise more men there; Warwick marched towards London. For the first time in ten years, Jasper's bravery and loyalty to the Lancastrian cause were to be rewarded. Few had been as steadfast as he in upholding the cause of his half-brother against heavy odds and despite repeated failure. Needless to say, his young nephew, Henry Tudor, did not figure at all prominently in his mind – except perhaps that he should be taken from Herbert custody in Raglan Castle and that his earldom of Richmond should be restored to him (and the earldom of Pembroke to Jasper) when the Lancastrian monarch was again on his throne.

After the Battle of Edgecote and the death of William Herbert, Henry Tudor may have stood in some danger, protected only by Herbert's widow. She took him to her family's home at Weobley in Herefordshire, perhaps for greater security. Margaret Beaufort now seized the opportunity to try to recover custody of her son from the Herbert family. But she may not have been able to transfer him to her own household before Edward IV himself was forced to flee into exile at the approach of Warwick and Jasper Tudor. At some point in these months, Sir Richard Corbet, who was married to a niece of Herbert's widow, took the boy under his protection and conveyed him to Hereford, where Henry was handed over to Jasper when he arrived in the city. Uncle and nephew were to spend the period of Henry VI's restoration in one another's company, getting to know one another and forging that close relationship which persisted right up to the end of Jasper's life a quarter of a century later.

6 A False Dawn, 1470–1

Edward IV was in Yorkshire when the Lancastrian army disembarked on the coast of Devon. Hopelessly outflanked and with little chance of reaching London before Warwick, the king's position was desperate, and on 2 October 1470 he fled to Holland. Four days later, Warwick entered London unopposed. He promptly released Henry VI from the Tower and restored him to the throne.

No one was better equipped than King Henry's half-brother, Jasper Tudor, to shoulder the task of consolidating the Lancastrian position in Wales. Prince Edward was only a boy and still in his mother's care in France. Jasper therefore took the prince's place in Wales as his 'general lieutenant'. But he did not stay there long. After being re-united with his nephew Henry at Hereford, he presumably took the boy with him to London before the end of October. On this visit, Henry joined his mother and her husband, Henry Stafford. On 28 October 1470 Jasper Tudor and Henry Stafford sat down to dinner together at Stafford's house, and two days later Margaret and her son rode from London to the Beaufort residence at Woking, where they stayed for over a week. Then Henry travelled with his mother and step-father to Maidenhead and Henley-on-Thames before parting from them on 12 November, presumably to rejoin his uncle Jasper. This may have been the last time that Henry, now thirteen, saw his mother before the victory at Bosworth in 1485.

According to several later writers, an extraordinary interview took place at about this time between King Henry and the young earl of Richmond, during which the saintly monarch foretold that the boy would one day succeed to the English throne. Is such an interview likely to have occurred?

It is not difficult to imagine that Henry VI would have received in audience the young son of his half-brother, Edmund Tudor. It is quite another matter to accept the story that Henry VI made such a prophecy. In the autumn of 1470, the long-term hopes of the Lancastrians centred on the king's own son, Prince Edward, who had yet to return from France. In any case, one or two other English noblemen had Lancastrian blood in their veins – notably the dukes of Exeter and Somerset – and George, duke of Clarence may have been promised the succession after Henry VI's own descendants as the price of his alliance with Warwick and Margaret of Anjou. And yet the old king, who had had very few relatives about him throughout his life and was fully conscious of the slender thread by which his dynasty hung, may well have regarded Henry Tudor, the son

Portrait of King Henry VI, by an unknown artist, c. 1518–23, though it is probably based on an original likeness. Edmund and Jasper Tudor were Henry's half-brothers.

of Margaret Beaufort, as an intimate member of the royal family. Some such acknowledgement by Henry VI at an audience with Jasper and his nephew could easily have been recalled after Bosworth, and invested with great significance, by those who were at the king's court fifteen years before – Jasper and Henry VII included. After 1485 it would have suited their purpose to represent Henry VI as a prophet as well as a saint.

Whatever the reality, there is no avoiding the fact that the first writer to report this supposed prediction by Henry VI is Bernard André, who was Henry VII's official historian and the author of an eulogy of the king which he penned towards the end of his reign. The story came to the notice of Polydore Vergil a few years later and then became part of the Tudor version of past events. According to Polydore Vergil,

> And so Jasper took the boy Henry from the wife of the Lord Herbert and brought him with himself a little after when he came to London unto King Henry. When the king saw the child, beholding within himself without speech a pretty space the haughty disposition therefore, he is reported to have said to the noble men there present, 'This truly, this is he unto whom we and our adversaries must yield and give over the dominion'.
>
> Thus the holy man showed it would come to pass that Henry should in time enjoy the kingdom.

Important practical matters were being decided in London at this time by Warwick and the restored Lancastrian government. Parliament was summoned and it sat from 26 November until Christmas. This Parliament dismantled much of Edward IV's work, and for Jasper Tudor this meant restoration to his earldom of Pembroke. As well as recovering his former title and estates, Jasper was also richly rewarded with other lands, especially the very extensive properties of the Herbert family in South Wales and the Marches. But his greatest windfalls came in 1471, when he was granted the substantial estate of Lord Powis and later, in conjunction with Warwick, the Welsh lordships of the duke of Buckingham. Both Powis and Buckingham were under age. All these grants immeasurably increased Jasper's wealth, prestige and territorial power. He now dominated a great triangle of land with its apex at Welshpool in North-East Wales and its other corners at Pembroke in the west and Gloucestershire in the east. Jasper's nephew was not so fortunate. Although he had enjoyed the title of earl of Richmond all along, the Richmond estates were still in the duke of Clarence's hands and, despite the efforts of Margaret Beaufort and her husband, they remained there during Henry VI's brief restoration. Not even Jasper's standing in the new régime could overcome the risks involved in forcing Clarence to transfer these lands to the young Henry Tudor.

Meanwhile, Jasper Tudor was busy in South Wales and the border shires. The Severn Valley was of special concern to the newly restored régime of Henry VI. It was probably felt that whereas much of Wales itself would rally to Jasper Tudor and the house of Lancaster, the loyalty of Herefordshire, Gloucestershire and the countryside of South-East Wales was uncertain. This region had been dominated by some of Edward IV's most trusted supporters – the Herberts of Raglan and Abergavenny, the Vaughans of Tretower and Bredwardine, and

Chepstow Castle, Gwent, from the east. This view shows the gatehouse of the castle, protected by the great Marten Tower. Chepstow became the initial refuge of Jasper Tudor following the Lancastrian defeat at Tewkesbury in 1471.

the Devereux family of Weobley and Bodenham. So, in the winter of 1470–1 Jasper was given extensive administrative and military powers there, including custody of Gloucester Castle.

After ten years spent in exile and in poverty, success doubtless was sweet, and as the king's half-brother Jasper had every expectation of continued royal generosity. Unfortunately, Henry VI's restoration was short-lived and its collapse bloody. On 12 March 1471 Edward IV returned from the Continent, landing in Yorkshire; he marched south, reaching London on 11 April. Three days later he defeated and killed Warwick at the Battle of Barnet, a little way north of the capital. He was then able to take custody of King Henry VI and immediately the entire Lancastrian régime was placed in serious jeopardy. Oblivious of these events and believing it to be safe to cross from France, Margaret of Anjou and her son, Prince Edward, had arrived at Weymouth on the very day of Warwick's defeat and death. She was devastated by the news from London. Nevertheless, Margaret, who was nothing if not resolute, set about gathering forces in the West Country and marched northwards towards the Welsh borderland, presumably in order to join forces with Jasper Tudor. Realising the seriousness of the situation and determined not to lose the initiative, Edward IV set off in pursuit of Margaret. They joined battle a little to the south of Tewkesbury on 4 May 1471. The day went to the house of York. Queen Margaret's army was routed and cut to pieces. Her son, Prince Edward, Henry VI's only heir, was one of those killed; his mother was captured very shortly afterwards. This was an utterly shattering defeat for the Lancastrian cause. With both Henry VI and Queen Margaret in captivity and the heir to the throne slain, the house of Lancaster was leaderless and Edward IV in an unassailable position.

While these decisive events were taking place, Jasper Tudor was moving up from South Wales with his forces. He was unable to reach Queen Margaret's army in time to prevent its destruction. Indeed, Jasper was still only near Chepstow when he heard news of the disaster. Henry Tudor was evidently with him, but his mother and step-father had already deserted the Lancastrian cause and had thrown in their lot with Edward IV. After a brief period of good fortune, the surviving Tudors faced a bleak future. Jasper was on the run once again, and this time Edmund's son was also a fugitive, with no one but his uncle to protect him.

7 The Years of Exile

The Flight to Brittany

The decisive defeat of Queen Margaret and her forces at Tewkesbury on 4 May 1471 was a disaster for the house of Lancaster – perhaps the greatest disaster it suffered during the Wars of the Roses. On hearing the devastating news from the battlefield, Jasper would have realised that the death of Prince Edward, only child of King Henry and Queen Margaret, and the execution of the childless Edmund Beaufort (whom the Lancastrians called duke of Somerset) left Henry Tudor as one of the few surviving male relatives of Henry VI. But worse was to come. During the night of 21 May, within hours of Edward IV's return to the capital in triumph, Henry VI died in mysterious circumstances in the Tower of London. Apprised of these facts, and in order to seek immediate personal safety for himself and his nephew, Jasper resolved to flee to France. Louis XI had befriended him in the past and had given him shelter when the future seemed bleak. Now that Jasper and Henry had to seek asylum, there was no better place than France in which to find it, and King Louis quickly recognised the value of the two noblemen as thorns with which to prick England's side.

Without waiting to challenge the victorious Yorkists, even though Edward IV soon left Tewkesbury for the Midlands, Jasper retreated with at least part of his army to the walled town of Chepstow, perched high on the Welsh bank of the River Wye. Sir Roger Vaughan of Tretower Court in Breconshire, a veteran Yorkist retainer, was sent by King Edward to capture the fleeing Tudors so as to reinforce his success at Tewkesbury. But Jasper turned the tables on Vaughan: the pursuer became the captive at Chepstow and was promptly beheaded. This drastic and ruthless act is said to have been in revenge for Vaughan's execution of Jasper's father, Owen Tudor, ten years before.

This settling of scores may have given the retreating Lancastrians some modest satisfaction, but it did not delay their flight westward to Jasper's lordship of Pembroke. At Pembroke, Henry's birthplace, the Tudors are said to have been besieged by Morgan ap Thomas, the grandson of Gruffydd ap Nicholas, who had dominated South-West Wales in the 1450s. Morgan and his men dug ditches and trenches around Pembroke to cut communications with those inside

Harbour and Castle Hill, Tenby, from a lithograph by G. Reinagle, c. 1830. The town, extending to the right, was strongly defended by Jasper Tudor, and from the harbour Jasper and Henry sailed for France in 1471.

and to discourage a break-out. After about eight days of hardship, relief came in the shape of Morgan's young brother, David, who was a long-time friend of Jasper and had managed to assemble 2,000 men to rescue him. It may seem surprising that Morgan, who had earlier shown himself to be loyal to the Lancastrian régime like his father and grandfather before him, should suddenly have turned on the Tudors in 1471. But he was married to one of Sir Roger Vaughan's daughters, and outrage at the treatment of his father-in-law in Chepstow may have superseded traditional family loyalties in Morgan's mind. The fugitives may also have encountered other hostile elements in South-West Wales, for William Herbert II, earl of Pembroke, and Lord Ferrers were despatched late in August to deal with Jasper Tudor and the other Lancastrians, and by October these commissioners were in Carmarthen. Nevertheless, Jasper and Henry were able to escape from Pembroke to the town of Tenby, whose walls Jasper had helped to reconstruct a dozen years before and whose port offered an opportunity for them to sail to France.

At Tenby Jasper hired a barque for himself, young Henry, and a number of friends and servants, and they set sail for the French coast sometime in early or mid-September. There is a strong tradition in Pembrokeshire that the small ship was made available by either Thomas White, the mayor of Tenby in 1471, or his son John. The Whites were prominent local merchants whose family may have been associated with Jasper in rebuilding Tenby's massive town walls and gateways which to this day retain some of the atmosphere of a heavily fortified medieval Welsh town. The beautifully carved and well preserved effigies of

Thomas and John White on their tombs in St. Mary's Church, Tenby, are eloquent witness to their wealth and prominence in the town in the late-fifteenth century. At sea, the Lancastrians ran into bad weather and storms soon blew them off course. After putting in briefly at the island of Jersey (or so tradition has it), they landed in Brittany, at the small fishing port of Le Conquet on the westernmost tip of the peninsula. News of their arrival had certainly reached London before the end of September.

The implications of the Tudors' flight were quickly appreciated at the English court. Whilst most were convinced that it was highly desirable for Edward IV to get his hands on the fugitives, many believed that skilful diplomacy alone could not achieve this result. Some were more sanguine and thought that Louis XI (whose friend and later biographer, Philippe de Commynes, was at the duke of Brittany's court and was able to inform his master about the new arrivals) would try to protect them and ensure that they had their freedom. Doubtless there were others who knew that Francis II, duke of Brittany, would look upon the Tudors as a valuable diplomatic weapon to be used in negotiations with both England and France. Indeed, soon after landing, Jasper made his way to the ducal court to seek asylum for himself and his nephew. As Philippe de Commynes later testified, Francis treated his guests with every courtesy; they were given the honours appropriate to English noblemen of royal blood, and they were assured that they could move freely about the duke's dominions. They were welcomed to Nantes, the great port and capital of Brittany in the south-east

Alabaster Tomb Effigies of (left) *Thomas White (d. 1482) and his son John (d. c. 1507) in St. Mary's Church, Tenby. Merchants and mayors of Tenby, their effigies show them dressed in townsmen's garb. One or both helped Jasper and Henry Tudor to escape to France in 1471.*

of the duchy, and from there they travelled west to Vannes, the charming hill-top town near the south coast where they were lodged in the duke's palace, the Château de l'Hermine. The speech of welcome which Francis II is said to have delivered to Jasper and his friends was turned into verse and published in 1562.

Diplomatic Pawns

From 1471 until Edward IV's death in April 1483, Jasper and Henry Tudor were relatively minor pawns in the conduct of diplomatic relations between England, France, Brittany and, to a certain extent, Burgundy. They were sought after by two kings and protected by a duke.

Edward IV regarded their presence in Brittany with intermittent concern, and on several occasions he sent envoys across the Channel to negotiate their return to England. Edward's trump card was the diplomatic, military and financial help which he could offer Francis II in his never-ending quest to maintain his duchy's independence from the French state.

In April 1472 Edward's valiant and talented brother-in-law, Anthony Wydeville, Earl Rivers, was sent to Brittany with a detachment of soldiers for the duke's service. They helped to throw back a French invasion and Rivers also negotiated a treaty with Duke Francis, at Châteaugiron on 11 September, which would be the prelude to an Anglo-Breton invasion of French territory. But English reinforcements sent over to Brittany at the end of the summer ran into disaster. Many of the soldiers fell ill and by November 1472 the rest were

Francis II (d. 1488), duke of Brittany, from his tomb effigy in Nantes Cathedral, Brittany. Duke Francis was Henry Tudor's most consistent protector during 1471–84. The tomb was carved c. 1502–7 by Michael Colombe and placed in the Carmelite Monastery; after the French Revolution it was transferred to the cathedral.

Château of Suscinio, on the Rhuys Peninsula, which encloses the Gulf of Morbihan in Southern Brittany. Jasper and Henry Tudor were placed in this secure fortress on a wild site by the sea in 1472–3. Built in the thirteenth century, it was used by the dukes of Brittany as a summer residence.

expected home any day. Meanwhile, the Norfolk knight, Sir John Paston, reported from London on 4 November that Breton envoys, led by Guillaume Guillemet, had arrived in England, apparently to negotiate more military aid for Brittany. So sensitive and delicate were relations with Brittany at this juncture that a rumour that Francis II had suddenly died spread like wildfire through the city. For their part, English ambassadors were well treated in Brittany, but Duke Francis showed no inclination to release the Tudors. He declared, with less candour than grandeur, that he could hardly hand them over in view of his earlier promise to protect them – an expression of chivalric virtue that was nothing more than a diplomatic counter. Francis did concede, however, that he would henceforth keep uncle and nephew under close surveillance and would restrict their movements. This was designed to mollify Edward IV, at least a little, and the king wrote to Francis promising more money and aid in return for such a welcome arrangement.

Louis XI was just as anxious as Edward IV to get his hands on the Tudors, who might be useful in putting pressure on Edward, especially in view of the latter's *rapprochement* with Charles the Rash, duke of Burgundy. The French monarch issued a stern rebuke to Francis II for detaining his unexpected visitors. In 1474 he sent to Francis's court, Guillaume Compaing, dean of the church of St. Pierre-en-Pont in Orléans. Compaing expressed Louis's strong objections to Breton negotiations with the English and also his outrage that

Francis should be holding prisoner Jasper Tudor, whom Louis had taken into his household in the 1460s and to whom he had given a pension. Compaing's orders were to secure the release of the Tudors, stressing their blood relationship with Louis himself, their original intention in 1471 to sail to France, and the significance of Jasper's pension. Francis replied with spirit that they were his enemies and the enemies of his ally, England; in any case, he added testily, they had not obtained a safeconduct to enable them to land and travel in Brittany. Louis, not unreasonably, denied that Jasper, as a royal pensioner, needed a safeconduct in any part of France, and he went so far as to say that the seizure of the Tudors was tantamount to a declaration of war on Louis himself. Moreover (the king reminded the duke), their landfall in Brittany had not been a hostile act but an accident and they ought to be as safe in Brittany as they undoubtedly would be in Paris. To cover all possibilities in this diplomatic exchange, Louis stated that if any of the English exiles should happen to commit a hostile act in Brittany, reparations were the appropriate answer, not the arrest of Jasper and Henry; after all, Louis stated, Edward IV, rather than Jasper and Henry, was the enemy of France. Finally, the French envoys demanded that if Francis II would not release them, he should keep them under strict control to prevent Edward IV from kidnapping them. This was the very least that Louis would accept and beyond this his envoy's efforts were unavailing.

To preserve his advantage and fulfill his promises to both Edward IV and Louis XI, Francis did place the Tudors under tighter control. By about October 1472 they had been taken to the secluded château of Suscinio, at Sarzeau on the Gulf of Morbihan, near St. Gildas's Abbey. This château belonged to the admiral of Brittany, Jean de Quelenhec, who fully supported Duke Francis's determination to protect Jasper and Henry, especially when it was rumoured that English envoys had instructions to kill Henry if they could not secure his extradition. The two noblemen stayed at Suscinio for about a year; after that, they were moved to Nantes because Suscinio seemed too easy of access from the sea. Early in 1474, when the diplomatic pressure from France and England intensified, Francis decided to separate uncle and nephew and to replace their English servants, who had gone into exile with them, with Breton guards. Jasper was lodged some twenty-five miles from Vannes in the fortress of Josselin, (which had recently been abandoned by the Vicomte Jehan de Rohan, who had entered Louis XI's service). Henry was sent not too far away to the château of Largöet, an immense seven-storeyed octagonal tower some 144 feet high known as the Tour d'Elven, which had only recently been rebuilt in the 1460s and was still not complete. Largöet belonged to the marshal of Brittany, Jean IV de Rieux, who treated his young guest with honour and consideration. The marshal's family included two sons who were doubtless able to make Henry Tudor feel at ease in his quarters on the sixth floor of the great *donjon*. If not quite enduring the rigours of imprisonment, Jasper and Henry can be regarded in the 1470s as being in Francis II's protective custody at the request of Edward IV and Louis XI and in the interests of the Tudors themselves and of their protector.

Gatehouse of the Château of Largoët, not far from Vannes, Brittany. The château belonged to Marshal de Rieux, one of Francis II's councillors, and Henry Tudor was kept in its massive keep, the Tour d'Elven, which rises behind. The gatehouse dates from the fifteenth century.

The Pace Quickens

During the late 1470s, the English and French kings were somewhat better placed to press their demands for the surrender of Jasper and Henry Tudor. For one thing, the failing health of the duke of Brittany led to personal and political rivalries at his court which affected Breton attitudes to the exiles. Although neither Brittany nor Burgundy had given practical assistance to the English expedition against France in July 1475, Edward IV was able to bring King Louis to the negotiating table. In effect, Louis bought off the English army with French gold at the treaty of Picquigny, which the two kings sealed on 29 August. Edward returned to England without military glory, booty or recaptured territory, but he had obtained a handsome pension, a seven-year truce, and the establishment of machinery by which to discuss future differences between England and France. Edward also extracted a promise from Louis that he would not attack Brittany. In the hope that Duke Francis would be grateful, Edward resumed his diplomatic offensive to get the Tudors into his hands. The matter had become a little more urgent as a result of the death of Henry Holand, duke of Exeter, whilst he was returning with the king's army from France. Exeter was a grandson of King Henry IV's elder sister, but in 1475 he had no surviving

Tour d'Elven, the octagonal keep, 144 feet and 6 storeys high, of the Château of Largoët, where Henry Tudor was kept in 1474–6. Built in the 1460s by Jean IV de Rieux, it was still not finished in 1475.

children, with the result that yet another offshoot of the Lancastrian royal house had perished. King Edward, therefore, had an added incentive to induce the duke of Brittany, with gifts and promises, to hand Henry Tudor over.

The English envoys to Brittany, their pockets full of gold, tried to persuade Francis to surrender the Tudor captives. This time they were the more persuasive because they claimed that Edward IV simply wanted to marry Henry Tudor to an English lady. Henry's mother, Margaret Beaufort, may have favoured this proposal, though for rather different reasons. After 1471, Margaret seems to have adopted a realistic attitude to her son's future in the hope that he would at least be allowed to return to England to recover his father's earldom of Richmond and inherit her Beaufort estates – not to speak of the lands of her own elderly mother, Margaret Beauchamp. As early as May 1472 Edward IV had acknowledged that some of Margaret Beaufort's estates should revert to her son when she died. Whether Edward was sincere in approving this arrangement or whether he was bent on getting Henry into his clutches by any available means may never be known. But the suggestion in 1476 that Henry should be found a suitable bride in England may have been part of the scheme his mother had in mind. If true, we may be sure that Edward had a reliable Yorkist lady in prospect as a wife for Henry Tudor, perhaps even one of his own daughters, so that he could bring this surviving Lancastrian nobleman under his control through matrimony, a stratagem that Edward had used on a number of other occasions in the past. As before, the envoys who carried this proposal to Brittany were courteously received, but Francis II proved as coy as ever in responding to overtures which he may or may not have found convincing.

Eventually, however, the duke gave way to persistent lobbying by Robert Stillington, the bishop of Bath and Wells. In about November 1476, by which time Henry and Jasper Tudor had been transferred under guard to Vannes, Francis II commended Henry Tudor to King Edward, apparently believing that he would treat the young man honourably and marry him to his own daughter, Elizabeth of York. With an English ship waiting off the north coast of Brittany, the jubilant envoys travelled with their precious charge to the port of St. Malo, there to embark for England. Their journey was interrupted because Henry suffered – or feigned – illness at St. Malo. It was a providential delay.

After several years of refusing to release the Tudors, Francis II had relented, partly because one of his most influential advisers who was also sympathetic to the Tudors' plight, Jean de Quelenhec, admiral of Brittany, happened to be away from court when the English envoys pressed their case most forcefully. When de Quelenhec returned, he remonstrated with Duke Francis, not least because the duke had broken the oath he had given to Jasper and Henry on their arrival in Brittany five years before. Francis had evidently succumbed to the combined pressure of the English ambassadors and those of his own councillors who hoped for greater personal and political rewards from a grateful English king. After de Quelenhec's return, other counsels reasserted themselves. Francis accordingly ordered his treasurer, Pierre Landais, to pursue the English party to St. Malo and to stop the ship from taking Henry to England. He arrived in the nick of time. Already delayed by Henry's illness, the envoys engaged in a long and difficult discussion with Landais. This gave Henry the opportunity to slip away and seek sanctuary in one of St. Malo's churches, possibly the cathedral. When the Englishmen made frantic efforts to winkle him out, the townsmen, who resented any threat to violate the privilege of sanctuary, sprang to his defence. A cavalier attitude to sanctuary rights may have been common in England towards the end of the fifteenth century, but it was not acceptable in Brittany.

When Henry returned to the Breton court, Francis II, who had recovered his health and his mastery of affairs, reassured him that he would not be handed over to Edward IV after all. The English envoys, having spent their money and lost their prize, complained bitterly. As a sop to their feelings, Landais agreed to do his best to make sure that Henry either was kept in sanctuary, out of harm's way, or else was placed in the duke's personal custody. Edward IV, in the person of his representatives, had gained custody of his quarry for only three days, and this short-lived success made him all the more bitter when his envoys reported the failure of their mission. Reassurances from Brittany were small comfort.

Henry Tudor was taken to the Château de l'Hermine in Vannes, where he

Château of Josselin, on the River Oust in Southern Brittany. Rebuilt in the 1370s, it passed to the de Rohan family in the fifteenth century, and after Jean II de Rohan joined Louis XI's service, it was in Francis II's hands. Jasper Tudor was kept here in 1474–6. The remains of the great keep are on the right. The Flamboyant additions date from c. 1500.

was joined by his uncle Jasper from Josselin. Some say that Henry went back to Largöet, though the accounts of the receiver of the château there make it clear that he was not in residence by 1481.

In the meantime, Louis XI continued to exert his pressure on Duke Francis. He sent envoys to Brittany, partly to urge the release of the Tudor exiles. The admiral of Guienne, Guillaume de Soupplainville, led an important mission to Nantes just before Christmas 1476, probably in response to news that at St. Malo Henry had only narrowly escaped repatriation. Louis demanded that he be handed over to de Soupplainville, but the envoys returned empty-handed to France at the beginning of 1477. Nevertheless, Francis II was in an increasingly precarious situation in relation to his two powerful neighbours, England and France, whose pressures upon him were becoming more and more intense.

Francis sent his own envoy, Jacques de Villeon, seneschal of Rennes, to England in 1479 to secure an assurance of Edward IV's friendship: inevitably, a further request for the surrender of Jasper and Henry was made. And new English envoys crossed to Brittany in 1482. They took with them 3,000 *livres* in silver bullion, and on 20 February Edward informed Francis that he was prepared, at a month's notice, to send 4,000 archers from Plymouth and

Prison Tower of the Château of Josselin, Brittany, with part of the stout curtain wall attached. Jasper Tudor may have lived in this tower during 1474–6.

Dartmouth to serve in Brittany for three months at his own expense; thereafter the duke would have to foot the bill for their wages and expenses.

At the same time, Edward IV and Margaret Beaufort, for different reasons, did not abandon hope of enticing Henry home by dangling rich estates and an attractive bride before his (and Duke Francis's) eyes. It had almost worked in 1476. In June 1482, the arrangements made in 1472 for the disposition of the Beaufort estates in the event of Margaret's death were confirmed and approved by Edward; but he tightened the screw. If Henry were to return to England and be admitted to the king's favour, he would receive an even larger share of his mother's lands, worth about £400 a year; but if he did not return, he would have none. As to a suitable marriage, in the 1470s Edward IV and Margaret Beaufort discussed (so several people recalled later) their close blood relationship which was an impediment if a marriage between Henry and Elizabeth of York were to be contemplated.

Matters stood thus when Edward IV died on 9 April 1483. The position of Francis II – and therefore the safety of Jasper and Henry – was yearly becoming more difficult to sustain. But the personal circumstances of the Tudors seem to have been tolerable enough. Henry had grown into a personable teenager, under some gentle restraint, it is true; but he was nevertheless welcome at the ducal court. The Burgundian chronicler, Jean Molinet, writing some twenty years later, described him as a 'pleasant and elegant person' and a fine ornament of the court of Francis II. Uncle and nephew enjoyed personal allowances to enable them to live with their own households in reasonable comfort and they were assigned Breton guardians who were well paid for their services. Jasper's custodian by 1476 was Bertrand du Parc, one of Duke Francis's commanders and master of his artillery. In 1481–2 Bertrand was being paid 600 *livres* a year for the expenses of Jasper's household, including 40 *livres* which went on Jasper's personal needs. Henry was placed at first in the charge of Vincent de la Landette, but he soon had two guardians, Jehan Guillemet, one of the duke's retainers, and Louis de Kermené. In 1481–2 these two men received the much larger sum of 2,000 *livres* to cover the expenses of a household that reflected Henry's dynastic significance; as much as 620 *livres* were assigned for Henry's own use. When, on 1 October 1482, de Kermené was replaced by Jean de Robihan, Francis II increased Henry's allowance even further, to 2,200 *livres* a year.

The Crisis in England

Edward IV's death in April 1483 and the accession of his twelve-year-old son as Edward V were followed by the *coup d'état* of the new king's uncle, Richard, duke of Gloucester, and by Richard's seizure of the throne on 26 June. None of this initially affected the Tudors in Brittany. Nevertheless, the political instability which these events created in England led both Francis II and Louis XI to believe that the Tudor exiles could be used to exert greater pressure on England's new ruler. When news of Edward's death became known in Brittany, Francis eased further the conditions of Henry's custody and restored his freedom of movement, something which must have disturbed the government at Westminster. Moreover, early in May 1483, at the height of the struggle between Richard of Gloucester and Queen Elizabeth Wydeville and her family, Sir Edward Wydeville and an English fleet slipped out of the Thames and made for Brittany, though only two of the ships actually joined Sir Edward in exile there. It was natural, therefore, that when Richard of Gloucester seized the throne in June he did not tarry long before sending ambassadors to establish cordial relations with Francis II and, if possible, to secure what had always eluded Edward IV, the extradition of Jasper and Henry Tudor. Richard also wrote in friendly fashion to Louis XI, who responded on 21 July with an effusive offer to do whatever he could for the new king of England.

Richard's envoy to Nantes, Thomas Hutton, one of the king's clerks and a canon of Lincoln Cathedral, was given his commission on 13 July. The letters which he carried from the king authorised him to renew the truce between England and Brittany and to improve commercial relations between them. What was more to the immediate point, Hutton was instructed to discover Francis II's intentions with regard to Sir Edward Wydeville and his ships, and in particular whether any hostile action was being planned against England. It is inconceivable that Hutton would have let slip the opportunity to raise the question of the Tudors, but for the moment there were more immediate

Portrait of King Louis XI (d. 1483) of France, attributed to Jean Bourdichon, the court artist from Tours. It conveys something of his physical unattractiveness and even of the scheming nature that earned him the nickname of 'Universal Spider'.

irritations in Anglo-Breton relations and the establishment of friendly relations with Duke Francis was Richard's priority.

Hutton's mission was matched by a visit to England by Francis's secretary, Master François Dupon. Then, on 26 August, Georges de Mainbier was sent to King Richard's court. Though he rose to become Francis's secretary in 1485, de Mainbier was not a particularly prominent servant of the duke in 1483 and Francis felt it necessary to explain his appointment as an envoy by saying that the Breton Estates (or Parliament) were about to meet and a more senior diplomat could not be spared at the moment. Lest Richard and his ministers take offence, Francis assured them that additional ambassadors would be sent to England as soon as the Estates had been prorogued. In the meantime, de Mainbier related Francis's view that, in relation to Henry Tudor, Richard should remember that King Louis XI was still threatening Brittany and that, as in Edward IV's time, Francis needed English archers, 4,000 paid for by the English government and a further 3,000 whom the duke would himself pay. This was a pointed reminder to the new king of England that he could not afford to offend the Breton duke unless he were prepared to see the French swarming into Brittany and occupying the coastline directly opposite England. In these circumstances, Henry Tudor seemed no less secure in Brittany in the summer of 1483 than he had during Edward IV's later years. Nor did he seem a greater threat to the Yorkist dynasty than in the past.

Margaret Beaufort may have been more sanguine about the future of her son and heir, and perhaps just as anxious to secure his return to England as she had been all along. The mid-sixteenth-century chronicler, Edward Hall, claims that after Richard III's accession she discussed with the new king's closest confidant, Henry Stafford, duke of Buckingham, whom she knew well as the elder brother of her third husband, Henry Stafford, the earlier proposal that Henry Tudor should marry one of Edward IV's daughters, presumably the eldest, Elizabeth of York. However, their blood relationship remained an impediment to such a match. At various times since the early 1470s, high-ranking ecclesiastics and lawyers, including Archbishop Rotheram of York, Bishop Morton of Ely and Bishop Alcock of Worcester, had been overheard discussing the question, sometimes in the company of Margaret Beaufort's servants. Such discussions are likely to have continued in 1483, as Margaret Beaufort strove to engineer the return of her son to his rightful place among the ranks of the English nobility. At the same time, they may well have begun to take on more startling significance as the deep rifts within the Yorkist royal family unfolded during the early summer of 1483.

8 Claimant to a Throne

The situation was dramatically altered by the consequences of Richard III's usurpation: the disappearance of his nephews, Edward V and Richard, duke of York; the rumours of their death that were current in London by the end of July 1483; and by the rebellion of the duke of Buckingham in October, followed by his execution on 2 November.

Buckingham's Conspiracy

In the late summer of 1483, Henry Tudor became the focus of at least two conspiracies against Richard III. These conspiracies had independent origins and need not initially have had identical aims; but their common antipathy towards the king enabled them to combine in an elaborate and secret plot. They sprang from Richard's violent seizure of the crown, the summary and illegal executions which accompanied it, and above all the growing belief that 'the Princes in the Tower' had been murdered.

One conspiracy was hatched in Brecon Castle by Henry Stafford, duke of Buckingham, and John Morton, bishop of Ely. In 1483, Buckingham, Henry Tudor and King Richard were the sole surviving adult males in England of the Plantagenet dynasty. The duke's frame of mind in August and September 1483 is not easy to gauge. Historians nowadays discount the traditional theory that he resented the way in which Richard III refused to grant him those lands of the earldom of Hereford which Buckingham's grandmother had conceded to the Lancastrian royal family in 1421 and to which he had a good claim since that family's extinction in 1471. Richard III in fact did restore these estates to him on 13 July 1483, but the king's grant was never formally enrolled. Furthermore, it ultimately depended on an act being introduced in Parliament, and Buckingham was awarded the estate's income only from Easter 1483. Whether this was sufficient to cause the duke to rebel is a moot point. As an alternative explanation for the rebellion, we may wonder whether Buckingham feared for his own safety in Ricardian England, having had an excellent opportunity to assess the results of the usurpation and the bloody methods which Richard was prepared to use. Moreover, if Richard's actions were to result in a major uprising against him, Buckingham may well have concluded that he should offer himself as an alternative king in the absence of Edward IV's sons. When

Yorkist Royal Family, from the north-west transept window of Canterbury Cathedral. Edward IV and his queen, Elizabeth Wydeville, appear with (left) *their sons Edward V and Richard ('The Princes in the Tower'), and* (right) *five of their daughters, led by the eldest Elizabeth, who married Henry VII. The window may date from the last few years of Edward IV's reign.*

Buckingham said his farewells to Richard at Gloucester on about 2 August 1483 – the king to continue his tour of Midland England and Buckingham to visit his castle at Brecon – the duke may have had the seed of a plot germinating in his mind. If so, it was carefully nurtured by Bishop Morton.

This prelate had been arrested by Richard III at the dramatic Council meeting in the Tower of London on 13 June 1483 that was the prelude to Richard's seizure of the crown. Morton was placed in Buckingham's custody, for not even Richard dared execute a prince of the church at such a precarious stage in his career. Opinions differ as to who took the initiative in the plotting at Brecon. Sir Thomas More, who much admired Morton and who had lived in his household as a youth, gives considerable prominence to the bishop and records in his *The History of Richard III* that it was Morton who induced Buckingham to turn against the king. On the other hand, Polydore Vergil, the Italian historian who was employed by Henry VII and Henry VIII, had no such special loyalty to cloud his vision. He suggested that it was Buckingham who first broached the subject of rebellion, and that the suspicious Morton thought it a device to engineer his downfall and accordingly pleaded for his life. But (continued Vergil) when Morton realised that Buckingham was serious, he readily co-operated.

If Buckingham's motives are elusive, his precise plan is no easier to reconstruct. Both Sir Thomas More and Polydore Vergil record that it centred on the claim of Henry Tudor to the English crown and the prospect of uniting the royal houses of Lancaster and York by a marriage between Henry and Edward IV's daughter, Elizabeth of York. However much they differed about Morton's role, both More and Vergil were avowedly Tudor propagandists who popularised the idea that there was a consistent plan to put Henry on the throne from the summer of 1483 onwards. It seemed logical to them to maintain that Buckingham endorsed it. Yet there must remain some doubt as to whether Buckingham supported such a plan from the outset, rather than advancing his own dynastic claim. Would he have abandoned the king he had helped to the throne and who had patronised him handsomely only to subordinate his own interests to those of a future Tudor monarch? His father's sympathies may have been Lancastrian, but in the summer of 1483 it was far from clear that Buckingham could best serve himself and his family by supporting Henry Tudor. What may have changed an initial attitude was the news that a second conspiracy existed, and its aim was undoubtedly to bring Henry to England and put him on Richard's throne.

The Beaufort-Wydeville Conspiracy

Soon after Richard's coronation on 6 July 1483, there was a small disturbance in London organised by some of Edward IV's servants. Their aim was to set fire to part of the city, rescue the two princes from the Tower (presumably in order to restore Edward V to his throne) and communicate with Henry and Jasper Tudor in Brittany, perhaps to encourage them to return to England. The common belief some weeks later that the princes were dead immediately shot Henry to prominence as a prospective king himself. Early in August, his mother's half-brother, John Welles, led another rising at the Beaufort residence at Maxey in Northamptonshire, and when it failed he fled to join Henry in Brittany.

Contact between Buckingham and a 'Tudor movement' seems to have been made by Bishop Morton and his friends. According to Polydore Vergil, Morton managed to summon to Brecon a servant of Margaret Beaufort, who had been attempting to safeguard her son's interests for the past twelve years. This servant was Reginald Bray, whom Margaret and Buckingham knew long before when he was receiver-general of the estates of her third husband, Henry Stafford. After visiting Brecon, Bray was able to inform Margaret of the plans which Buckingham and Morton had been laying. For his part, Bray may have been able to tell them of a separate conspiracy that was beginning to form in and around the Beaufort household. At what point Margaret turned from seeking the restoration to Henry Tudor of his English inheritance to plotting his accession to the throne is unclear. But the disappearance of the princes was probably a crucial factor in making up her mind.

It was an enormous asset to this conspiracy to be able to attract the support of Edward IV's widow, Queen Elizabeth Wydeville. Rumours of her sons' deaths were bound to inflame the dowager-queen and alienate her from Richard III. This gave Margaret Beaufort and Elizabeth Wydeville a common cause. Contact between them was established by Margaret's physician, the Welshman Lewis Caerleon. A noted doctor with degrees from the University of Cambridge, he was even more distinguished as an astronomer and mathematician. He was a

Portrait of Lady Margaret Beaufort at prayer, from a painting in St. John's College, Cambridge, which she patronised. Her arms and the Beaufort portcullis are behind her, the Tudor rose above. Although Margaret was prepared to come to terms with Edward IV to secure her son's return from Brittany, after Richard III's usurpation she plotted for Henry's accession and remained his close confidante until he died shortly before Margaret herself (1509).

prolific writer in both these fields, and a number of his books and his commentaries on other people's works can still be seen in the libraries of Oxford and Cambridge. He had been patronised by some of the leading intellectuals at Henry VI's court; and in an age when the study of astrology was compulsive, his observations of the stars and their movements and of the sun's eclipses may have led him to make predictions about the fate of Richard III just as he had offered a horoscope to Henry VI in 1441. By 1482 Lewis was practising medicine in London and it is not at all surprising that he was consulted by both Margaret Beaufort and Queen Elizabeth; indeed, in 1494 he was still serving the queen's eldest daughter, by then herself a queen. Presumably because of his treasonable activities in the summer of 1483, Richard III clapped Lewis Caerleon in the Tower and seized all his possessions, though he continued to write and to observe the heavens from behind the walls of the Tower. He was rewarded by Henry VII for his professional and other services, and among the latter we may confidently include acting as an intermediary between Margaret and Elizabeth Wydeville in 1483.

When Dr. Lewis visited Queen Elizabeth Wydeville in sanctuary at Westminster (whence she had retired as Richard of Gloucester approached London from the north at the beginning of May 1483) it was relatively easy for him to carry messages to and from Margaret Beaufort on the subject of a marriage between Henry Tudor and either Elizabeth of York or, if Elizabeth should die, her younger sister Cecily. Elizabeth Wydeville was much in favour of Margaret's proposal – it had, of course, been in the air for years already – and sent an encouraging message to the London inn of Margaret's fourth husband, Thomas, Lord Stanley. Elizabeth Wydeville promised to urge her own and Edward IV's friends and servants to give it their support too, aware that it implied an attempt to replace Richard on the throne. As for Margaret, she used her agent, Reginald Bray, to attract others into the conspiracy, especially young servants of Edward IV from Southern England like Sir Giles Daubeney, Richard Guildford, Thomas Rameney and John Cheyne, each of whom swore an oath to adhere to the ladies' plan.

A wife and a crown are two of the weightiest obligations any man can undertake, and it was essential in 1483 that Henry Tudor be informed as soon as possible of the details of the conspiracy organised in his name. As her agent, Margaret sent to Brittany Christopher Urswick, a young priest whom she took into her household on the recommendation of Lewis Caerleon. The intention was that he should go to Brittany to tell Henry all about the alliance with Queen Elizabeth Wydeville and the nature of the conspiracy that was designed to place him and Elizabeth of York on the throne. Henry was well aware that his name had been linked with that of Elizabeth in the past, but the dynastic significance of the latest proposal was a new dimension.

Before Urswick could leave on his mission, Margaret Beaufort received news, *via* Reginald Bray, of what was happening at Brecon. Accordingly, she stopped Urswick leaving and instead sent a more urgent, practical mission, led by another of Edward IV's former servants, Hugh Conway. The choice of Conway as Margaret's confidential messenger may have been an exceptionally significant one. He came from North-East Wales, where the Stanleys had long been

Wood-Panel Painting of Elizabeth Wydeville (d. 1492), queen of Edward IV. The rumoured death of her sons, Edward V and Richard, duke of York, in 1483 led her to conspire with Margaret Beaufort to bring Henry Tudor to England and marry him to her daughter Elizabeth. This may be a copy of a painting by John Stratford painted at the time of Elizabeth's marriage to Edward IV in 1464.

Sir Reginald Bray (d. 1503), in the window which he probably gave to Great Malvern Priory Church, Worcestershire, c. 1500. Bray moved from the employ of the Stafford family to serve Margaret Beaufort; he was one of her agents communicating with Henry Tudor in Brittany. He became an intimate adviser of Henry VII after 1485.

dominant. Margaret Beaufort was not only married to Thomas, Lord Stanley, but she had conducted her secret correspondence with Queen Elizabeth Wydeville from Stanley's London inn. The Conways' principal seat was at Bodrhyddan in Flintshire, and the family owned property in the small colonial borough founded at Rhuddlan by Edward I. Hugh was the son of the elder John Conway, who died in 1486. By 1456, John had married as his second wife Jonet, the daughter of Edmund Stanley of Ewloe, and this marriage may have brought young Hugh into the Stanley circle in North-West England and the Welsh borderland. Some years later, Hugh moved to the king's court, and by 1464–5 he was a servant in Edward IV's household, where he prospered – as did Lord Stanley. As a result, he married a high-born wife, Elizabeth, the younger sister of the Lancastrian earl of Devon who had been executed in 1461. In 1481, still as one of King Edward's servants, he was given a tenement in Mark (or Mart) Lane in the city of London. Thus, by 1483, Hugh was in the Stanley circle (and therefore came in contact with Margaret Beaufort) and had spent twenty years at the Yorkist court (and hence came to know Queen Elizabeth Wydeville). After Richard III's *coup d'etat*, he was an ideal agent to be used by both women. Hugh was accordingly highly favoured by Henry VII, who appointed him keeper of his great wardrobe for life within a month of the Battle of Bosworth. And Hugh retained his connection with the Stanleys, serving on a commission in 1486 with Lord Thomas, now earl of Derby.

In 1483, Hugh took with him to Brittany a large sum of money raised by loans negotiated by Margaret Beaufort in the city of London and elsewhere. He was instructed to urge Henry Tudor to come as soon as possible and land in Wales, where substantial aid could be expected, notably from the duke of Buckingham. Lest a hitch occur, two other messengers from Kent were sent posthaste after Conway: Richard Guildford, whose father had been controller of Edward IV's household, and Thomas Rameney took essentially the same message and seem to have reached Henry almost simultaneously. The link between the Beaufort-Stanley household and the Edwardian-Wydeville retinue seemed to be working well, and the various agents gave Henry his first clear sign that, after twelve years, his exile might soon be over and that a realistic plan was afoot to bring him to England in triumph – and to claim what previously can hardly have been more than a dream, the English crown.

The Risings of October 1483

On 24 September 1483, the duke of Buckingham himself wrote to Henry Tudor, indicating his association with the Beaufort-Wydeville conspiracy, even though his and Henry's interests where incompatible in some particulars. Despite the assertions of sixteenth-century writers, it would be rash to assume that Buckingham endorsed Henry's claim to the throne or the marriage with Elizabeth of York as a means of ending the Wars of the Roses and deposing Richard III. When he wrote the letter, he may have had more immediate concerns in mind; he may have felt that he could tackle the thorny question of who should have primacy in the kingdom once Richard was out of the way. Thus, when he wrote to Henry on 24 September, he informed him that his own rebellion would begin on 18 October and he invited him to join in. He made no pretence of acknowledging Henry as the next king of England or of welcoming his marriage to Elizabeth of York. In the fraught circumstances of 1483, with conspirators as far apart as Brecon, London and Southern Brittany, precise political and constitutional aims were difficult to discuss, let alone reconcile; in any case, conspiracies and secret negotiations and messages were naturally imperfectly known to contemporaries and to chroniclers. Knowledge of the eventual outcome – the failure of Buckingham's rebellion and the accession of Henry Tudor and Elizabeth of York – may have warped the perceptions of later writers and created in their writings an irresistible Tudor chronology out of what were the confused and crowded events of the summer of 1483.

After Henry had received his mother's envoys and the letter from Buckingham, he conferred with Duke Francis II, whose approval and assistance were essential if he were to return to England or Wales. In his enthusiasm, Henry promised to repay whatever Francis gave him; he may even have undertaken to transfer to the duke the honour of Richmond, which dukes of Brittany had enjoyed until the end of the fourteenth century. Despite the

Tomb of John Morton (d. 1500), bishop of Ely (1478), archbishop of Canterbury (1486) and cardinal (1493). Servant of Lancastrian, Yorkist and Tudor kings, he played a crucial role in the conspiracies against Richard III in 1483–5. The carved symbols round his tomb in Canterbury Cathedral include the Beaufort portcullis, the Tudor rose and crown, and his own eagle on a tun.

exchange of envoys with Richard III, Francis promised to support Henry's venture; according to Polydore Vergil, he did so willingly. Meanwhile, in England many were expectant: some were restless and seditious; others, prompted by Bishop Morton, formed an underground network of messengers to alert any who had cause to fear or hate King Richard.

Richard III seems to have been taken by surprise by news of Buckingham's defection and therefore he had no army ready to suppress a serious rising. The disturbances of the summer could be put down to resentment at the usurpation. Even at the end of September, Richard may not have had any inkling that the duke was about to desert him. His dismissal on 23 September of Bishop Morton's nephew, Robert, from his post as master of the rolls at the royal Chancery, and his seizure of the worldly possessions (as opposed to the spiritual authority) of Bishop Wydeville of Salisbury the same day, may simply have been a wise precaution against two families that were known to be hostile to him. But not long afterwards, hearing from his informants that something more serious was afoot, Richard summoned the duke of Buckingham to him. Knowing all too well King Richard's record for ruthless treatment of his enemies, Buckingham feigned a stomach illness so that Richard had to send a more sternly-worded order for him to come to court. Buckingham refused and prepared for a confrontation. At last, by 11 October, when he was in Lincolnshire, Richard was fully informed as to Buckingham's intentions and he hastily set about assembling a force of men. He had probably been alerted by a premature outbreak of violence in the Weald of Kent, for on 10 October the duke of Norfolk reported from London that the city was under threat of attack from the Kentishmen. According to the government, a series of risings was scheduled to begin on 18 October, and it is possible that the to-ing and fro-ing of agents and messengers had succeeded in co-ordinating them. Yet Richard III did not allow the shock he undoubtedly felt at being betrayed by his most intimate collaborator to dictate all his actions. He carefully advised loyalists not to 'rob, spoil or hurt any of the tenants, officers or other persons belonging to the said Duke . . . so that they raise not nor made commotions or assemblies'. This policy of calculated restraint was eminently successful.

The duke of Buckingham assembled a force at Brecon and elsewhere on his estates in the March of Wales; but he encountered difficulties because many of his tenants were reluctant to join a rebellion against a Yorkist king. Thomas Grey, marquess of Dorset, the son of Queen Elizabeth Wydeville by her first husband, had escaped from sanctuary at Westminster and appeared in Yorkshire, although he soon made his way south. At Exeter on the eighteenth, he led a rising with Sir Thomas St. Leger, Edward IV's brother-in-law, Sir Robert Willoughby, a loyal West Country knight, and the Courtenays, Edward, the dispossessed heir of the Lancastrian earldom of Devon, and his cousin Peter, bishop of Exeter. Elsewhere on the eighteenth, a group assembled at Maidstone in Kent and over the next few days made their way to Rochester, Gravesend and Guildford under the command of two of Edward IV's knights, Sir John Guildford and Sir George Browne, and the latter's step-son, Edward Poynings. Other rebels met simultaneously at Newbury in Berkshire, led by two more knights from King Edward's household, Sir William Noreys and Sir

William Berkeley of Beaverstone, and by Sir Richard Wydeville, the queen's brother. Again on the eighteenth, there was a rising at Salisbury under John Cheyne, one of King Edward's esquires, and Sir Giles Daubeney. By this stage, however, Richard III had raised a large army and he determined to strike wherever the traitors could be found.

The weakness of the rebellion was at its core. Buckingham's tenants in the Welsh March were reluctant recruits to his force and they seem to have had little respect and less liking for their lord, a sentiment unusual among Welsh communities in the fifteenth century. Many of them deserted, and some attacked the duke's estates as soon as he left South-East Wales. Thomas Vaughan of Tretower Court (whose father had been executed by Jasper Tudor at Chepstow in 1471) and his prolific kin harried the countryside round Brecon, while Sir Humphrey Stafford of Worcestershire destroyed some of the bridges across the Severn and guarded the rest with a strong force. Buckingham, therefore, found his advance hampered and his men disloyal. Making his way to Weobley in Herefordshire, he was himself betrayed and in a desperate situation. Together with Bishop Morton and other friends and counsellors, he disguised himself and fled, leaving his loyal men to fend for themselves. He sought refuge in the house of a servant from his childhood, Ralph Bannaster (some later writers mistakenly call him Humphrey), until he could escape to Brittany and perhaps raise a new army there. He was discovered at Bannaster's home, partly because of suspicion aroused by the large quantities of provisions taken in to sustain a duke and his entourage, and partly because Bannaster betrayed his old master to the sheriff of Shropshire. Buckingham was seized and taken to Shrewsbury, where he was handed over on 31 October to Richard III's staunch supporter, Sir James Tyrell, and to Christopher Wellesbourne, one of Tyrell's men, and several other gentlemen. Together with Ralph Bannaster, they took him to Salisbury, where Richard III had strategically stationed his army so as to deal with all wings of the rebellion.

Fascinating details of the rising in the Welsh borderland are given in an account written for Buckingham's son, Edward, about twenty years later from information supplied by the servant who looked after him during the dangerous days of October 1483. Elizabeth Mores was a servant in the household of Sir Richard de la Bere at Kinnersley in Herefordshire. She later married her employer and presumably recalled her experiences in 1483 at Duke Edward's request. A copy of her story was discovered in 1575 among his archives at Thornbury Castle, Edward's favourite residence.

According to Elizabeth, Edward's father and mother and their two sons arrived at Weobley from Brecon; here the duke spent a week assembling and talking to the local gentry. In his absence, Brecon Castle was seized and plundered by Thomas Vaughan and his brothers, even though they were the duke's retainers. The duke's two daughters and their gentlewomen were carried off to the Vaughan house at Tretower. News of this calamity caused the duke to retire from Weobley, but he left his young son Edward in the charge of Sir Richard de la Bere, Sir William Knevet, one of the duke's leading councillors, and a nurse who took him for safety to de la Bere's house. The duke's younger son, Henry, stayed with the duchess. As a result of Richard III's proclamation offering generous rewards for the capture of the duke and his family, Buckingham was betrayed and taken to Salisbury by Sir James Tyrell. After his execution, the Vaughans searched high and low for Edward Stafford and his protectors; but Sir William Knevet and young Edward, his nurse Elizabeth Mores and one of de la Bere's Welsh servants went into hiding near Kinnersley, the Stafford heir dressed as a girl. Tyrell and the king made further efforts to find Edward and his nurse, who eventually reached the city of Hereford, where the boy was left in a widow's care. The duchess was conveyed from Weobley to London, and Sir William Knevet made his peace with the king.

This account is entirely plausible, and at those points where it can be checked – Richard III's proclamation and the transfer of the duke to Salisbury – it is an accurate account of what took place. Bannaster was later rewarded on 13 December for his treachery towards his former lord with one of Buckingham's forfeited Kent manors; by then he could be described as Richard's servant. The royal proclamation of 23 October offered large rewards of £1,000-worth of land for the capture of the duke himself, 1,000 marks or 100 marks of land (a mark being worth two-thirds of a pound) for the marquess of Dorset or any of the bishops involved, and 500 marks or £40-worth of land for the capture of any of the rebellious gentlemen. It stressed, too, the personal immorality of the marquess of Dorset in that 'holier-than-thou', puritanical style that made Richard 'the first king to use character assassination as a means . . . of moulding popular opinion' (Charles Ross). And along with Dorset, it named Buckingham's principal confederates as the bishops of Ely and Salisbury (Lionel Wydeville), Sir William and John Noreys, Sir Thomas Bourgchier (nephew of the archbishop of Canterbury and one of King Edward's knights), Sir George Browne, John Cheyne, Walter Hungerford (another of Edward IV's household servants), John Russh and John Harcourt. These and others had their estates and possessions seized on the day Buckingham was executed. Similar proclamations were sent to the sheriffs of every county in Central and Southern England.

News of Buckingham's capture led to the collapse of the other risings. The leaders sought sanctuary or went into hiding or else fled to Brittany. Most joined Henry Tudor. The rebels from the south-west found it easiest to secure a ship. Among them were Edward Courtenay, the bishop of Exeter and his brother Walter Courtenay (who had been in the service of the king's brother, the duke of Clarence, executed in 1478); the marquess of Dorset himself and his young son, Thomas Grey; Sir Robert Willoughby; Sir Thomas Arundell of Cornwall, whose sister was married to another rebel, Sir Giles Daubeney; and Richard Edgecombe, together with William Frost from Liskeard and John Halewell from Combe in Devon. They were helped by West Country merchants whose continued contacts with Brittany led to an investigation in October 1484. The leading rebels around Salisbury also managed to escape: Bishop Wydeville, Sir Giles Daubeney, John Cheyne and his two brothers, and Edmund Hampden of Fisherton in Wiltshire. And several who had risen in Kent got away, including the East Anglian brothers, William and Thomas Brandon, and Richard Guildford and Edward Poynings, whom Polydore Vergil regarded as one of the principal captains of the rebel force. The escape route followed by Sir William Berkeley and John Harcourt, who had tried to rouse Newbury, was the most

Tomb Chest allegedly of Henry Stafford (d. 1483), duke of Buckingham. The table tomb, partly mutilated, stands in Britford Church, near Salisbury, where the duke was executed on 2 November 1483. It may originally have stood in Ivychurch Priory, not far away, until the Dissolution of the Monasteries. The Stafford arms are on one of the tomb's shields.

hazardous of all, but they also eventually reached Brittany, where the two earlier fugitives, Sir Edward Wydeville and John Welles, met them. Two others, Bishop Morton and Christopher Urswick, whose role may have been confined to the preparatory plotting, took an independent course to Flanders. Richard III was convinced that another able cleric, Richard Fox, canon of Salisbury Cathedral, had joined Henry by 22 January and become one of his advisers. For a few the exile proved unusually short: John Harcourt died in Brittany in June 1484, and Bishop Wydeville's death by the following November may have occurred in France (though tradition says that he was buried in his diocese of Salisbury).

Richard III made strenuous efforts to prevent this exodus of traitors to his crown and recruits to Henry's cause, but he was largely unsuccessful. Only with Buckingham did he have good fortune. At Salisbury, the duke was closely questioned, but he was denied an interview with the king who had been his collaborator and whom he had utterly betrayed. On 2 November this self-conscious descendant of Edward III was executed by the axe, a final concession to his noble blood. The failure of Buckingham's rebellion and the duke's execution on 2 November 1483 were critical events for Henry Tudor. His sole rival as claimant to the English throne was removed at a stroke, for Buckingham's son and heir was only six.

Fiasco at Sea

Henry Tudor's contribution to the risings of October 1483 was late and ineffective. Whatever his precise hopes and their relationship to Buckingham's aims, the rising presented Henry with an opportunity to return to England after twelve years in exile. Through Pierre Landais, he gained Francis II's support for an expedition, and this was publicly demonstrated at a solemn oath-swearing ceremony in Vannes Cathedral in the presence of the duchess of Brittany, whose chaplain, Master Arthur Jacques, officiated at the mass. The duke provided Henry with ships, including three great vessels. According to Polydore Vergil, fifteen vessels in all were made ready to carry 5,000 Breton soldiers to England. The accounts of Francis II's receiver-general record the precise composition and cost of at least part of this fleet. Seven ships are named, manned by about 515 men. Two ships were from St. Malo; another was supplied by Alain de la Motte, lord of Les Fontaines and vice-admiral of Brittany; two more came from Brest and Auray, and a third belonged to the admiral of Brittany himself, Jean Dufou. Dufou was in fact the commander of the flotilla, which was being assembled in Henry's service during the first half of September – presumably in response to the messages from Margaret Beaufort and Queen Elizabeth Wydeville, and well before Henry received the letter which Buckingham wrote on 24 September. The commissary-general of the duke of Brittany, Yvon Millon, provided Henry and Jasper Tudor with 13,000 *livres* during October and November for the wages and provisions of their expedition, in addition to a loan of 10,000 *écus d'or*.

The flotilla probably did not set sail before the end of the month, for on 30 October Henry was still at the fishing town of Paimpol, on the north coast of Brittany, where he received Duke Francis's very welcome loan. The bay at Paimpol was large enough to accommodate a dozen or so ships and from there the voyage to England was just about the shortest possible. But soon after the ships put to sea, a storm blew up and before evening they were being tossed hither and thither and separated, some running towards Normandy and others returning to Brittany for shelter. Henry's own vessel was buffeted all night in the severe gales and early next morning, in company with one other ship, it came in sight of the Dorset coast near Poole Harbour.

Meanwhile, King Richard left Salisbury for Exeter, which he had reached by 8 November, evidently controlling the countryside in between. So when the Breton ships eventually anchored outside Plymouth Harbour to enable Henry to assess the state of things ashore, Richard's men had the situation well in hand. Henry and his men saw soldiers on the shore and wisely forbade a landing until the other ships reappeared after the storm. He did send a boat to reconnoitre and the men it carried were encouraged to land by the soldiers, who claimed that they had been sent by Buckingham to await Henry's arrival and that Richard had been defeated. Henry Tudor learnt the virtue of caution that day. None of his scattered ships found their way to Devon waters and news soon arrived of Buckingham's execution. Henry hurriedly put to sea. A few of the Bretons were left behind and taken prisoner; weeks later, just before Christmas, four of them were released to go home and arrange their own ransom and the ransoms of their fellows who had to stay behind in English hands.

Henry and his luckless ships encountered further storms at sea, but at last they reached the northern coast of France, far to the east of Brittany: one put in at Dieppe, the second at St. Vaast-la-Hogue on the Cotentin Peninsula. Of the rest of his flotilla, some vessels had reached Calais and even Flanders. Henry and those who were with him rested for three days before setting out on the journey overland through Normandy back to Brittany. He sent his battered ships home to Brittany ahead of him. The English continued to patrol the Channel and in December Richard III was still trying to stop any vessels returning to Brittany from Flanders; on 20 December all available ships – even small ones – were ordered to sea when the weather permitted to apprehend and, if possible, destroy them. Henry needed a safeconduct from the new French king, Charles VIII, to enable him to travel through Normandy in safety. His envoys to Charles's court returned with permission and even some money to meet expenses. In view of Louis XI's persistent attempts to get his hands on Henry and Jasper Tudor, it is significant that the opportunity was not now grasped to escort Henry to the French court. Louis's death on 30 August 1483 and the political uncertainty that followed may have paralysed the new king's ministers. Perhaps, too, the fiasco of Henry's expedition disillusioned the French that he could be used to threaten Richard III and England. More to the immediate point, though, was the substantial sum of money sent by Margaret Beaufort to purchase the safeconduct for her son, and the representations of Pierre Landais, whom the new French government wished to cultivate as an ally inside Brittany. Whatever the explanation, Charles VIII allowed Henry and his entourage to return to Francis II's protection; he took pity on their plight rather than advantage of it. An escort was provided by Henri Carbonnel, an esquire from King Charles's stable and the son of Jean de Carbonnel, who was lord of Sourdeval and the king's chamberlain. He accompanied Henry as far as the abbey of Saint-Sauveur at Redon, on the road to Vannes.

If Henry's prospects in October 1483 had never seemed so bright, a month or so later, following his ignominious return to Brittany, they can hardly have been dimmer. The French had not thought it worthwhile to intercept him. His value as a weapon in Francis II's diplomatic armoury had been seriously diminished; and, as Philippe de Commynes reported, Henry himself feared that Francis might now become reconciled with Richard III. His effectiveness had been shown to be the effectiveness of an impoverished exile whose allies in England had been soundly defeated. The only ray of hope and source of consolation lay in the groups of fugitives from England who sought out Henry when they arrived in Brittany. Henry learned that the marquess of Dorset and a large number of Englishmen had reached Vannes in search of him, and although Henry lamented the failure of their rebellion, he was at least cheered to see so many flocking to his cause – perhaps as many as 500. They made him realise that he must soon mobilise his scant forces again if whatever momentum remained in his cause were not to be irretrievably lost and Francis II abandon him, perhaps even hand him over to King Richard.

Accordingly, Henry assembled the exiles and strove to restore their morale and to inspire them with a sense of mission. He called a meeting at Rennes with Dorset and others. The discussion took several days and at Christmastide 1483,

Portrait of Elizabeth of York (d. 1503), queen of Henry VII. It was painted by an unknown artist in the sixteenth century and has a certain mechanical quality. But it is based on an earlier, contemporary portrait which existed by Henry VIII's reign. The queen is shown holding the white rose of York.

in Rennes Cathedral, their mutual oaths were confirmed. Henry solemnly promised to marry Elizabeth of York once he became king, thereby blending the Wydeville conspiracy with his own. For their part, all those present swore homage to Henry as if he were already king of England, placing their lives and their modest possessions at his disposal in his quest to win King Richard's crown.

The next task was to persuade Francis II to support a second expedition to England. Money was the priority, since the recent fiasco had exhausted the exiles' resources, including subventions from the duke and other friends in Brittany. Henry again promised to repay whatever was provided, and Duke Francis agreed to help assemble another flotilla. The French government appears to have encouraged Francis to support Henry's new venture, probably because of Richard's vigorous retaliation against both French and Breton shipping in the months following Henry's return to Brittany. On 5 April 1484, a high-ranking embassy was sent to Brittany in King Charles's name: it was led by three of Charles's councillors, the bishop of Périgueux, the lord of Torcy and the lord of Argentan. They assured Francis that the integrity of Brittany was as close to Charles's heart as was his own kingdom; they promised that the king would give all aid necessary to preserve it – though Francis was too wily a statesman and too experienced a Breton to fall for such talk. More immediately, and cynically, Charles hoped that another expedition would distract England and weaken Francis's traditional support against any future French advance into a duchy whose duke had no heir save his daughter Anne. According to Francis's receiver-general, the new flotilla consisted of no more than six ships, carrying 890 men. The vessels came from Morlaix, St. Pol de Jean and Brest, and the admiral of Brittany as well as the lord of Auray lent their ships. To judge by the payments made to the men and the provisions collected, the ships were fitted out during March and the early part of April 1484. Yet nothing came of the enterprise and instead the English exiles bided their time at Vannes.

A Community of Exiles

Henry and his followers formed a curious colony of exiles. They had been deprived of whatever position and wealth they had previously enjoyed in England; they were separated from their families and friends; they were largely cut off from English news and gossip; and they had prices on their heads. To them Henry Tudor felt a profound sense of obligation which he acknowledged as soon as the Battle of Bosworth was won. He recorded publicly his appreciation of the dangers and hardships they had experienced for his sake, both overseas and in the final challenge for the crown. These exiles can be observed fleetingly in the accounts of Jean Avallenc, the procurator of the chapter of Vannes Cathedral. They attended mass in the cathedral, led by Henry Tudor, Dorset, and the bishops of Exeter and Salisbury; they made offerings at the high altar on 8 February, 15 August and 8 September 1484 during high mass; and these glimpses suggest that they were at liberty and living comfortably, if in a state of frustrating expectancy. Philippe de Commynes noted that they were a financial burden on Duke Francis, and when their numbers were considerably swollen by fugitives from Buckingham's rebellion it became a particularly heavy one; for example, in June 1484 he paid 3,100 *livres* to the Englishmen in Vannes. At the same time, the burgesses of the city gave credit to their impoverished English guests which Francis guaranteed to the sum of 2,500 *livres*. The Vantois gave loans, too, including 200 *livres* by the canons of Vannes Cathedral which had not been repaid a decade and a half later. The duke gave personal gifts to the leaders of the exiles: to Dorset and his men 400 *livres* a month, to Sir Edward Wydeville 100 *livres* a month, to John Halewell 200 *livres* and to the Willoughbys another 100 *livres*. Nor were the English always well behaved and trouble-free. On one occasion the duke had to indemnify to the tune of 200 *livres* a poor Vantaise widow, Georget le Cuff, whose husband had been killed by one of Henry's friends.

Of the several hundred who gathered round Henry in Vannes, rather more than a hundred can be identified by name, largely because they took part in the successful expedition of 1485 and were rewarded after Bosworth. Doubtless others did not survive the journey or the battle, and perhaps a few remained in Brittany for reasons of their own.

City of Vannes, on the Gulf of Morbihan in Southern Brittany. St. Peter's Cathedral dominates the city, and the ducal Château of l'Hermine (of which only two towers survive) stood beside the ramparts. The medieval wash-houses are in the foreground beside the city ditch.

Prison Gate of Vannes, Brittany. Part of the ramparts begun in the thirteenth century, this gate and tower were inserted in the fifteenth century and lead up to the heart of the old city where the English exiles lived in 1483–5.

Many of Henry's companions were drawn from the ordinary rank and file of rebels in 1483 and little or nothing is therefore known about their antecedents, their loyalties and any relatives they may have had still living in England. But such details are available for about a third of them, and these show that the exiles were the remnants of the noble retinues recruited to the conspiracies in Southern England in the late summer of 1483. As far as one can judge, none of Buckingham's retinue escaped to Brittany. This tends to confirm the lack of enthusiasm shown by his tenants and servants and perhaps, too, the suggestion that his plans did not regard Henry Tudor as having first claim on the English crown.

Queen Elizabeth Wydeville's role is reflected in the presence in Brittany of her son Dorset, and her brothers Lionel, Edward and Richard. In their company was a significant number of loyal servants of her husband, Edward IV, who were doubtless outraged by the deposition and disappearance of Edward V. These included Sir Giles Daubeney, an esquire for the body who was created a knight of the Bath in 1478; John Cheyne, another esquire for the body and the king's standard-bearer, his master of the horse and, in 1478–9, the master of his bodyguard; William Brandon, who had held the latter post in 1473–4; and William Knight, a yeoman of King Edward's crown. Richard Guildford's father, John, who was executed in 1483, had been controller of Edward's household. These leading exiles were attended by their own servants and retainers. This was certainly the case with John Welles and Edward Poynings, and Sir Giles Daubeney had at least five yeomen in his entourage in Brittany. The retinue of William, Lord Hastings, Edward IV's bosom friend whom Richard III summarily executed in June 1483, was represented overseas by John Harcourt. Of even greater interest is the group connected with Margaret Beaufort and her husband, Lord Stanley. Their presence suggests that the latter was neither ignorant of, nor unsympathetic towards, his wife's plot in the interest of her son. Bishop Morton, John Cheyne, Richard Pigot and John Browne were involved in the arrangements made by Margaret and Lord Stanley in 1482 for the inheritance of Margaret's estates. Reginald Bray served in Margaret's household, and so too did Christopher Urswick. He may have been one of the Urswicks of Rawcliffe in Lancashire, a family associated with the Stanleys in the fifteenth century. Other exiles, notably Sir John Risley, Seth Worsley and John Edward, can be connected with Stanley with even greater certainty. And at the centre of these interlocking retinues was Bishop Morton. Among the guests at his enthronement as bishop of Ely in August 1479 were John Cheyne and William Brandon's father, while Sir Robert Willoughby had granted a manor in Dorset to Morton the previous year. All this evidence of service, connection and loyalty helps to substantiate chroniclers' reports of plots and rumours of plots during the summer of 1483; it suggests that a conspiratorial network did actually exist, linking Buckingham, Beaufort, Stanley, Wydeville and Edward IV's servants. A substantial part of this network crossed the Channel to Brittany, where the solemn oath-swearing in Rennes Cathedral at Christmastide 1483 amounted to a public dedication to Henry's cause. When Henry Tudor eventually landed in Wales in August 1485, he could present himself as the unifier of the warring houses of Lancaster and York, and to claim that he, above all others, was the true surviving heir of both dynasties.

The majority of the exiles were in Brittany for no more than a year. Although they all seem to have lived in or near Vannes, they did not have time to integrate with the local population or to be other than a distinctive colony, speaking a foreign language and with leaders who formed a miniature court about Henry Tudor. None is known to have courted or married a Breton lady; perhaps the Englishmen's doubtful prospects were a deterrent. Illicit relationships may have flourished, but (as Henry VII's biographer, S. B. Chrimes, has shown) the later tradition that Roland de Veleville was Henry's own bastard born in Brittany is false. It is true that after fighting for Henry at Bosworth, de Veleville was rewarded with a knighthood and the ancestral Tudor lands at Penmynydd in Anglesey, and in his will de Veleville asked that he be buried at Llanfaes Friary, the mausoleum of the earliest Tudors. But as far as Henry is concerned, he was simply and genuinely expressing deep gratitude to a Breton friend who had stood by him when support was short. Most of Henry's English companions were men (not one woman is known to have fled to him in 1483) of about Henry's own age or just a little older. To that extent, they formed a vigorous

entourage bent on improving their fortunes and prepared to risk much in order
to regain their wealth and influence in England. Older, more experienced heads
– like Jasper Tudor and Bishops Wydeville and Morton – were rare, but in the
younger clerics, Richard Fox and Christopher Urswick, Henry had at his
disposal intelligence and discretion.

Richard's Offensive

With many of his enemies beyond his reach, Richard III took what measures he
could to neutralise Henry Tudor and the dynastic threat he represented.
Richard's actions were harsh and conciliatory by turns. First, while he was still in
Exeter, Richard ordered Sir Thomas St. Leger and Thomas Rameney to the
scaffold; in London, Sir George Browne and seven of Edward IV's yeomen of
the crown were beheaded; and after the king returned to London, Sir Roger
Clifford was tried and executed. A few weeks later, in mid-December,
commissioners were sent to every county from Yorkshire southwards to
investigate the recent risings and the property and possessions that should be
forfeited to the king. All this was preliminary to a meeting of Parliament, which
had been summoned on 9 December. Its purpose was both to denounce publicly
and to attaint all rebels, especially those who had escaped. When the Parliament
opened on 23 January, they were condemned as traitors and all their possessions
were seized. It is difficult to believe that Richard did not suspect Lord Stanley of
complicity since rumours were widespread that his wife, Margaret Beaufort, was
deeply involved. But, like other kings before him, Richard may have hesitated to
challenge Stanley power in North-West England and North Wales. Rather did
he insist that Lord Stanley keep his wife under strict control, remove those
servants of hers who had taken messages between Brecon, London and Brittany,
and prevent her from having any further contact with her son and his friends.
Though Richard believed that Margaret deserved attainder, he did not want to
alienate Stanley irredeemably. Accordingly, he gave Stanley custody of his wife's
property for the rest of his life; after his death it would pass to the king and his
heirs. This was an humiliating arrangement for Margaret Beaufort, though it
meant that she escaped relatively lightly from the débâcle of 1483.

It may be that Richard consciously took a risk with the Stanley-Beaufort
household, offering reconciliation in order to wean some of Henry Tudor's
English supporters from his cause. This artful policy may also explain the
general pardon granted in January 1484 to two other conspirators, Reginald
Bray and Sir Richard Edgecombe. Then, on 1 March, the king tried to win over
Queen Elizabeth Wydeville herself. In the presence of his lords and the mayor
and aldermen of London, Richard formally assured her that he would protect
her five daughters if they would only come out of sanctuary and place themselves
in his care. He promised that they would be treated honourably as his own kin
(an astonishing change of heart after he had branded their father and mother as
adulterers), that they would not be sent to the Tower or any other prison (a vital
promise in view of their brothers' suspected fate), and that a pension would be
given to their mother and dowries set aside for them. These steps were matched
by military moves when news arrived of the naval preparations in Brittany (even

Gateway of the Château of Nantes, Brittany. These two towers – (left) the Hind's Foot Tower and (right) the Bakery Tower – were built by Francis II, and the château was visited on several occasions by Jasper and Henry Tudor during their exile.

though these proved abortive in the event). On 1 May Richard alerted every county in the kingdom so that his officers would be ready should another rising occur.

On the diplomatic front, Richard sent a series of missions to the French, Breton and Papal courts. Ostensibly to inform Pope Sixtus IV and King Charles VIII of his accession, the experienced diplomat, Thomas Langton, bishop of St. David's, was instructed in March 1484 to negotiate peace with the French government on his way to Italy, though it was several more months before he arrived in Paris. Relations with Brittany were more delicate, but Richard opened negotiations with Francis II and these all but succeeded in achieving what had eluded Edward IV – the surrender of Henry Tudor. The news that a new expedition was being prepared in Brittany spurred him on and he made promises and offered financial inducements to make Duke Francis more amenable. He sought the aid of Maximilian, duke of Austria and husband of the

Burgundian ruler, to put pressure on Francis. By 8 June 1484 Richard was able to announce the end of hostilities with Brittany and two days later he approved a truce which would last until 24 April 1485. Richard went even further. Two weeks later, on 26 June, he undertook to send 1,000 archers from Southampton to Brittany under the command of John Grey, Lord Powis, as a tangible sign of his wish to repair relations with Francis. These precautions and negotiations were designed to give Richard security against rebels who were beyond his reach. Henry Tudor had reason to fear that they might result in his being handed over to his enemy and returned to England.

Richard's efforts were assisted by Francis's uncertain health, for at this juncture he was too ill to deal personally with special messengers from Richard III. The initiative instead passed to his treasurer, Pierre Landais, who seems to have concluded that his own and Brittany's best interests would be served by an alliance with Richard. Aside from anything else, this would enable him to strengthen his personal position against some of the Breton nobility who resented his influence over Francis. Landais may also have suspected that Henry Tudor was considering approaching the new French government for assistance. At some point in the summer of 1484, two young esquires from the Wiltshire-Dorset area, William Collingbourne and John Turberville, allegedly offered £8 to a messenger to travel to Brittany and encourage Henry to return in force before mid-October and to land at Poole in Dorset where sympathisers would meet them. Apparently the messenger was also told to urge Henry to send John Cheyne, one of his most reliable lieutenants, to Charles VIII to plead for his aid in the venture. Charles might be persuaded to help if he were told that Richard was planning to delay and deceive Charles's ambassadors in England until the winter was passed and then he would launch an invasion of France. As it happens, one day in mid-August an Englishman, who was on his way to Brittany, was captured by the French after he had landed by mistake on the Normandy coast. On the orders of Charles VIII, he was treated gently, partly because he was on his way to visit Henry Tudor and partly because he had interesting news from England. Whether or not this misdirected Englishman was Collingbourne's messenger, and whether or not he ever reached the exiles at Vannes, cannot now be known. But the seriousness and plausibility of the allegations against Collingbourne and Turberville are indicated by the powerful commission of enquiry appointed by Richard on 29 November 1484. (There was, in addition, the more famous charge that Collingbourne had posted on the door of St. Paul's Cathedral on 18 July the slanderous rhyme against King Richard and his three henchmen, Viscount Lovell, Sir Richard Ratcliffe and William Catesby: 'The Cat, The Rat and Lovell our Dog, Rule all England under an hog'.)

It was in this atmosphere that Richard III continued his discussions with Pierre Landais, presumably in the hope that Henry Tudor would be repatriated to England. Richard's intimate counsellor, William Catesby, was in Brittany by September 1484 (when he made an offering in Vannes Cathedral at the tomb of the duchy's newest saint, Vincent Ferrier), and probably on this occasion Richard offered to restore the earldom of Richmond to Duke Francis and grant him certain other lands. For his part, Landais obtained Richard's assurance that he would protect him from the Breton nobility if Landais urged the duke to accept Richard's proposals.

Henry Tudor was extraordinarily lucky. Bishop Morton, who was spending his exile in Flanders, got wind of the discussions between Richard and Pierre Landais from agents at Westminster, most notably a member of the bishop of St. Pol de Leon's mission who was evidently less than happy at the progress of the Anglo-Breton negotiations. Morton warned Henry of what was afoot. He sent his protégé, Christopher Urswick, who was also in Flanders, to Brittany to advise Henry Tudor to flee into France. Urswick found Henry at Vannes and was promptly sent by him to Charles VIII's court to discover whether he would be offered asylum there. The king agreed and as soon as Urswick had returned Henry began planning his flight.

Historical Sources

This description of Urswick's mission is the most detailed of the accounts of the secret communications of 1483–5 to be given by Polydore Vergil in his *English History*. When put beside Vergil's earlier reference to Urswick's role in Morton's conspiracy of 1483, it suggests that one of Vergil's informants was Christopher Urswick himself. A comment on Vergil's chronicle as a unique source of knowledge for the events of these years is appropriate at this point.

Polydore Vergil, whose home-town was Urbino in Central Italy, first arrived in England in 1502. He was then about thirty-two years old and an ordained cleric. Later on, he recorded his reception at court:

> Then [in 1502] I first came to England, as Adriano Castelli's deputy in the collection of papal revenue, which office he held at that time. This after they called the Papal Collectorship. I was most courteously received by the king and ever after was entertained by him kindly.

Polydore prospered in the English church, but his greatest claim to fame is as a humanist scholar. He already had three books in Latin to his credit by the time he reached England, and he quickly became interested in the peoples of these islands and their history. Henry VII had a similar project in mind, and he saw Vergil as the ideal man to undertake it. Henry wanted a large-scale, modern history of England from the earliest times to his own day. Polydore started work seriously in 1506 and the first draft was written during 1512 and 1513; it culminated in the great English victory over the Scots at Flodden Field in September 1513. This draft in the author's own hand is now in Rome in the Vatican Library, where it was deposited in two fine volumes by Polydore's grand-nephew in 1613.

Polydore Vergil was uniquely placed to tell the story of Henry's own life. Not only did he have access to the English court, but his intellectual circle, focussed on the dining club known as Doctors' Commons, included several key actors in the events of 1483–5. Although John Morton had died in 1500, one of his protégés was Thomas More, who knew Vergil and began his *History of Richard III* just when the Italian was finishing the first draft of his *History*. Reginald Bray was still alive when Vergil came to England and Richard Fox lived on until 1528.

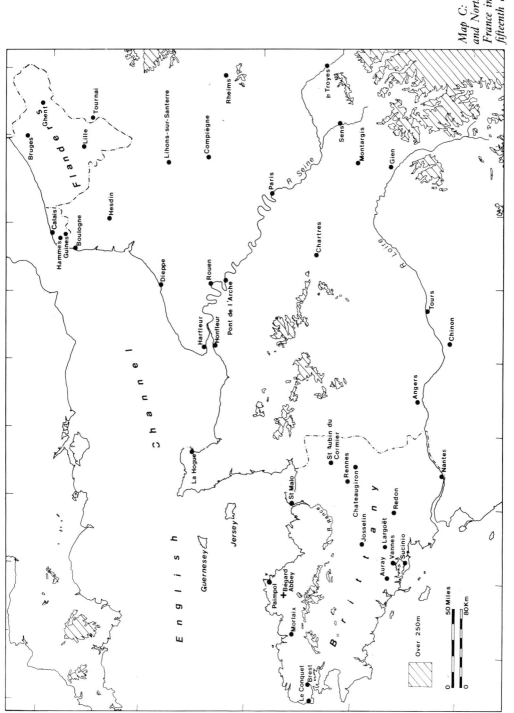

Map C: Brittany and North-West France in the later fifteenth century.

Memorial Brass of Christopher Urswick (d. 1521). He was Margaret Beaufort's confessor and her secret agent during the conspiracies of 1483–5. A prominent figure at Henry VII's court, he may have been Polydore Vergil's main informant about Henry Tudor's movements in France. The brass is in Hackney Church, London.

Fox is likely to have known Vergil well and both he and Bray could have provided oral history for Vergil's work. But, above all, Christopher Urswick is likely to have been the most informative and reliable of sources; he was Vergil's friend and we may imagine him recalling his travels between the conspirators in England, Flanders, Brittany and France. The result is that Polydore Vergil's account of Henry Tudor's experiences before Bosworth is of the highest historical value; at almost every point where its details can be checked, they are found to be accurate and full. Indeed, Vergil's chapter on Richard III's reign reads very much like an account of the opposition in England and France; there were, after all, few in Henry VII's service who were able to provide Vergil with details about the domestic affairs of Richard's reign.

At this point, it is worth considering two other sources which reflect the secrecy and intrigue of the two years prior to the Battle of Bosworth. Their main defect is that they were written much later than the events they claim to describe, and for this reason distort and confuse reality. The 'Song of the Lady Bessy' was a ballad popular round about 1500 but which survives today only in versions written 100 years later. It tells of a conspiracy by Elizabeth of York ('Lady Bessy') and Thomas, Lord Stanley to bring Henry Tudor back to England. The world of spies which it recreates is the world of Queen Elizabeth Wydeville, Margaret Beaufort, Buckingham and Morton. It is difficult to imagine that Elizabeth of York, who was only seventeen in 1483, had a major part to play; the ballad may cast her in her mother's role. But Lord Stanley's involvement is strongly hinted at in other sources. According to the ballad, he sent a messenger to Henry Tudor, Humphrey Brereton of Malpas in Cheshire, whose family may have been the source of the ballad itself. The Breretons of Shocklach and Malpas were connected with the Stanleys during Edward IV's reign, and one of the two Humphrey Breretons alive at this time could have been sent as a Stanley agent to Brittany. The ballad says that he set sail in one of Stanley's ships from or near Liverpool, where the Stanleys had a house. He took with him a large sum of money for Henry, whom he found at the Cistercian abbey of Bégard, not far from Paimpol on the north coast of Brittany. Henry had certainly been in the vicinity in October 1483. Questionable though some of the other details may be, a mission (or missions) from Lord Stanley is quite credible in the period before August 1485.

The second source, a biography of Sir Rhys ap Thomas, the most powerful gentleman in late-fifteenth-century Carmarthenshire, was written by one of his descendants at the beginning of the seventeenth century. It glorifies Rhys to the point of eulogy, and there is more than a hint that it inserts fanciful details of his life into the general history of 1483–5 as published by sixteenth-century historians. And yet, Rhys's refusal to join Buckingham's rising in 1483 because he resented the duke's ambition to dominate Carmarthenshire parallels the reaction of other Welsh gentlemen to the duke. And the claim that Henry Tudor sent appeals to various people in England and Wales, including Rhys, is likely to be true. Such a letter was among the confiscated archives of Rhys's family when the Banqueting Hall of the Palace of Westminster and the official documents in its basement went up in flames in 1619. In the British Library, there are several copies of a similar letter, which is the only known communication from Henry Tudor to his friends in England and Wales before he returned in 1485.

9 The Die is Cast

The Flight into France

According to Polydore Vergil, Henry Tudor's flight from Brittany into France in 1484 was planned in great secrecy. Only a few of Henry's intimates were 'in the know'. Having decided the best route to follow, at some point early in September Henry sent ahead a few English noblemen, led by his uncle Jasper. He was instructed to give the impression that the riders intended to visit Francis II at Rennes, not too far from the French frontier. When they approached the frontier, Jasper and his companions made a sudden dash for it and arrived in the province of Anjou.

Meanwhile, Henry left Vannes two days after his uncle, accompanied by a small retinue on horseback (Polydore Vergil says there were five, a Breton chronicler thirteen); he pretended to visit a friend who owned a manor not far away. No suspicion was aroused because most of the English exiles were still in Vannes. Five miles from the city, Henry suddenly left the highway, went into a wood, changed into a groom's clothes and, with one of his servants acting as a guide, he rode swiftly towards the French frontier, stopping only to water the horses. Without taking leave of his protector, or seeking Francis's permission, Henry crossed into Anjou and joined his uncle and the other English noblemen.

Four days after Henry's departure, Pierre Landais was still raising a force, ostensibly to assist Henry's return to England though in reality to convey him and the other English nobles to prison. When he heard that Henry had escaped he sent men in all directions to find him and bring him back; indeed, as Henry crossed the frontier, his pursuers were only an hour's ride behind.

Henry's flight placed the rest of the English exiles in Vannes – about 410 of them – in jeopardy. Out of either compassion or a sense of guilt, Francis II took pity on them and in a remarkable gesture he allowed them to rejoin their leader. Sir Edward Wydeville, John Cheyne and Edward Poynings were summoned to Francis's presence and the duke promised that he would help them to travel to France. Each of these leaders was given 100 *livres* to cover his expenses. The 400 or so other Englishmen and their servants had received 20*s*. each for their maintenance in Vannes, and the last payment was made in September 1484. In all, Francis spent 708 *livres*, a genuine token of regret for his minister's mistreatment of Henry and his companions. Henry was deeply grateful and sent a message of thanks to the duke who, once again, had shown himself to be an honourable man, but one who was no longer fully in control of his own duchy.

Henry Tudor and the French Court

The presence of Henry Tudor in France transformed the diplomatic scene at a stroke. It gave France an advantage it had been seeking for more than a decade, but it worked to the disadvantage of both England and Brittany. The French government was certain to be a more enthusiastic supporter of Henry's political and dynastic claims than ever Francis II had been; and it was equally certain to use its guests in the negotiations which it was currently having with Richard III. (On 13 September Richard allowed certain French envoys and a large entourage of about 200 to enter his realm.) To Francis II, Charles VIII's control over the Tudors was just as unwelcome. He no longer had a lever by which he could extract aid from England to preserve Breton independence. Fortunately for Francis, the government of Charles VIII was so weakened by personal and political rivalries that it could not exploit its advantages to the full.

When Louis XI died on 30 August 1483, his son Charles was only thirteen years of age. In the past royal minorities had always led to argument about how the king's authority should be exercised and to disputes about who should control his government. The situation was no different in 1483. The queen mother, Charlotte of Savoy, had been firmly excluded from politics and government by the late king; in any case, she was in poor health and died a few months later on 1 December. A struggle ensued between King Charles's older sister, Anne, and the senior prince of the blood royal, Louis, duke of Orléans, the husband of Charles VIII's younger sister. Anne was married to Pierre, lord of Beaujeu, brother and heir of the duke of Bourbon. She was a formidable and capable woman of twenty-two who took after her ruthless father. Her Beaujeu party triumphed in the struggle, and among relatives and sympathisers whom it brought to the French court were the new king's aunts and uncles from Savoy.

The Orléans party resented its eclipse and forged an alliance with those Breton nobles who had fallen foul of Pierre Landais and had fled to France. On 7 April 1484 these Breton noblemen had broken into the ducal palace in Nantes, and others made for Landais's country house in order to arrest and try him. He escaped and the failure of the nobles' plan forced them to flee to the fortified Breton town of Ancenis, on the French frontier. In Nantes, Landais seemed as powerful as ever. Towards the end of September 1484, the Orléans faction also made overtures to the Breton government, with the aim of reconciling Francis II and his dissident noblemen; indeed, it succeeded in making an alliance with Francis with Landais's approval. In order to win Richard III's support and thereby to discourage Richard's negotiations with Charles VIII, Landais prepared to hand Henry Tudor over to the English. It was news of this plan – and perhaps of Richard's negotiations with Maximilian of Austria and Burgundy – that led Henry to flee to France. A diplomatic combination of Brittany, Orléans, Burgundy and England would discourage any French advance on Brittany, and it would give welcome security to Richard's régime. But unless he escaped, it would also put Henry Tudor in grave jeopardy. The French

Portrait of Anne of Beaujeu (d. 1522), from the Triptych in Moulins Cathedral, by the Master of Moulins (possibly Jean Perréal, the court painter), c. 1488–91. Anne, eldest daughter of Louis XI and wife of Pierre II de Bourbon, governed France during the minority of her brother, Charles VIII. It was her support which enabled Henry Tudor to plan his expedition to Wales in 1485.

government responded by welcoming Henry to the French court and supporting his invasion of England. That would preoccupy Richard III, deprive Francis II and Landais of their foremost ally, and undermine the Orléans's plots against Anne of Beaujeu. Henry was a diplomatic pawn, to be moved about the chess board by Bretons and French alike. He had survived for fourteen years by courtesy of Duke Francis; he was to be made king of England by courtesy of King Charles.

Safe in Anjou, Henry sent to Charles VIII the much-travelled Christopher Urswick, for whom a safe-conduct had already been obtained. Charles was some considerable distance away to the east at Montargis when, on 11 October, he was informed of Henry's arrival in his kingdom. An envoy was straightway sent to greet him in the person of Gilbert de Chabannes, lord of Curton and governor of the province of Limousin. He was authorised to receive Henry and to arrange lodgings for him in the towns through which they had to pass on the way to the great cathedral city of Chartres. Charles VIII had ordered him to be taken there so that the two could meet. De Chabannes was given 20,000 *francs* to meet the expenses of the journey, which took about ten or eleven days. Henry thanked Charles for his indulgence, explained why he was throwing himself on his mercy, and sought aid for his return to England. Charles VIII was sympathetic and positively encouraged Henry's enterprise, though he was less keen to commit himself to sustained financial support for the entourage that had followed Henry out of Brittany. On 4 November arrangements were made to lodge about 400 of these followers at the town of Sens (some distance to the north-east of Montargis) but at a cost that was reasonable. A fortnight later, Charles authorised a grant to Henry of 3,000 *francs* so that he could clothe his men, but it was made clear that this would not be repeated. When it came to raising an army, Charles was prepared to allow him to recruit mercenaries. The French court spent the rest of the autumn in the Loire Valley, near Montargis, and then it travelled north to Paris with Charles's newest guests, Henry being treated with honour on the journey. The party had reached the capital by 4 February 1485.

Richard's Alarm

Relations between England and France deteriorated sharply during the winter of 1484–5. Richard III responded to news of Henry's welcome at the French court with the same mixture of anger and conciliation as in the previous year. At the beginning of December, he learned with alarm that the exiles, 'now confedered with our ancient enemies of France', were sending letters to England 'to provoke and stir discord and division between us and our lords'. On 6 December Richard alerted the mayor of Windsor (and doubtless many other officials) and ordered him to arrest and punish the distributors of any such letters that might come into his hands. At least one of these letters did come to light and although it has since disappeared, it was copied several times in the seventeenth century, usually alongside the letter to Windsor's mayor. One of the earliest copies of this letter (if not the earliest of all) makes fascinating reading in the light of the tense circumstances of 1484–5. It is undated and without a specific address, but it evidently carried Henry Tudor's autograph – the elaborate 'H' which he continued to use until 1492 (but which the copyist has probably misread as 'HR').

> Right trusty, worshipful and honourable good friends, I greet you well. Being given to understand your good devoir and entreaty to advance me to the furtherance of my rightful claim, due and lineal inheritance of that crown, and for the just depriving of that homicide and unnatural tyrant which now unjustly bears dominion over you, I give you to understand that no Christian heart can be more full of joy and gladness than the heart of me, your poor exiled friend, who will, upon the instant of your sure advertising what power you will make ready and what captains and leaders you get to conduct, be prepared to pass over the sea with such force as my friends here are preparing for me. And if I have such good speed and success as I wish, according to your desire, I shall ever be most forward to remember and wholly to requite this your great and moving loving kindness in my just quarrel. Given under our signet   H
> I pray you to give credence to the messenger of that he shall impart to you.

Within a further twenty-four hours, Richard had reacted with his own propagandist appeal. On 7 December 1484 he issued his first major proclamation against the leaders of the exiles in France, Bishop Courtenay of Exeter, the marquess of Dorset, Jasper Tudor, the earl of Oxford (who had recently joined the rebels, as we shall shortly see), and Sir Edward Wydeville. They were denounced for choosing as their 'captain' Henry Tudor, who had the effrontery to style himself earl of Richmond and even to use the royal style. The entire proclamation was skilful propaganda for domestic and overseas consumption. The duke of Brittany, with whom Richard was negotiating, was portrayed as spurning the promises the rebels had made in order to obtain Francis's support. In contrast, Charles VIII, 'calling himself king of France', was described as England's ancient enemy to whom Henry had surrendered all claim to the French throne, for which English kings had fought for 150 years, to Gascony, which had been English from the twelfth century until its loss in 1453, and even to Calais, which was still English territory. To bring the horrors of a future Tudor régime home to his subjects, Richard warned that once in the realm these rebels would commit 'the most cruel murders, slaughters, robberies and disinheritances that were ever seen in any Christian Realm'. On this platform Richard appealed for help to resist the despicable rebels. It was powerful and persuasive material, appealing to the fears and pride of Englishmen and to their sense of justice.

This condemnation was accompanied by elaborate orders for special commissioners to muster armed men at short notice in every shire, to organise them in companies, and to raise cash for their payment. For these and for other precautions on the coasts, Richard sought loans in February 1485, and during the next two months careful arrangements were made for their repayment. At the same time, he offered inducements in the shape of general pardons to certain leading rebels. On 11 December Bishop Morton received one, and Sir Richard Wydeville, the queen's younger brother, had another on 30 March 1485.

On the diplomatic front, the king continued his negotiations with Brittany, while Maximilian of Austria and Burgundy used his powers as a mediator to bring the two sides together. By 20 December, Francis II was ready to authorise an embassy, led by the bishop of St Pol de Leon and the duke's secretary, Master Jean Mauhegeon, to discuss an extension of the truce with England. The importance which Richard attached to these discussions is indicated by the standing of his own representatives nominated on 20 February: Bishop John Russell of Lincoln was chancellor of England, and John Gunthorp, dean of Wells, was keeper of the privy seal, two of the most senior officials of the government. An extension of the Anglo-Breton truce was agreed relatively quickly, and on 2 March 1485 Richard announced that it would last until 1492. This was the longest extension in recent times and one of its terms provided that neither side would support the rebels of the other. To the French king's Council these steps seemed like a threat, and even before Christmas 1484 it thought that an English attack on France was a distinct possibility.

Hammes Castle, 5 miles south of Calais, photographed prior to its destruction in the first world war. It was in the form of a pentagon with a round tower at each angle. Here the earl of Oxford was held prisoner until he escaped to join Henry Tudor in 1484.

The Earl of Oxford's Escape

An incident which occurred near Calais highlights the place of Henry Tudor in international affairs during these winter months. When Louis XI died in August 1483, Lord Dynham, who was then at Calais, emphasised how vulnerable the colony and its frontiers were. In order to protect them from the French, he strongly advised an alliance with Brittany and Maximilian of Austria and Burgundy. As relations with France deteriorated, not only did Calais become more vulnerable but so also did John de Vere, the Lancastrian earl of Oxford. He was an important prisoner of state who had been locked up in 1475 in Hammes Castle, a fortress in the Calais March close to the French frontier. Oxford was to play a role of significance for both Richard III and Henry Tudor, and his escape from Hammes heightened the tension between England and France.

Oxford was in the charge of the custodian of Hammes, James Blount, and the porter of Calais, John Fortescue. These two English officers were persuaded to desert their posts, release their captive and join Henry Tudor. According to the Burgundian chronicler, Jean Molinet, Lord Stanley's advice was decisive in making up Blount's mind. It is significant that Fortescue had been friendly with Bishop Morton, who was living in Flanders; and along with one of Stanley's acquaintances, John Riseley, Fortescue was accused of causing disturbances in the Home Counties at the time of the breakout from Hammes.

The desertion of Blount and Fortescue seems to have been precipitated by King Richard's order that Oxford should return to England. The earl had tried to escape before (or to commit suicide): in 1478 he jumped from the castle walls but ended up in the mud of the moat with water up to his chin. Now, on 28 October 1484, the king ordered William Bolton, a yeoman-usher of his Chamber, to travel to Hammes. He was to accompany Oxford and James Blount to a ship and to wait with them until Oxford had embarked for England. The strict instructions given to Bolton betray not only Richard's anxiety to put Oxford in more secure custody but also, perhaps, some doubt about Blount's loyalty. Richard was justified in his suspicions because Blount preferred to declare for Henry rather than comply with Richard's wishes.

Henry Tudor was delighted to welcome the new recruits, not least because Oxford and his family had been Lancastrian supporters in the past and the earl was popular with discontented Yorkists. But their flight had been a hasty one, and Blount was forced to leave his wife behind in Hammes with most of the garrison. Richard tried to retain their loyalty by offering a general pardon in November to Blount and fifty-two of his men.

To Richard the desertions were alarming. He therefore sent part of the Calais garrison to take control of Hammes Castle. But the rebels inside appealed to Henry for aid and Oxford himself returned to help the besieged. He encamped not far away, while Thomas Brandon, one of the exiles of 1483, and a detachment of thirty men entered the castle undetected across the marshes and gave new vigour to the garrison in its skirmishes with the besiegers. With Oxford sniping at their rear, the Calais force offered terms whereby the besieged would retire from the castle under a safe-conduct, taking their weapons and their baggage with them. Oxford, whose sole purpose had been to rescue his friends (and especially Blount's wife) rather than to hold an exposed fortress against overwhelming odds, accepted these terms and withdrew without loss to Paris. Richard tried to avoid calamity by hastily sending his staunch aide, Sir James Tyrell, to Flanders, probably to gain assistance there from the sympathetic Maximilian of Austria and Burgundy. Shortly after his return, on 13 January Tyrell was appointed to take charge of Guisnes Castle nearby and preparations were made to ship a force across from Dover to Calais. In a way typical of Richard's approach to crises, he again combined resolution with conciliation in order to avoid disaster. On 27 January a general pardon was offered to Elizabeth Blount, to her husband's kinsman, William Blount, to the leader of Oxford's relieving force, Thomas Brandon, and to the enlarged garrison of seventy-two at Hammes.

The entire episode was a boost to Henry's morale and a demonstration to Richard that loyalties were fragile and that disloyalties could be embarrassing and dangerous. Even at Calais, several of the garrison were sympathetic to Henry's cause and were promptly ejected from the fortress.

Nor were these the only Englishmen to desert to Henry in the months before his return to England. Some, like John Riseley, stole away from England itself to join him in Paris. English students at the University of Paris offered their services, the most prominent among them being Richard Fox, who was later to be a leading figure in Henry's court and government. A London draper, William

Henry Tudor as a young man, possibly while still in exile. One of a series of drawings by Jacques le Boucq (d. 1573), Hainault Herald, now in the city library at Arras, but presumably based on an earlier portrait.

Bret, personally delivered to him several suits of armour costing £37 (though he was not paid until after Bosworth). Yet others stayed in England but vowed to support Henry when the opportunity came – men like Piers Curteys, one of Edward IV's household servants, who lived in fear as he cowered in sanctuary at Westminster hoping for Henry's return.

'King Henry'

These events encouraged Henry Tudor and his advisers to make more explicit both his plans and his claims. All along, Henry had considered himself to be earl of Richmond, as his father's heir, and Francis II and two French kings had so regarded him. Although, as a lad of five, he had been deprived of the earldom of Richmond in February 1462, Henry had not been attainted until Richard III's Parliament of January 1484; thereafter, Richard referred to him (at best) as 'Henry, calling himself earl of Richmond'. Probably from the summer of 1483, he regarded himself – and was regarded by the Beaufort-Wydeville conspiracy in England – as right claimant to the English crown. But when he acknowledged receipt of Francis II's loan on 30 October 1483 at Paimpol, he still signed his name as 'Henry de Richemont', after the habit of English nobles. (Kings signed

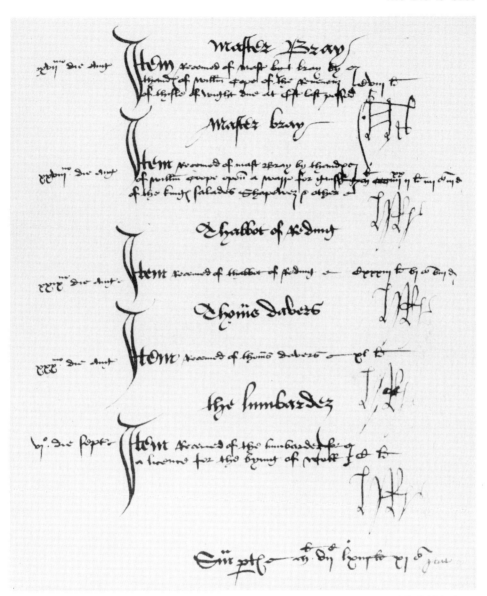

Extract from the Book of Receipts of Henry VII's Chamber, 1492 (P.R.O., E101/413/2/2 f.36). It shows the king's initials beside each entry and how, on 28 August, he altered his signature from the one he had used since 1484–5 to a more cursive one.

otherwise: Henry VI as 'R H' or 'Rex Henricus'; Edward IV as 'R E' or 'Rex Edwardus'.)

The flight to France and the quickening pace towards invasion produced a change of attitude and style. According to the Burgundian chronicler, Jean Molinet, he was now urged by the earl of Oxford and, from England, by Lord Stanley to use the title of king. Henry's appeal to his friends in England, sent sometime in November 1484, appears to have carried a new, royal signature, 'H', which he continued to use until well after he gained the English throne. Richard III was well aware of this piece of pretension after one of Henry's letters reached the king's eyes. On 7 December the king's proclamation against the rebels noted that Henry, 'of his ambitious and insatiable covetousness ... encroacheth upon him the name and title of Royal estate of this Realm of England, whereunto he hath no manner interest, right, or colour, ...' The propagandist pretence of actually being king might encourage waverers and the faint-hearted to declare themselves when the time came. No sooner had Henry landed, therefore, than he signed letters with the simple, regal 'H', a style he was to use until 1492. The canons of Rouen recorded the offering which Henry made to their cathedral in the spring of 1485 as if it had been made by the king of England. It was the same pretence that led him to date his reign from the day before the Battle of Bosworth, as if he were already king when the God of Battles delivered his judgement. The solemn ceremonies and oath-swearings in the cathedrals of Rennes and Vannes in 1483–4 and his acclamation by hundreds of Englishmen in exile could be cited as a public justification for this daring decision. No previous claimant to the English throne – neither Henry Bolingbroke in 1399 nor Edward of March in 1461 – had gone so far as to call himself king before the decisive moment. Henry Tudor dared so much.

Richard's Last Chance

Richard became increasingly desperate in his attempts to disrupt and demoralise the ranks of the exiles in Paris. His queen, Anne Neville, died in March 1485, but there were already rumours circulating that he was planning to replace her with his own niece, Elizabeth of York, or else with Elizabeth's younger sister, Cecily, both of whom were in his custody. The rumours were officially denied, but they may have been close to the truth. When they reached Henry, whose role as the unifier of Lancaster and York partly depended on his own marriage to Elizabeth or Cecily, he feared that dissident Yorkists would desert him.

Richard would probably be able to browbeat Queen Elizabeth Wydeville into agreeing to such a marriage with one of her daughters, but the presence in Paris of her son Dorset and her brothers Edward and Richard was an embarrassment. The queen was persuaded to induce Dorset to desert Henry and to return to Richard's court. The marquess may have been preparing for flight as early as February 1485, when he sent Roger Machado on several missions to Bruges, Ghent and elsewhere in the Low Countries. Machado had been one of Richard III's heralds, but in 1484 he joined the rebels in France, entering Henry Tudor's service as Richmond Herald. (Whatever his business on behalf of Dorset had been, he returned to England in 1485 and became Richmond King of Arms at King Henry's court.)

When he was ready, the marquess left Paris secretly at night and made for Flanders. Because he knew all the rebel plans which had been under discussion during the past few months, Henry pleaded with Charles VIII to stop him. With Charles's agreement, two of the English party, Humphrey Cheyne and Mathew Baker, were sent posthaste in pursuit. They overtook him at Lihons-sur-

Santerre, some distance beyond Compiègne and before he could reach France's northern border. Dorset was persuaded – or compelled – to return to Paris. Nevertheless, when, on 21 June, Richard issued his second proclamation denouncing the rebels, he purposely omitted the name of Dorset.

Meanwhile, Richard withdrew his ships from their Channel station and stood down some of the soldiers who were on watch along the English coast. But he was fully aware that an invasion was coming. On 22 June he ordered the commissioners who had been nominated in every county the previous winter to muster their men, and to make sure that they were properly paid and ready for service at an hour's notice. The sheriffs were to hold themselves available, and beacons were set up along the coast to signal instantly when and where the invasion occurred. Richard's new proclamation, though based in part on the earlier one of 7 December, betrays the urgency of the moment. He heaped extra personal abuse on Jasper and Henry Tudor, and especially on Henry, 'for he is descended of bastard blood both of father's side and of mother's side'. Henry's subservience to the French king was graphically emphasised by alleging that he planned to remove the lilies of France from the arms which English kings had borne since Edward III's day. And the oppression which Englishmen could expect from a Tudor régime was now likened to a conquest: Henry would overturn the laws of England and seize men's property; had he not already granted bishoprics, earldoms and other inheritances to foreigners? This was Richard at his most inventive and robust as an unashamed propagandist – but then the aim was to rouse Englishmen swiftly in order to resist an imminent Tudor landing.

Richard also kept an eye on the most dangerous elements in England, notably the Beaufort-Stanley household. He became suspicious when, round about July 1485, Lord Stanley told the king that he wanted to visit his home and family in Lancashire whom he had not seen for some time. So suspicious was Richard that he would only agree if Stanley left his eldest son, George, Lord Strange, as a virtual hostage at the court. By 1 August, Strange was in Richard's company at Nottingham and Stanley was in the north-west.

The Invasion

In these tense circumstances, Henry pressed Charles VIII to support his invasion plans. Richard's bold response showed how urgent it was for Henry to make his move and how vital that Charles VIII should come to a final decision about the aid that was so crucial. Henry was in close touch with the French court during these months, and at some stage had at least one lengthy conversation with Philippe de Commynes, the veteran diplomat. It may have taken place when Henry accompanied Charles and his court to Normandy in March 1485 to make a solemn, ceremonial entry to Rouen on 14 April, prior to the opening of the Norman Estates (or Parliament). At this assembly on 4 May, Charles requested financial aid to assist Henry to recover the realm to which (Charles assured the Norman representatives) he had a better right than anyone else living. A large sum of money was needed to pay for the help which Charles had already undertaken to provide. Well satisfied with the response, the king had returned to

Terracotta Bust of King Charles VIII (d. 1498), c. 1494–5. It is now in the Bargello Museum, Florence. Though a minor, Charles accompanied Henry Tudor to Normandy in 1485 to raise men, ships and finance for the expedition to England.

Paris by 3 June – presumably with Henry in his entourage, though some preliminary preparations may already have been made for the assembling of a fleet at the mouth of the River Seine.

In view of the possibility that Richard might deprive Henry of his Yorkist bride, Henry sought an alternative. The choice of a daughter of William Herbert, earl of Pembroke, one of Edward IV's most trusted councillors who had died in battle in 1469, harks back to Henry's own childhood in the Herbert household. But it also reminds us that few major Yorkist magnates in England were yet prepared to desert Richard III. The Herberts' Yorkist credentials were impeccable and so, too, were their Welsh blood and connections. There was little point in Henry approaching – either for a marriage or for support in South Wales – the present head of the Herbert clan, for William II, earl of Pembroke, was a man of limited intelligence who had recently married Richard's bastard daughter, Katherine, and was the prince of Wales's chamberlain. In any case, he had been forced by Edward IV to exchange the earldom of Pembroke for the earldom of Huntingdon. But, as the earl of Oxford apparently noted, Huntingdon's younger brother, Sir Walter Herbert, was of a different caste. Alert, energetic, and with military experience and a powerful presence in South

Wales, he seemed a better man to approach. Walter was also married to Anne, the daughter of Henry Stafford, duke of Buckingham, whose rebellion Henry Tudor had tried to join in 1483.

Henry had known Walter in the 1460s when both were boys, and in his will of 1469 the earl of Pembroke had arranged that Henry should marry Walter's sister, Maud. Now, in 1485, Maud was no longer available, since she had married Henry Percy, earl of Northumberland; but Jane, Cecily and Katherine Herbert were still unmarried. Henry, therefore, sent his trusty messenger, Christopher Urswick, to seek out the earl of Northumberland in Northern England and enlist his help in arranging a marriage. As it happens, Urswick never delivered his message and he returned empty-handed to Henry. It is impossible to say how Northumberland would have reacted to such an overture – and whether his behaviour at Bosworth would have been more decisive if Henry's agent had in fact reached him.

The naval and military preparations at Harfleur in the early summer of 1485 neared completion. Charles VIII gave a grant of 40,000 *livres*, and Henry borrowed more from the king and others, including local merchants of Rouen and Barfleur. All told, Henry seems to have raised about 4,000 men, who embarked on a flotilla at anchor off Honfleur. The French government provided the ships and a vice-admiral to command them, Guillaume de Casenove, whose nickname was Coulon. According to Jean Molinet, at first 1,800 men were assembled for the expedition, with another 1,800 at Honfleur immediately prior to departure. The total included about 1,500 discharged soldiers from the new French military base at Pont de l'Arche, a little way up the Seine from Rouen, whose commander, the elderly marshal of France, Philippe de Crèvecoeur, lord of Esquerdes (or Cordes, as he was known in England), later prided himself that he played such a central role in assisting Richmond's enterprise. When Philippe de Commynes commented that most of the Frenchmen were 'the worst kind which could have been found anywhere', he may have been referring especially to those recruited at the eleventh hour.

The French soldiers were commanded by Philibert de Chandée, a young nobleman from Savoy. Philibert probably arrived at Charles VIII's court in the train of the queen mother's relatives following the death of Louis XI; Philippe de Savoy, count of Bresse, was her brother and became King Charles's close confidant. If de Chandée was related to the count of Bresse and his family, Henry was justified in referring to him as 'our dear kinsman, both of spirit and blood', thereby recording their kinship through the French royal family and his debt to the man who commanded the French soldiers at Bosworth. Henry regarded de Chandée with special affection, as well he might. He gave him the novel title of earl of Bath on 6 January 1486 and 100 marks a year which Philibert continued to draw until Easter 1488. Although he also acted as one of Charles VIII's envoys in England, soldiering was his first love. Philibert and Sir Edward Wydeville decided to take their retinues to Spain to fight for King Ferdinand and Queen Isabella against the Moors of Granada. Wydeville was at the fall of the Moorish town of Loja in May 1486, when he managed to have his front teeth knocked out; but Philibert may not have left England until March 1487. Thereafter, he had an eventful military career in France. He was King

Bernard Stuart, lord of Aubigny, from a drawing by Jacques le Boucq (d. 1573), though probably based on a contemporary portrait. Stuart commanded Charles VIII's Scots guard, a contingent of which sailed with Henry Tudor in 1485. Stuart was treated with honour by Henry when he himself later visited England.

Louis XII's chamberlain, and by 1494 was given command of a company of soldiers. He was prominent in the French invasion of Milan in 1499, but at the battle of Cerignola in Southern Italy in 1503 he was slain by the victorious Spanish forces. Henry VII freely acknowledged that the march to Bosworth Field in 1485 owed much of its success to the French troops whom Philibert de Chandée commanded.

Henry also had with him about 400 English exiles, who formed the core of his invasion force. These men were under the command of Richard Guildford, who had fled to Brittany in 1483. On 8 August, the day after the landing in Milford Sound, Guildford was made master of Henry's ordnance and he continued to occupy this office after Bosworth. Charles VIII contributed the artillery pieces in his charge. There were some Bretons, too, in the expedition, men like John Perret, who accompanied Henry in his flight from Brittany in 1484. And according to some Scottish writers, who may have had their information from fellow countrymen who fought at Bosworth, Henry's force was stiffened by the presence of about 1,000 Scots. They are said to have been commanded by Sir Alexander Bruce of Earlshall and John of Haddington. If this was so, most of their men are likely to have been recruited from the companies brought from Scotland in 1484 by Béraut (or Bernard) Stuart, lord of Aubigny, whose family had settled in France earlier in the century. Stuart had been in Scotland to negotiate a truce between Scotland and France, and the soldiers were sent by King James III to serve with the armies of Charles VIII. Bruce of Earlshall was a member of Henry VII's household in 1485 and he was rewarded by the king for services that might well have included help at Bosworth. Later writers have claimed that Bernard Stuart himself had a command at Bosworth, but it is unlikely that Scottish chroniclers would have mentioned Bruce and Haddington and forgotten the more distinguished Stuart if he had in fact been there. Henry did not lavish any rewards on him immediately after his accession and in any case Stuart, like many others, soon found military diversion in Spain fighting against the Moors. Yet Henry did not forget the service which his Scottish troops did him in August 1485 and, as we shall see, opportunity arose more than twenty years later for him to do honour to their commander, Bernard Stuart.

Leaving John Bourgchier and the marquess of Dorset (who was no longer a reliable ally) as security for the money he had borrowed, on 1 August 1485 Henry and his army embarked at Honfleur and the flotilla emerged slowly from the shelter of the Seine. The wind was fair and southerly, and there was no opposition in the Channel. After six days, the ships entered Milford Sound on 7 August, just before sunset. The army probably landed in the small haven of Mill Bay, at the tip of St. Anne's Head, just inside the Sound and a few miles south of the settlement at Dale. After his experiences off the south coast of England in November 1483, Wales is likely to have been Henry's actual destination. The sea journey was admittedly not the shortest that could be contemplated, but promises of aid – and hope of Herbert support – may have been crucial. Recent messages had come from John Morgan, a Welsh lawyer, who reported that Rhys ap Thomas, the most powerful Welshman in Carmarthenshire, and John Savage, a Cheshireman who was Lord Stanley's nephew, were committed to Henry's cause, and that Reginald Bray had collected a large sum of money to recruit more men. Morgan advised Henry to make straight for Wales as soon as possible. He arrived on 7 August. A London chronicler, writing some twenty years later, heard that on landing Henry knelt down and, overcome with emotion, began the psalm 'Judge me, Lord, and fight my cause'. Then, he kissed the soil of Pembrokeshire, made a sign of the Cross and commanded those with him to follow him boldly in the name of the Lord and St. George.

10 The March through Wales

The Battle of Bosworth Field in 1485 ranks with the Battle of Hastings in 1066 as a battle which every British schoolchild knows about. It was, indeed, the first battle since Hastings during which the monarch was slain by the forces of a pretender to his throne. Nor does the comparison stop there. On both occasions, the pretender used a mainly French army to defeat the much larger defending forces of the English. And in both 1066 and 1485 the victor was unknown to most of his new subjects and largely ignorant of them and the realm he acquired. For these and other reasons, Bosworth, like Hastings, has been regarded as one of England's decisive battles almost from the day it was fought. We may set aside the naive and superficial view that this brief encounter could alter the entire course of English history – culturally, religiously, constitutionally and economically as well as politically. Nevertheless, there is much to be said for the view that the twenty-four-year reign of Henry Tudor as King Henry VII did see a decisive shift in several aspects of the story of England and Wales. Practically all kings leave the impress of their personality, intelligence and character on the institutions and development of their realm. Henry VII did so indelibly because of the man he was after fourteen years spent in exile, and because the condition of his new kingdom after twenty years of civil war demanded vigorous government.

Our Informants

It is extraordinary that such a battle, which brought such a man to the throne and inaugurated such a reign, remains so obscure to us now. So far as we know, none of the participants at Bosworth described their experiences. The London chroniclers, who were the city reporters of their day, were too far distant to grasp any of the details of the fighting that were later given to them. In any case, the confusion of the battle – of any medieval battle – largely defied rational description. For the supporters of the dead Richard III, it was too painful to recall and too dangerous to write about publicly. As to the companions of the victor, the days, weeks, months and years ahead raised more pressing concerns than the wish to record the unpredictable, confused and bloody details of Monday, 22 August. Therefore, the sources available to us to reconstruct the course of the battle and the events of the weeks beforehand are meagre in the extreme, though this fact has not prevented numerous writers from the sixteenth century onwards from producing a plurality of interpretations, no two of which are precisely alike. Only in the last few years have historians shown the caution in interpretation which the sketchy evidence regrettably makes necessary.

The only near-contemporary person to provide a detailed account of what happened between Henry Tudor's landing in Milford Haven on 7 August and the battle he fought at Bosworth two weeks later on 22 August is Polydore Vergil, the Italian historian whom Henry VII himself employed. Even he was writing twenty years after events which he had not witnessed. But, as we have seen already in relation to the years of Henry's exile, some of Vergil's intellectual friends had been with Henry in Brittany and France; they may not have been the sort of people who actually fought at Bosworth, but they were almost certainly – Urswick, Fox and Bray amongst them – in Henry's company as he marched from Pembrokeshire into the heart of England. The temptation to use Polydore Vergil's *English History* to retell the story of these weeks is a strong one simply because it is the only detailed and coherent account to survive; but in addition to that, his acquaintances and his skill as a historian justify any trust placed in him.

It is true that, as earlier, we have two other sources that give a narrative of certain events in 1485, including the Battle of Bosworth; but, as we have also seen, each was written down much later and surveyed matters obliquely from one particular standpoint only. The ballad known as 'The Song of the Lady Bessy', written about 1600 from an oral tradition current in the Stanley household and dating from about 1500, continues its story of Henry's career after he landed at Mill Bay. A similar ballad, 'Bosworth Field', which was also popular in the Stanley circle, deals exclusively with the battle and its prologue. Naturally, both ballads record events mainly from the Stanleys' viewpoint and we need to remember that they were composed after the rebellion and execution in 1495 of one of the participants at Bosworth, Sir William Stanley, with the intention of highlighting the Stanley contribution to Henry's victory.

The second source is the biography of Sir Rhys ap Thomas, which was written at the beginning of the seventeenth century by one of Sir Rhys's descendants in order to cultivate the reputation of his family after it, too, had been tarnished by the disgrace and execution of Sir Rhys's grandson in 1531. This account is predictably written from Sir Rhys's standpoint and with the unmistakeable purpose of exaggerating his role in Henry's successful march to Bosworth Field. Nevertheless, when all is said and done, this tradition and that of the Stanleys are as likely to incorporate peculiar knowledge and special details concerning their principal actors as they are to exaggerate their heroes' contribution to the eventual outcome. It should be noted, too, that whereas Sir Rhys's biography is woven into the popular history that Tudor historians like Polydore Vergil provided, the Stanley ballads were probably being sung and recited before Vergil wrote and are all the more likely therefore to have nuggets of independent information embedded in them.

Only two writers alive in 1485 have left more than perfunctory impressions of the Bosworth campaign, and even they have serious drawbacks. A chronicle composed at Crowland Abbey in Lincolnshire in 1486 includes a short account of the battle. Its author – an intelligent cleric with access to Richard III's court –

may not have witnessed the fighting himself, and his information is mainly confined to activity in Richard's camp. Then, earlier this century there came to light a most unlikely contemporary source for the violent events in England in 1485. Early in 1486 an old and distinguished adviser of the king and queen of Spain reported to Their Catholic Majesties news which he had just heard from certain merchants recently returned from England. His letter was written in Spanish by a Spaniard who was trying to make sense of news brought by other Spaniards who may not have spoken English and were bystanders recalling what they had heard in Bristol or Southampton. In these circumstances, some curious misunderstandings are to be expected.

When put together, these several sources – and other more minor ones – throw up occasional inconsistencies. But it is worth emphasising that Polydore Vergil's account, though written under Tudor patronage some twenty years after Bosworth, is confirmed in several particulars and is rarely contradicted in anything important. We are now ready, Polydore Vergil in hand and the other sources at our elbow, to follow Henry Tudor from Mill Bay in South Pembrokeshire to the victory at Bosworth Field.

The Landing

The choice of Mill Bay as Henry's landing place was a fortunate one. It lay out of sight of Dale Village and Castle, which were about a mile and a half due north. The soldiers who had been stationed at Dale the previous winter, as one link in Richard's chain of coastal protection, had been withdrawn before August 1485. As a result, Henry Tudor was able to begin disembarking his men and unloading their weapons and artillery undetected. According to a Scots chronicler, who may have obtained his information from Scotsmen in the expeditionary force, there were faint hearts in the company and Henry had to burn one of the ships to deter others from sailing away as soon as they arrived. After all, most of the 4,000 or 4,500 men – especially the foreigners among them – were about to take a step literally into the unknown.

That same evening Henry led the first contingents up from the bay and along the lanes to the small settlement of Dale, around which they spent the night. Polydore Vergil takes up the story. At day-break on 8 August, the army moved off from Dale along the road towards the well-fortified borough and castle of Haverfordwest, some twelve miles or more to the north-east. Henry and his lieutenants were well aware of the need to secure a major centre quickly and it seems that they achieved their goal and reached Haverfordwest just about the same time as news of their landing reached the town! Now a second piece of good fortune came Henry's way: there was no resistance in Haverfordwest and the townsmen welcomed the invaders.

The first question that arises is why Henry made for the northern shore of the great waterway of Milford Sound that snakes its way into the very heart of Pembrokeshire at the extreme south-western tip of Wales. The explanation is not a simple one, but it shows the nature of the exiles' intelligence in France, the extent of the preparations they had made in Wales, and the quality of the strategic plans which Henry and his advisers had laid. In 1485 there was to be no

Red Dragon of Cadwaladr, from King's College Chapel, Cambridge, whose building was resumed by Henry VII in 1507, according to the plans of his step-uncle, Henry VI. Henry adopted the dragon as one of the supporters of his arms to stress his alleged descent from British kings. It also appeared on his banner at Bosworth.

repetition of the fiasco two years earlier when Henry's and Jasper's flotilla made for the Dorset coast, where it was prevented from landing by patrols of soldiers, with King Richard himself not far away. Instead, it was decided to land at the most westerly point of Jasper's old earldom of Pembroke, where he and his young nephew had sought refuge in 1471 and where there might still be people who sympathised with the deposed earl. The northern shore of Milford Sound seemed less risky as a landing site than the southern shore. There would be fewer castles to confront and a better chance of breaking out to the north or east than there would be in the narrow, more confined peninsula south of the Haven. To land much further east, in Carmarthen Bay, would be even more risky.

The south coast of Wales seemed firmly under Richard III's control. Two of his devoted agents in particular had such extensive powers as to deter any Tudor landing along most of the coastline. Richard Williams, a gentleman-usher of Richard's chamber, had wide-ranging authority in the south-west. He had custody of the castle, town and lordship of Pembroke, the castle at Tenby, the castle and lordship of Manorbier, and the lordship of Llanstephen. Although he also was constable of the castles and steward of the lordships of Haverfordwest and Cilgerran in North Pembrokeshire, the core of Richard Williams's authority was the area between Carmarthen Bay and Milford Sound; if effective, it could insulate much of Pembrokeshire from Tudor attack. Even the town of Tenby seemed uninviting in 1485. Aside from Williams's men in the castle overlooking the harbour from which Jasper and Henry had sailed in 1471, Thomas White, who may have helped the Tudors to escape, was now dead and his son John was regarded as Richard's servant in February 1484 when the king gave him lands in the town worth £20 a year. Another of Richard's agents, Sir James Tyrell, had comparable control over the coastal region towards the south-east of Wales. Tyrell was one of Richard's closest counsellors, and in 1485 the lordships of Gower, Glamorgan and Newport answered to his authority.

The second question that arises is why Henry led his army northwards into the centre of Wales rather than through the coastal lowlands of South Wales or along the Roman road into Carmarthenshire and east to Brecon and the English border at Hereford. The more southerly route was quickly eliminated because Richard's agents controlled most of the lordships through which the army would have had to march on its way to Gloucestershire and the Severn crossing. The Carmarthen-Brecon route, too, had serious drawbacks. Following the execution of the duke of Buckingham in 1483, his lordship of Brecon had fallen into the hands of Sir Thomas Vaughan, who was no lover of the Tudors. Builth lordship to the north was in Sir James Tyrell's orbit; and Richard Williams, no less, had custody of Goodrich Castle which overlooked the plain of South Herefordshire. This route, too, was effectively barred to an invading force. As for Carmarthenshire, Henry learned while he was still at Haverfordwest that the leading landowner of the Tywi Valley, Rhys ap Thomas, could not be trusted. There was no practical alternative to a march northwards.

The countryside in this direction, for all its mountains, had more positive merits. Although the royal counties of Carmarthen and Cardigan, with their large castles at Carmarthen, Cardigan and Aberystwyth, were part of the dominions of Richard III as king – the southern part of his principality of Wales

Freestone Effigy of Sir Rhys ap Thomas (d. 1525), from his tomb in St. Peter's Church, Carmarthen, Dyfed. It originally stood in the Franciscan Friary, Carmarthen, where Sir Rhys was buried, but after the Dissolution of the Monasteries it was transferred to St. Peter's. Despite his equivocation in 1485, Rhys was the most powerful Welshman in the early Tudor period.

– he found it difficult to enforce his authority in them. The duke of Buckingham had been his viceroy in both counties at the time of his rebellion in 1483; but thereafter he was not replaced with Richard's agents and the local Welsh gentry were left to themselves. In any case, Cardiganshire had been very difficult for the Yorkist régime to subdue after 1461, and its persistent Lancastrian loyalty made it good ground for Henry Tudor's march in 1485.

Henry also expected much from North Wales and Cheshire, where the Stanleys ruled. Sir William Stanley was the king's justiciar or chief lieutenant in Anglesey, Caernarfonshire and Merioneth, the northern part of the royal principality of Wales; Cheshire and Lancashire amounted to a fief belonging to Sir William's elder brother, Lord Stanley. Chroniclers hint that as soon as he landed at Mill Bay, Henry sent messengers to his step-father so that they could co-ordinate their movements. If this were so, a meeting of their forces would be more practicable in the northern borderland than in the south.

Henry had been in touch with various friends and sympathisers before ever he left the River Seine. The Stanleys and the Savages in North Wales and Cheshire are mentioned by name, and we can assume that others included not only Rhys ap Thomas in the south but certain Welsh gentlemen in the north. After the landing on 7 August these were probably contacted by messengers. The letters which Henry sent to them have since disappeared as sensitive, confidential messages have a habit of doing. But by pure chance one was copied into the *History* of the Wynn family of Gwydir of Caernarfonshire, written by Sir John Wynn (died 1627). The original letter was sent to his forebear, John ap Maredudd ab Ieuan ap Mareddud, a notable and influential squire who lived in the area of Eifionydd in South Caernarfonshire.

It was calculated to appeal to the Welsh gentry of the north, 'the nobles and commons of this our principality of Wales'. It was written in the royal style which Henry had recently adopted and it was introduced with the characteristic phrase 'By the king'. Henry posed as a monarch fighting for his crown against an odious tyrant and usurper. He had already received aid from certain of 'our loving friends and true subjects', and he expressed his great confidence in the people of the principality of Wales, which he had just entered when he crossed the River Teifi at Cardigan. To encourage John ap Maredudd (and presumably other gentlemen to whom he wrote), he declared that it was not only his aim to restore the realm of England to its ancient state but also the principality of Wales to its ancient freedoms, a reference most probably to the legal restrictions placed on Welshmen at the time of the Glyndŵr Revolt. In these skilful terms, Henry called on John ap Maredudd and his men to come to him armed without delay.

> Right trusty and well beloved, we greet you well. And where it is so that through the help of Almighty God, the assistance of our loving friends and true subjects, and the great confidence that we have to the nobles and commons of this our principality of Wales, we be entered into the same, purposing by the help above rehearsed in all haste possible to descend into our realm of England not only for the adeption [recovery] of the crown unto us of right appertaining, but also for the oppression of that odious tyrant Richard late duke of Gloucester, usurper of our said right, and moreover to reduce as well our said realm of England into his ancient estate, honour and prosperity, as this our said principality of Wales, and the people of the same to their erst [original] liberties, delivering them of such miserable servitudes as they have piteously long stand in. We desire and pray you and upon your allegiance straitly charge and command you that immediately upon the sight hereof, with all such power as ye may make defensibly arrayed for the war, ye address you towards us without any tarying upon the way, unto such time as ye be with us wheresoever we shall be to our aid for the effect above rehearsed, wherein ye shall cause us in time to come to be your singular good lord and that ye fail not hereof as ye will avoid our grievous displeasure and answer unto at your peril. Given under our signet...

We do not know what John ap Maredudd's response was to Henry's letter, but other Welshmen did join the pretender's army and fought for him at Bosworth. Their motives are not easy to gauge. Henry had reason to believe that he would be welcomed in the principality counties of Wales. Welsh writers of the nineteenth and twentieth centuries have frequently pictured a population,

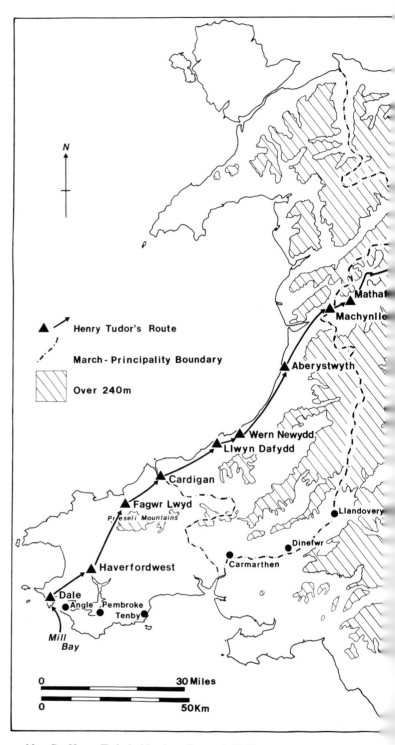

Map D: Henry Tudor's March to Bosworth Field.

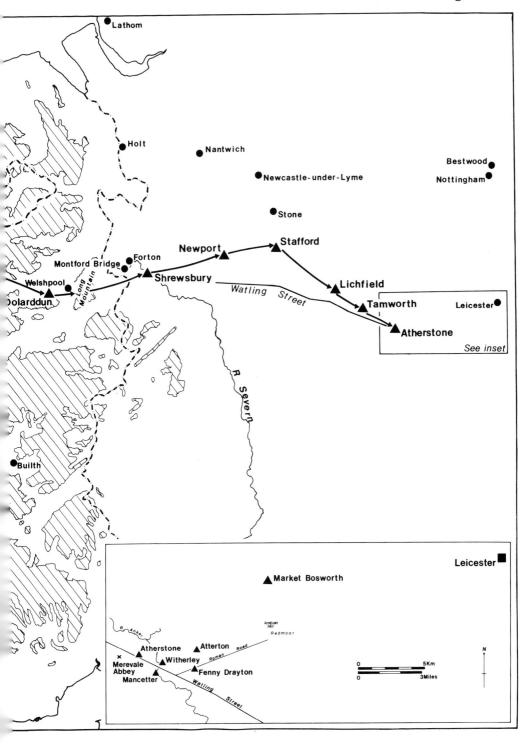

especially the influential gentry, waiting impatiently for the return of the Tudors to fulfil the prophecies of their nation, strike a blow for Welsh nationhood, and at last impose their rule on the English after a millennium of defeat and conquest. It is said that such expectations were nourished by Welsh poets patronised by these self-same gentlemen. But it is unlikely that these poets and their hard-headed patrons interpreted the political realities of the late fifteenth century simply and precisely in terms of these immemorial prophecies. No doubt there were some who regarded any prominent Welshman as a potential scourge of the English; not for nothing did Henry, in his letter to John ap Maredudd, assure the people of the principality that he would release them from their servitudes. Others composed their poems in the heat of the moment, when Henry Tudor was approaching in 1485 or had actually arrived and had to be flattered and entertained. And yet others may have produced their verses to generate enthusiasm, express solidarity or create a sense of mission, manipulating an audience in a time-honoured fashion that still works well at football matches, union meetings and political rallies.

Since the 1460s, several Welsh poets had been singing the praises and lamenting the exile of Jasper Tudor and, more recently, of his nephew Henry. We know who the authors of these poems are, but we do not know precisely when or why they wrote them, or who commissioned them. Some longed for the return of two pre-eminent Welsh noblemen, whose family was the first to enter the English peerage. Poets like Ieuan ap Rhydderch of Cardiganshire yearned for their return to pre-eminence and power in the tradition of Owain Glyndŵr. Some saw the Tudors as prominent leaders of the defeated Lancastrian dynasty. But unless they were true seers, they could not have regarded Henry – and certainly not Jasper – as an alternative to King Richard III before the summer of 1483. And very few can seriously have cherished the hope that Henry Tudor would harness Welsh resentment against the English conqueror on a national level; his letter to John ap Maredudd, with its overriding emphasis on his claim to be the true king of England, gave the lie to that.

These sentiments may have been alive in various parts of Wales, particularly in the principality counties, and even if the exiled Tudors could not encourage them directly, Henry's messengers in 1483–5 may have helped to point them in a Tudor direction as useful propaganda. The Carmarthenshire poet, Lewis Glyn Cothi, longed for the return of the familiar figure of Jasper Tudor. To the summer of 1484 or 1485 probably belong poems which impatiently expected him to come to cast the Yorkists from the English throne:

> In what seas are thy anchors, and where art you thyself?
> When wilt thou, Black Bull, come to land; how long shall we wait?
> On the feast of the Virgin, fair Gwynedd, in her singing, watched the seas.

Poetry in praise of Henry Tudor in the context of ancient prophecies flourished most vigorously after, and not before, the Battle of Bosworth. One of the most distinguished writers and seers was Dafydd Llwyd of Mathafarn in Western Montgomeryshire. If his reported reaction to the arrival of Henry Tudor on his doorstep in August 1485 reflects his attitude at all accurately, he signally failed to identify Henry as the fulfiller of the prophecies. When Henry asked Dafydd whether or not he would be successful at the end of his march, Dafydd hesitated and asked for time to think before answering. During the night, he consulted his wife who advised him to answer in the affirmative. She pointed out that if Henry were victorious against Richard III there was a good chance that he would reward a true prophet; if he were unsuccessful, he would be unlikely to pass their way again! Practically all Dafydd Llwyd's poems in honour of Henry Tudor were addressed to him as king, after his victory at Bosworth. Nor can we regard the Welsh poets as preparing the ground for a landing in Milford Sound. If there was one part of Wales where the siren songs of the poets struck no chord it was the Anglicised region of Southern Pembrokeshire.

The Long March

While he was at Haverfordwest on 8 August, Henry Tudor received disturbing news. Rhys ap Thomas, the most prominent of Carmarthenshire gentlemen, and John Savage, nephew of Lord Stanley, were not prepared to give Henry their support. This was a bitter blow because both men had led Henry to believe that they would support him once he had landed, and assurances of this sort had played a part in making South Wales the invaders' destination. Rhys was cautious, as others would be before Bosworth was won. Despite the best efforts of his biographer to persuade posterity that Rhys was one of the first and foremost to greet Henry as he stepped ashore in Mill Bay, delivering a grand speech of welcome and placing his retainers at the pretender's disposal, such scenes are imaginary. Rhys declined to renounce his loyalty to Richard III at this stage and he did not do so until Henry was just a few days away from Shrewsbury. Rhys's biographer may unwittingly provide us with an explanation of this caution. In response to a demand from Richard III that Rhys should swear an oath of fealty and send his only son Gruffydd, a mere boy, to court to ensure his father's good behaviour, Rhys replied from Carmarthen Castle in 1484 reassuring the king of his loyalty and expressing sorrow that it should ever have been questioned. Rhys's letter was included in his descendant's biography, and it may have been the long arm of Richard III that dictated Rhys's cautious attitude in 1485. As for John Savage, he too had felt the weight of Richard's authority. In May 1485, Savage was arrested at Pembroke where he may have been intriguing on Henry's behalf. Richard ordered Richard Williams, as steward of Pembroke, either to keep him locked up or to send him to the king immediately. He must have been released soon afterwards, but the experience made him hesitate until the very eve of the Battle of Bosworth before fulfilling his earlier promise to Henry Tudor. King Richard's grip on South Wales seemed effective.

On the other hand, Henry also received more cheerful news while he was at Haverfordwest. The men of Pembroke, the capital of Jasper's earldom and Henry's birthplace, announced that they were ready to serve their old lord and his nephew. This welcome news was brought by Arnold Butler, who was the first officer beyond Haverfordwest to declare for Henry Tudor. Thus encouraged,

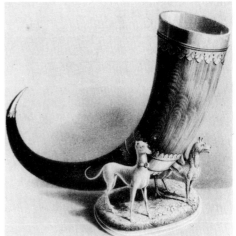

The Hirlas Horn, supposedly given by Henry VII to Dafydd ab Ieuan of Llwyn Dafydd, Dyfed, as a reward for his hospitality during Henry's march through Wales in 1485. The earliest known (1684) representation of it (left) shows a drinking horn on a silver mount flanked by Henry's supporters of a dragon and a greyhound, with the Beaufort portcullis and Tudor roses on the rim. The horn passed to the Vaughans of Golden Grove, Dyfed, and then to the Earls Cawdor. In the process it seems to have been lost or destroyed and was replaced early in the nineteenth century by the present horn (right) in the possession of Earl Cawdor.

he and his men set out from Haverfordwest later that day, or on 9 August, along the road that led north-eastward to Cardigan.

From this point on, we have precious little concrete information about Henry's march until he reached Machynlleth, some ninety-two miles north of Dale, at the lowest crossing point on the River Dyfi. There, on 14 August, Henry wrote the only letter of his that has survived from the entire journey between Pembrokeshire and Bosworth Field. These ninety-two miles were covered in seven days, a moderate pace of march during which Henry was presumably sending out appeals for support as he entered the principality of Wales at Cardigan. The only details we have of this week's march come from Polydore Vergil, supplemented by Welsh traditions which may or may not be well founded.

After crossing the bare and craggy Preseli Mountains, Henry's mainly infantry army needed a rest. According to tradition, Henry himself spent the night some seventeen miles north of Haverfordwest at a house called Fagwr Lwyd, near Cilgwyn in the parish of Nevern. The fertile valley of the River Nevern, above the small haven of Newport, provided a good camp-site. Next day, probably 10 August, they covered the next eight or nine miles to the River Teifi and the walled town of Cardigan, where the soldiers were allowed to relax. Henry supposedly slept at The Three Mariners Inn. There, too, word came that confirmed the wisdom of following this northerly route. It was reported that Sir Walter Herbert was approaching from Carmarthen with a large force. Henry's men jumped to arms and prepared for their first trial of strength since landing. Scouts were sent out, but when they returned they reported that the rumours were false. Nevertheless, that Henry was so uncertain of the loyalty of the man whose sister he had thought of marrying only a few months before indicates the dangers the insurgents believed were ahead of them even in Wales and the apprehension with which they faced them. Yet once again there was encouragement. At Cardigan, Richard Griffith, whose family had estates in West Wales as well as in Staffordshire, suddenly appeared with John Morgan of Gwent, who had been a royal officer in Carmarthenshire and Cardiganshire in the 1470s and may have continued to have interests in the locality. They declared their support for Henry, and after the Herbert alarm this was bound to raise the spirits of Henry's men. Richard Griffith had earlier joined Sir Walter Herbert and Rhys ap Thomas, and perhaps it was his approach that had deceived Henry's scouts into thinking that the main Herbert force was coming to block Henry's path. In fact, Richard Griffith and a small company had deserted Herbert and set out to find Henry's forces. According to his biographer, Rhys ap Thomas was friendly with both Richard Griffith and John Morgan, and perhaps their presence in his camp enabled Henry to keep in touch with Rhys himself and negotiate terms for his desertion of King Richard later on.

Without wasting too much time, perhaps on 11 August Henry moved further north, hugging the coast and crossing numerous streams and small vales which must have slowed him down. Here, in central Cardiganshire, tradition provides him with no fewer than two beds, only a few miles apart, though the evidence for these visits is too fascinating to ignore. About fourteen or fifteen miles north-east of Cardigan, Henry's army is said to have halted near the house at Llwyn Dafydd of a Cardiganshire man called Dafydd ab Ieuan. A remarkable memorial of the visit is the famous Hirlas Horn, a handsome drinking horn which Henry, after he became king, is supposed to have sent to Dafydd in gratitude for his hospitality. The Hirlas Horn passed to the Carmarthenshire landowning family of the Earls of Carbery in the mid-seventeenth century and then, in the eighteenth century, to the family of the present Earl Cawdor. The horn was supported by two beasts, a greyhound representing the Wydeville family of Henry's queen, and the dragon representing his Welsh forebears. The rim of the horn was decorated with the portcullis of the Beauforts and with the unique Tudor rose, distinctive emblems which appear on Henry's own tomb in Westminster Abbey. That tradition seems convincing enough, although the Hirlas Horn now in Cawdor Castle is most likely an early-nineteenth-century replica of the original, which may have been lost in a great fire towards the end of the seventeenth century at the Carmarthenshire house inherited by the Earls Cawdor.

Another tradition places Henry in a bed at the home of Einion ap Dafydd Llwyd, another Cardiganshire gentleman, at Wern Newydd in the parish of Llanarth, no more than four miles further along the road. Even today there is apparently an inscription in an old house at Wern Newydd that recalls the visit. Hospitality, of course, need not always extend to a bed for the night, though Henry could be pardoned for becoming exhausted on such a march. At least we may assume that Henry Tudor and his army rested along the road from

Cardigan before reaching the town and castle of Aberystwyth, and the ancient monastery of Llanbadarn Fawr close by, on 12 August.

According to Polydore Vergil, there were fortresses to be attacked and garrisons won over as he marched, and presumably these included Cardigan and Aberystwyth Castles, the only substantial royal fortresses in Cardiganshire. He noted, too, that Henry's scouts reported that Sir Walter Herbert and Rhys ap Thomas were continuing to shadow his advance, but that Henry determined to press on. It was becoming clear by this stage that Henry's best route into England lay across the mountains of Mid-Wales to Welshpool and the Shropshire plain beyond. If he planned to join forces with the Stanleys and others from North Wales, they needed to be informed in plenty of time of the route he proposed to follow and the general timetable he had in mind. Lord Stanley, as we shall see, probably set off from Lathom in Lancashire on 15 August and so Henry must have taken these decisions and established contact with him while still in Cardiganshire. We know of the letter he sent to John ap Maredudd soon after he reached Cardigan, and Polydore Vergil records that he also wrote to his mother, the Stanleys and Sir Gilbert Talbot. He evidently told them that he intended to cross the River Severn at Shrewsbury and to make his way to London; he would inform them later when and where they should join him.

On he pressed. Presumably on 13 August, Henry and his men travelled the seventeen or so miles to Machynlleth, where the change in the direction of the march would take place. There Henry seems to have taken steps to ensure that his passage eastwards to the lordships of the Welsh March would not be hindered. Fortunately, we have a letter, still in private possession, which Henry wrote and signed at Machynlleth on 14 August, the day after his arrival in the town. It is addressed to Sir Roger Kynaston, the influential Shropshire knight who was the uncle of John Grey, Lord Powis and temporarily in charge of Grey's estates during his absence. According to Henry, Grey was another who had promised him his aid. It is not known when such a promise was made. It may have been during the journey north from Pembrokeshire. But there is another – more intriguing – possibility. Lord Grey had commanded the 1,000 men whom Richard III sent to Brittany in the summer of 1484 to serve with Duke Francis II. It may be that Grey met Henry during his mission and secretly indicated his readiness to help if he were to return. They had, too, something in common, for Grey was married to one of the Herbert girls whom Henry had known as a child. Now, on 14 August, Henry was claiming his due. Grey's help – or at least his neutrality – would be of enormous value in easing Henry's progress through the Welsh borderland to Shrewsbury, though he may well have approached other marcher lords at the same time. There were further excellent reasons why Henry should have approached Sir Roger Kynaston while at Machynlleth. The Kynaston family estates were at Knockin and Middle in Shropshire, which Lord Stanley's son, Lord Strange, had recently acquired by marriage, and what was more to the point, Kynaston was constable of Harlech Castle and sheriff of Merioneth, a county whose border lay very close to the route Henry was about to take.

Henry Tudor's Letter to Sir Roger Kynaston, dated 14 August 1485 at Machynlleth. The king's signature, which he continued to use until 1492, appears at the top.

H   By the King

Trusty and well beloved we greet you well. And forsomuch as we be credibly informed and ascertained that our trusty and well beloved cousin the Lord Powis hath in the time passed be of that mind and disposition that at this our coming in to these parts he had fully concluded and determined to have do us service, and now we understand that he is absent and ye have the rule of his lands and folks, we will and pray you and upon your allegiance straightly charge and command you that in all haste possible ye assemble his said folks and servants and with them so assembled and defensibly arrayed for the war ye come to us for our aid and assistance in this our enterprise for the recovery of the crown of our realm of England to us of right appertaining. And that this be not failed as ye will that we be your good lord in time to come and avoid our grievest displeasure and answer to us at your peril. Given under our signet beside our town of Machynlleth the 14 day of August.

We do not know what Kynaston's reaction was; but even if he did not send the men asked for, the insurgents were not to be deterred. Leaving Machynlleth, perhaps later on 14 August, Henry moved up the spacious and fertile Dyfi Valley and may have spent a night with the elderly poet-seer, Dafydd Llwyd, at Mathafarn, four miles from Machynlleth. If the traditional account of this visit is accurate, Henry left next morning mightily encouraged by Dafydd's prediction that his march would be crowned with success. Crossing the bleak watershed between the Dyfi Valley and the valley of the Upper Banwy, his army eventually reached the vicinity of Welshpool. Henry himself, says a local tradition, spent a night along the way at Dolarddun, near Castell Caereinion, only a few miles west of Welshpool. There he is said to have been presented with a fine white horse which carried him all the way to Bosworth and victory. We do not know exactly how long the thirty-mile sojourn took from Machynlleth to Welshpool through difficult country; but Henry's army is certain to have spent at least one night in the lonely valley beside the Banwy before descending to the rolling hills around Castell Caereinion.

These few days amid some of the most rugged mountains in Wales were physically the most taxing of the entire journey. No pretender to the English throne undertook such a task before Bonnie Prince Charlie – and he achieved far less for his pains. Paradoxically, this part of the march, between Machynlleth and Shrewsbury, saw Henry's messages and negotiations at last bearing substantial fruit. The sixteenth-century chronicler from Flintshire, Elis Gruffydd, who may well have heard reminiscences at home or among Welsh friends in London about the march to Bosworth, recorded that a great number of men from Gwynedd joined Henry before he reached Shrewsbury. One of them was Rhys Fawr ap Maredudd (Rhys 'the Mighty') from Golgynwal in the uplands at the head of the Conwy Valley; he raised a contingent for Henry that rode with him to Bosworth. These recruits brought with them food and stores, including fatted animals, oxen and cattle, a welcome sight after the experience of the last few days.

On the way to Shrewsbury, too, Rhys ap Thomas belatedly threw in his lot with Henry Tudor and offered him the services of his substantial force. Rhys's biographer, after weaving an imaginary tale of Rhys's speech of welcome to Henry Tudor at Mill Bay, seems to have charted accurately his independent journey from Carmarthen up the Tywi Valley to Llandovery, then east to Brecon in the valley of the Usk, and then northwards through the Welsh borderland to the neighbourhood of Welshpool. The meeting between Henry and Rhys is supposed to have taken place on Long Mountain, the high ridge overlooking Welshpool from the east. There they spent the night, probably of 16 August. Persistent tradition in Rhys's family put his force at between 1,800 and 2,000 men which, if true, swelled Henry's army considerably. Between them, they accounted for several influential gentlemen and local government officials from Carmarthenshire and Cardiganshire in the cosmopolitan army that was now being assembled. Polydore Vergil relates what Rhys's biographer silently omits: some hard bargaining preceded Rhys's decision to support Henry, but after promising Rhys a dominant role in a Wales under Henry's rule, the bargain was struck. Although, after the Battle of Bosworth, Rhys may not have got all he had wanted, he certainly acquired governmental and social pre-eminence in South Wales early in the new reign.

Henry was now nearing his first major test as claimant to the English throne. He was close to the English border and no more than fifteen or sixteen miles from Shrewsbury, gateway to the English Midlands. The ten days' march had not (so far as we know) been seriously contested, even if some leading Welshmen had been less than enthusiastic. The pace had not been a gruelling one, although the Welsh mountains, the French artillery and the nervousness that inevitably marks the opening of a lengthy campaign allowed no more than a moderate daily progress.

11 Bosworth Field

The March to Battle

On the day, 17 August, that Henry marched down the Roman road from Long Mountain to Shrewsbury, some of his emissaries returned with a goodly sum of money, which was essential if the mercenary troops were to be paid and kept under control. But at Shrewsbury itself Henry received a rebuff. The reasons are complex but not far to seek. The bailiffs of Shrewsbury in August 1485 were Thomas Mitton and Roger Knight. Both had been prominent figures in the town since the mid-1460s and bailiff several times; Mitton, indeed, was Shrewsbury's premier burgess. While in office in October 1483, Mitton had helped in the arrest and custody of the duke of Buckingham, and as a result King Richard had given him custody of Buckingham's castle at Caus and had also generously reduced the town's annual tax bill. Mitton, then, had his own reason for not wanting to let Henry Tudor into Shrewsbury and the town may have felt some attachment to Richard III. Moreover, townsmen faced with massed insurgents had a common fear of destruction and disorder at the hands of thousands of roughnecks in narrow urban streets. And the largely French, Scottish and Welsh followers of Henry Tudor, a mere pretender to the English throne, were even less appealing. Thomas Mitton accordingly refused Henry permission to cross the Severn and enter Shrewsbury from the west by the Welsh Gate; he pompously declared that if Henry marched through the town it would only be over his body. The town's chronicle describes the scene vividly.

> ... he came to the town of Shrewsbury where the gates were shut against him and the portcullis let down. So the said Earl [of Richmond]'s messenger came to the gate, to say the Welsh gate, commanding them to open the gates to their right king, and Master Mitton made and swore, being head bailiff and a stout wise gentleman, saying that he knew him for no king but only King Richard to whom he was sworn, whose life tenants he and his fellows were. And before he should enter there he should go over his belly, meaning thereby that he would be slain to the ground and so to run over him before he entered, and that he protested vehemently upon the oath he had taken.

Henry had no option but to withdraw and consider his position. If he were denied passage through Shrewsbury, he would have to make a lengthy and embarrassing detour round the town, and he would hardly be able to persuade other English towns to open their gates to him.

Henry and his company retreated about four or five miles to Mountford Bridge on the Severn and the village of Forton nearby. They camped that night on Forton Heath, while Henry himself stayed at a certain Hugh of Forton's house in the village. Next morning, he decided to send more conciliatory emissaries to plead with the town bailiffs, assuring them that, if admitted to the town, he and his men would march through quietly and in good order without causing any damage or injury to any, and they would respect the oaths of loyalty which the townsmen had sworn to Richard III. No doubt this went some way towards removing the townsmen's fears, but the crucial factor in changing the bailiffs' mind may have been the arrival of one of Sir William Stanley's men, Rowland Warburton. In response to Henry's messages, Sir William was already on his way to rendezvous with him; along the way, he seems to have been alerted to Shrewsbury's resistance. Sir William therefore sent Warburton to urge the bailiffs to open Shrewsbury's gates, though the colourful story of how he delivered his message – wrapped round a stone thrown over the town walls – is likely to be apocryphal. Realisation that the Stanleys were supporting Henry in his venture may finally have convinced the townsmen that it was wiser to allow the insurgents in than to continue keeping them out. Again the local chronicler captures the scene, with Mitton contriving to observe the oath he had sworn the previous day.

> . . . upon this they entered and in passing through the said Mitton lay along the ground and his belly upward and so the said Earl stepped over him and saved his oath and so passing forth and marching forwards . . .

Having opened the gate, the bailiffs escorted Henry and his men in battle order through the town; Elis Gruffydd later recorded that Henry rode in the middle of his columns of troops. As had been agreed, his army did not halt in Shrewsbury or stay the night, though there is a strong tradition that one of the fine fifteenth-century houses still to be seen on the street known as Wyl Cop gave Henry hospitality while he was in the town. A few doors away was the house of Thomas Mitton, who had had to eat humble pie on behalf of his town.

Henry's experience at Shrewsbury had been a sobering one and the solution to the *impasse* something of an humiliation for him. He had not extracted from the townsmen any recognition of his right to the crown of England. It was a reminder, too, that the difficulties facing him in the populous and prosperous English Midlands were of a new order. The accent now was on winning new supporters and joining up with influential friends.

Henry took the road through Shropshire towards Newport where, on a hill close to the town, he pitched his tent and spent the night of 18 August. The following afternoon, Sir Gilbert Talbot arrived with more than 500 armed men, one of a number of contingents that now began appearing from the English counties bordering Wales. However reluctantly, Shrewsbury itself had contributed some soldiers to Henry's force as it marched through the town, whilst among the men of Shropshire who joined him were 800 under Sir

Welsh Gate and Bridge, Shrewsbury, from a watercolour by Paul Sandby (d. 1809). Both were demolished by 1792, though a statue probably of the Black Prince was transferred from the Gate to the facade of the old Market Hall. Gate and Bridge proved major obstacles to Henry Tudor in August 1485.

Richard Corbet (whose step-father was none other than Sir William Stanley) and others led by Roger Acton. From Herefordshire came Thomas Croft, who had been brought up with Edward IV when both were very young; Croft's strong Yorkist leanings did not extend to supporting Richard III. Worcestershire was represented by John Hanley, who may have been one of the duke of Clarence's old servants, and his men. Further south in Gloucestershire, Robert Pointz set out to meet Henry on his march. And other companies came from adjacent Welsh marcher lordships like Caus, one of the duke of Buckingham's former estates, and Talgarth. This was the kind of substantial response from English knights and their retinues that Henry needed in order to carry conviction in challenging the king.

He moved rapidly forward the twelve miles to Stafford, and there potentially the most heartening meeting so far took place, with Sir William Stanley and a small advance retinue. They had a short talk and then Sir William returned to the bulk of his force some distance off. Sir William is certain to have told Henry that Richard III was based at Nottingham and that by a short march southwards the king would be able to bar Henry's path to London. A more rapid advance was therefore advisable and Stanley assistance crucial.

At this point, with the first appearance of the Stanleys, the ballads from the Stanley household can be used to flesh out the story which Polydore Vergil tells. According to 'The Song of the Lady Bessy', Sir William Stanley had set off from his house at Holt in Flintshire, less than thirty miles north of Shrewsbury. He made his way to Nantwich accompanied by large numbers of men from North Wales and Cheshire. As justiciar of the three counties of the principality in North Wales, he had authority to raise men in Gwynedd, but it had doubtless taken a little time and he is likely to have been responding to appeals from Henry Tudor in West Wales. The ballad goes on to say that on Tuesday morning [16 August] he set off to cover the twenty miles to Stone in Staffordshire, and that soon after this the meeting with Henry Tudor took place at Stafford. This date is almost certainly too early; if Sir William had arrived in Staffordshire as early as this, according to a pre-arranged plan with Henry Tudor, he had not bargained for Henry's delay at Shrewsbury and perhaps even a delay imposed by Rhys ap Thomas outside Welshpool. Hence Sir William's urgent message to Shrewsbury's bailiffs to let his confederate in. Rather did the meeting with Henry Tudor take place at Stafford on the evening of his arrival in the town, Friday, 19 August. In the discussion, Henry explained how much he needed Sir William's aid and that of Lord Stanley. Sir William is said to have reassured him but before nightfall he returned to his own camp at Stone.

Henry therefore pressed on, reasonably encouraged and presumably expecting Sir William to follow close behind. When Henry reach Lichfield, he decided to spend the night outside the walls of the cathedral city, rather than run the risk of his much enlarged force running amok and alienating the citizens and the cathedral authorities. Very early the following morning, 20 August, he entered the city and was well received. He learned that three days earlier Lord Stanley himself had reached Lichfield with a considerable army which was later put as large as 5,000.

Once again, the ballads supplement Polydore Vergil's account. Like his brother William, Lord Stanley had set out several days before Henry reached the English border. He apparently left his home at Lathom in Western Lancashire on Monday, 15 August, while Henry was still in Mid-Wales; he made his way to Newcastle-under-Lyme. His route was naturally independent of his brother's from Holt and although they may have kept in touch by scout and messenger, their armies were separate until the eve of Bosworth. Whereas Sir William waited at Stafford to meet Henry Tudor, Lord Stanley seems to have pressed on to Lichfield, and Polydore Vergil implies that when he heard that Henry's force was approaching, he moved rapidly along the main road that was Watling Street to Atherstone, perhaps to give Henry's main army room to billet. Vergil, however, also claims that Stanley kept his distance from Henry's army in order to demonstrate to King Richard's scouts that he had not abandoned the king, but rather was responding to Richard's summons to come with his retainers to support him. After all, Lord Stanley's eldest son, George, Lord Strange, was in Richard's custody, along with William Griffith, a prominent Caernarfonshire landowner. This created a dilemma for both Sir William and Lord Stanley in their relations with Henry and Richard in August 1485. Their sympathies, reflected in their promises, lay with Henry, but they dared not offend Richard lest they never see Lord Strange again. This explains their cautious and seemingly equivocal attitude on the way from the north-west, the distance Lord Stanley kept between his and Henry Tudor's army, and the anxiety that plagued Henry right up to the battle itself.

Lord Stanley was the first to arrive in the vicinity of Atherstone, near what was to prove to be the site of the Battle of Bosworth. His brother William reached Lichfield early on 20 August. He encountered some of Henry's men still at Worsley Bridge after they had spent the night outside the walls. On this Saturday morning, the ballad of 'Bosworth Field' describes the city as being *en fête*, with the armies of Henry and Sir William Stanley mingling with each other and guns firing 'to cheer the country', either in celebration or in boisterous anticipation. Sir William eventually passed through Lichfield and took up position outside the city pending further discussions with his brother and with Henry. Indeed, a messenger came from Lord Stanley at Atherstone to say that Richard III was near and that he could expect to be fighting within three hours. This was unduly alarmist, but Sir William accordingly pushed on to Tamworth and Atherstone, where he met his brother and made arrangements for a call to arms next day. What they decided at their meeting is not known. Did they decide to throw their weight openly behind Henry, as they had promised? Or did they decide to continue holding aloof in order to try to protect Lord Strange? Repeated instructions from King Richard and anxious pleas from Henry Tudor made their position increasingly delicate and yet they still refused to declare themselves publicly. Next day, Sunday, 21 August, the two Stanleys made their battle plans, and if 'Bosworth Field' is to be believed, these involved amalgamating their forces: Lord Stanley would command the vanguard, Sir William the rearguard and their brother, Sir Edward Stanley, the wing. This was their position when night fell on 21 August. Contact with Richard III's army could hardly be avoided on the morrow.

Meanwhile, Henry Tudor was moving somewhat gingerly towards Tamworth, about seven miles south-east of Lichfield. There, late in the evening of 20 August, Sir Thomas Bourgchier, Walter Hungerford and others who (as we shall see) had escaped from a royal force that was making its way from London to Nottingham, found Henry's encampment and joined his ranks. As the pretender's army approached Tamworth a curious incident took place which is related only by Polydore Vergil. Henry and about twenty of his personal bodyguard had fallen back a little. According to Vergil, they were gripped by doubts and uncertainty and, as news came in of Richard's presence at Leicester, they were worried because the Stanleys had still not offered unqualified support. When night fell, Henry's army was able to camp in the broad river plain in the shadow of Tamworth, but Henry himself was still three miles away and lost in the dark. Thoroughly alarmed, he and his companions remained where they were, waiting for dawn and making contact with no one lest they reveal their exposed position. The main army was naturally alarmed at the disappearance of its leader and his lieutenants, and when Henry reappeared in the grey dawn of 21 August he had to restore morale. He explained that during the night he had received some good news from secret friends, by implication the Stanleys, though Henry may have been referring to the renegades from London. That

Tamworth Castle, Staffordshire. Though altered since the fifteenth century, the Norman shell-keep still dominates the valleys of the Tame and Anker. It was vital for Henry Tudor to receive its submission in August 1485, and he may have been able to commandeer its stock of arms.

Polydore Vergil should have reported this incident in detail, and not entirely to Henry's credit, suggests that his informant recalled their acute nervousness at this juncture and the panic which Henry's disappearance began to cause; even if he had been in secret contact with the Stanleys, morale among his men was too fragile to justify him vanishing so suddenly and without explanation.

Whatever happened that night, Henry marched next day down Watling Street to Atherstone, there to rendezvous with Lord Stanley and his brother. Sometime during 21 August, Henry rode across the River Anker to meet his step-father and Sir William. 'Bosworth Field' relates how they heard someone coming through the woods and jumped to the conclusion that it was the king. They were doubtless much relieved to see Henry emerge from the trees. They shook hands and discussed how they would act when the fighting began. Henry asked his step-father to allow his right vanguard to join Henry's army, and Stanley may have been surprised that 'small is your company'. 'The Song of the Lady Bessy' makes it clear that Stanley was determined to keep overall control of his own men; but he did order four knights – Sir Robert Tunstall from Lancashire, Sir John Savage from Cheshire, Sir Hugh Persall, and the Staffordshire knight, Sir Humphrey Stanley – to reinforce Henry's vanguard. The meeting, then, seems to have been reasonably satisfactory to both sides, though Henry could have ridden back to his camp with a nagging doubt still in his mind. Before the day was done, his spirits were raised. Brian Sandford, Simon Digby and the younger John Savage, who had been induced to stay loyal to Richard earlier in the summer, managed to desert the king and appeared in Henry's camp with 'a choice band' of armed men. However, suspicions and doubts were not confined to the insurgents.

The King

Richard III was at Nottingham when he heard of Henry Tudor's landing in Pembrokeshire. He had been in the city or at the royal lodge of Bestwood in Sherwood Forest since early in June. The area served his purpose well. It was within easy reach of his friends and supporters in the North of England and yet it was well placed in the centre of England to enable him to react to any invasion the Tudors might launch. On 11 August, he received news that Henry had arrived in Milford Haven. Richard thought that the landing took place at Angle, on the south side of the entrance to the Haven, but the message seems to have been garbled or misunderstood and it is more likely that the Tudor landing had been *witnessed* by loyal observers at Angle gazing across the narrow waterway at the ships anchored outside Mill Bay. Richard had no doubts about the significance of the news, and to judge by one letter he sent from Bestwood Lodge on 11 August, summoning the Vernons of Derbyshire to his standard, he was fully determined personally to oppose the invader.

> ... our rebels and traitors accompanied with our ancient enemies of France and other strange nations departed out of the water of Seine the first day of this present month, making their course westwards been landed at Angle beside Milford Haven in Wales on Sunday last passed, as we be credibly informed, intending our utter destruction, the extreme subversion of this our realm and disinheriting of our true subjects of the same, towards whose recountering, God being our guide, we be utterly determined in our own person to remove in all haste goodly that we can or may.

According to the Croyland Chronicler, who may have been able to observe his moods, Richard was eager to get to grips with Henry Tudor and to destroy the threat that had hung over him for months past. This impression need not conflict with Polydore Vergil's report that to begin with his confidence was high because he had been told that Henry's initial position after landing was weak. That was largely true. Richard could justly feel that his agents in Wales – or most of them – were steadfast and prepared to resist the invasion; with any luck, the insurgents would be captured by Sir Walter Herbert and Rhys ap Thomas. Indeed, only by marching north-eastwards was Henry able to avoid them. As the days passed and news came in of Henry's steady progress through West and Mid-Wales, Richard's mood of optimism changed.

He had already summoned nobles and gentry to muster with their retinues at Nottingham as quickly as possible, in accordance with undertakings given in the autumn of 1484. Northumberland was summoned from the north, the duke of Norfolk from East Anglia. Sir Robert Brackenbury, lieutenant of the Tower of London, the king's main arsenal, was ordered to bring with him several important gentry who were in his custody, including two, Sir Thomas Bourgchier and Walter Hungerford, who had been under suspicion ever since their involvement in the revolts of 1483. These summonses were stern and uncompromising: punishment would be severe for any who failed in their duty. This had more point for Lord Stanley than for most others. Even if the full extent of his intrigues on behalf of his step-son were still not fully appreciated by Richard III, Stanley was bound to be mistrusted after he retired to Lathom in Lancashire in July 1485. Moreover, Henry was certain to be in touch with his mother as he made his way across Wales and moved closer to Lancashire and Cheshire. Stanley declined to answer the king's summons, pleading a bout of sweating sickness. But Richard had a hold over him and his family which might prevent them at least from supporting Henry Tudor with armed men. Not only had Lord Stanley's heir, Lord Strange, been sent by his father to Richard's court towards the end of July as an assurance of Stanley loyalty, but when Strange was captured trying to escape from Nottingham sometime in August he made a damaging confession about a sinister conspiracy. He admitted that, along with his uncle, Sir William Stanley, and Sir John Savage, he had intended joining Henry Tudor. The Croyland Chronicler, whose detailed recollection of these revelations suggests that he was at or near Nottingham at this time, wrote that Strange pleaded with Richard for mercy and, in return, promised to try to persuade his father to return to court. Probably under duress, Strange described to Lord Stanley the great danger he was now in and urged his father to help Richard, not Henry, in the present emergency. As for Sir William Stanley and Sir John Savage, they were publicly proclaimed traitors by Richard III as a warning to all who were thinking of supporting or welcoming Henry Tudor.

It was a nice judgement that Richard had to make: to outlaw two of the leading conspirators might deter others from joining Henry, but would the continued imprisonment of Lord Strange prevent the traitors themselves from giving Henry all the help they could? The gamble seemed to work for a time, but in reality it strengthened the Stanleys' resolve to throw their weight behind the invader.

News that Henry had reached Shrewsbury alarmed Richard. And when his scouts reported that, after marching eastwards from Shrewsbury to Stafford as if to confront the king near Nottingham, the insurgents had turned south along Watling Street, the road that ran close to Lichfield and on to London, Richard mobilised his assembled forces. Late on Friday, 19 August or early the next morning, he led them quickly south to Leicester as if to bar Henry's path to the capital. It is unrealistic and unfair to blame Richard III for inactivity at Nottingham and for failing to confront Henry Tudor sooner than he did. It would have been foolish to have moved his large army without being certain of his adversary's objective. In any case, it was wise of the king to continue recruiting for as long as possible, and sensible to draw Henry's men, most of whom had been on the hoof or on foot for two weeks without a substantial break, further into England and to tire them as much as possible before attacking them in battle.

Richard had probably assembled a larger army than Henry's, though we have no precise indication of its size. It moved south in square battle formation, with

Copper-gilt Processional Cross found at Bosworth in 1778. The Yorkist sun-burst badge appears on the reverse of the four Evangelists' plaques. The cross may have been carried to the battlefield by Richard's forces.

Richard and his personal guard preceded by two wings predominantly of horsemen. By sunset on 20 August, they had covered the twenty-three miles to Leicester, where they camped for the night; tradition has it that Richard stayed at The White Boar Inn in Northgate Street. And at Leicester, further recruits arrived. 'Bosworth Field' lists almost 100 nobles and knights who responded to Richard's summons and swore an oath to fight by his side. The majority were from Richard's beloved North Country, especially Yorkshire and Lancashire, and a cursory investigation suggests that the author of the ballad had an accurate list of some of the royal retinue-leaders in front of him. Others were members of the king's household and Council, or had come from London with Brackenbury, or marched from East Anglia with the duke of Norfolk and his son, the earl of Surrey. He may also have had the services of some Flemish mercenaries sent by Maximilian of Austria and Burgundy, and led by his Spanish-born commander, Salazar. What was disturbing was that Richard was unable to hold the loyalty of small groups of gentry who contrived to flee from his encampments to join Henry's forces in the days before the battle.

Next day, Richard III set off from Leicester westward along the road to the Cistercian abbey of Merevale, a mile to the west of Atherstone. As the Croyland Chronicler recalled, he came with great pomp as a true king of England. He wore his crown, which the awe-struck Spanish merchants heard was worth 120,000 crowns. He wore his surcoat embroidered with the royal arms of England; and his entourage included a goodly company of noblemen led, perhaps, by the beautiful processional cross, decorated with the Yorkist emblem of the sun-burst, which was discovered in 1778 near the battlefield. The Scottish ambassador, the bishop of Dunkeld, may have been present too. Richard's scouts discovered where the enemy lay, somewhere close to Atherstone; to judge by the damage done to the buildings, corn fields and pasture of the monks at Merevale, they had taken over the abbey. According to tradition, Henry himself stayed at The Three Tuns Inn in Atherstone itself. The Stanleys were located further to the north-east, across the river. Richard presumably chose as his camp for the night of 21 August a site in the broad plain of Redmoor, perhaps on or near the modest ridge that runs through it from east to west, never more than 400 feet in height. He ordered the tents to be pitched, allowed his soldiers to rest and, according to Polydore Vergil, exhorted them to victory in the battle that was bound to come on the morrow.

The Battle

If our sources for Henry Tudor's march to Bosworth are often vague and sketchy, they are positively skimpy when it comes to explaining the action on 22 August. Aside from Polydore Vergil, the Croyland Chronicler and the Stanley balladers, no one living within a generation of that day has left a record of its momentous events. Moreover, few late-fifteenth- and sixteenth-century writers had an eye for geography or topography, however hard they might try to describe the exchanges in a battle. Modern accounts begin with the study by William Hutton, the local historian and topographer whose *The Battle of Bosworth Field between Richard the Third and Henry Earl of Richmond, August 22, 1485*, 'wherein

is described the approach of both armies with plans of the battle, its consequences, the fall, treatment and character of Richard, to which is prefixed, by
way of introduction, a History of his life till he assumed the regal power', was
published after he had tramped the battlefield in 1788. Since then, poorly
recorded 'improvements' by enclosure, drainage, canal-cutting and railway-
laying have so transformed Redmoor Plain as to make a detailed topographical
interpretation now impossible. Local traditions, mostly recorded by Hutton, and
the occasional discovery of objects at various places on Redmoor and the hill
overlooking it are all that we have to supplement the written word.

Contemporaries referred to the conflict as taking place on Redmoor Plain.
During the sixteenth century it became common to identify it as the Battle of
Bosworth, after the small town to the north of the plain. The Welsh chronicler,
Elis Gruffydd, later commented that the two hosts met near Market Bosworth,
among the towns known as 'the Tuns' (surely those villages like Fenny Drayton,
Atterton and Dadlington whose cornfields were trampled by Henry's forces).
Nevertheless, many different accounts of this battle have been written, based on
topographical interpretation, 'inherent military probability', conjecture,
imagination and invention, and it serves no purpose to repeat them. When all is
said and done, we cannot be certain where the fighting took place, where the
adversaries were stationed beforehand, at what time the battle started and
finished, nor what the tactics of each side were. There is no sound alternative to
relying on the contemporary record, frustrating though that may be.

On the morning of 22 August Richard's camp was awake early, but the day did
not begin well for the king. As he told his friends, he had spent a disturbed night.
In a superstitious age, this was regarded as an ill omen, though we need not
follow Polydore Vergil's interpretation of Richard's sleeplessness as a sign of a
guilty conscience, or William Shakespeare's dramatic vision of the king's mind
plagued by ghostly victims of his misdeeds. The duke of Norfolk may have been
disconcerted, too, for early in the day he discovered a warning fixed to the
entrance of his quarters: 'Jack of Norfolk be not so bold, For Dykon thy master
is bought and sold'. The king rose so early that (according to the Croyland
Chronicler) there was no chaplain on hand to say mass and no breakfast ready.
Richard declared that the engagement which would take place that day would be
decisive for himself, for Henry and for England; for this reason, he wore his
crown throughout. Indeed, a later Scottish chronicler described how Richard
sent for his crown in his pavilion and with some ceremony put it on his head in
the presence of several lords and the bishop of Dunkeld who, though he left the
king's camp shortly afterwards, may have been the source of this particular
report.

Richard's host was assembled, armed and well organised. The vanguard of
horsemen interspersed with infantry stood in a long broad line, with archers in
front 'like a most strong trench and bulwark'. These archers were commanded
by the duke of Norfolk. Behind the vanguard came Richard himself with 'a
choice force', the flower of his army. No contemporary tells us precisely where
Richard's army was, but it is reasonable to suppose that it climbed the ridge on

Redmoor Plain and moved along it to the hill at its western end called Ambien Hill. This would give the king as good a view as could be obtained of the surrounding plain and any activity to north, west or south. If this was indeed Richard's position, it was a relatively narrow one but long enough to allow his 'battles' to advance one after the other.

Meanwhile, Henry Tudor was assembling troops for his advance. He asked Lord Stanley, who lay between the two main armies, to prepare his men too. Henry may have been shaken by the response. Despite the discussions the previous day, Stanley still could not bring himself to join forces with his step-son. He told the messenger that Henry should make his own men ready and Stanley would come with his; in other words, the two armies would remain separate. This made Henry very anxious as he ordered his men to their position sometime during the morning. His vanguard, which he had hoped Lord Stanley's men would strengthen, was relatively small: in the front were archers under John de Vere, earl of Oxford, a man of considerable experience and daring in warfare; the right wing was put in the hands of Sir Gilbert Talbot and the left under John Savage. Henry himself followed with a troop of cavalry and a small contingent of infantry. Nevertheless, it will not do to repeat Polydore Vergil's estimate of the size of the two armies. Chroniclers were innumerate when it came to handling large numbers and Vergil could not resist underlining Henry's achievement by underestimating the size of his forces. He put Henry's army at about 5,000 and the king's at more than twice that number. The Spanish merchants heard that Henry indeed had fewer men than Richard, but he is likely to have had more than 5,000 on 22 August. About 4–4,500 had landed with him at Mill Bay on 7 August, and even if some of these had fallen by the wayside during the next two weeks, substantial reinforcements from Rhys ap Thomas and the countryside through which he marched, not to speak of others raised at Shrewsbury and in the border shires, must have swollen his army considerably. Polydore Vergil put Sir William Stanley's force at 3,000 men.

We are no better informed about the composition of each force. Suffice it to say that the armies of both Richard and Henry had companies of cavalry and infantry, and were supplied with cannon and hand-guns as well as the more traditional bows and blades. According to 'Bosworth Field', Richard chained together 140 cannons called 'serpentines' to form a phalanx of artillery in support of his vanguard; a similar number of great 'bombards' were trundled to the battlefield; and his troops had hand-guns or arquebuses. On Henry's side, the artillery provided by the French king had presumably been carried through Wales and the West Midlands and it may have been supplemented by the guns that were fired, in joy rather than in anger, at Lichfield.

When the two vanguards saw one another, the men put on their helmets and sounded the call to battle. At what time of day this was and which way Henry advanced, we do not know. To judge by the compensation he later offered, Henry and his commanders led their men across the ripening corn fields belonging to the villages of Manseter, Witherley, Fenny Drayton and Atterton. Beyond that, we may simply conjecture that he was moving north-eastwards towards Ambien Hill; he advanced at a moderate pace, according to the Croyland Chronicler. The Spanish merchants heard that he tried to inspire his smaller and somewhat dispirited force to attack the king, and confidence was probably higher in Richard's camp than in Henry's because of uncertainty about the attitude of the Stanleys. Their active participation in the battle was more important to Henry than it was to Richard, whose gamble had so far succeeded in at least keeping them at bay.

Henry encountered marshy ground, perhaps as he neared the slope of Ambien Hill. The remains of a marsh still exist to the south and west of the hill and it seems likely that it was more extensive in 1485 than it is today after centuries of enclosure and drainage schemes. Henry's best way forward was to wheel left, leaving the marsh on his right hand to act as a barrier against any attack on his flank. (Jean Molinet attributes this manoeuvre to a plan by the French to outflank Richard's main 'battle'.) Henry's men therefore turned to face north or even north-west as they skirted the marsh and what may have been the western slope of Ambien Hill. Though we do not know precisely at what time these manoeuvres took place, if Henry's army had come from the further side of Atherstone, it must have been mid-day or later. This would explain why Polydore Vergil noted that the sun climbing in the August sky was now at Henry's back.

When Henry had passed the marsh, Richard saw his opportunity and ordered his men to attack. At the same time, he realised – and could probably see – that Lord Stanley showed no sign of joining him. Richard ordered Lord Strange to be beheaded. According to 'Bosworth Field' and 'The Song of the Lady Bessy', Strange managed to send one of his servants to tell his tenants and retainers what was to happen to him and to take a ring to his wife, asking her to take their son and flee abroad if the day proved to be Richard's. But Strange need not have worried; he was saved by the speed and confusion of the fighting. Once the vanguards were engaged, Sir William Harrington suggested to Richard that this was no time for executions. Even Richard became distracted by the heat of battle, and Strange's guardians left him more or less to his own devices.

After an exchange of shouts and arrows, the two sides fell to vigorous hand-to-hand fighting with axe, sword and pike, somewhere near the foot or on the slope of Ambien Hill. Oxford's French and English soldiers were apparently ranged against Norfolk's men. The tactical progress of the battle is now impossible to reconstruct. But 'The Song of the Lady Bessy' claims that Norfolk's line began to break under pressure from Rhys ap Thomas's men, and this may be the stage at which (according to Vergil) Oxford, fearing lest some of his men push too far ahead and be surrounded in the mêlée, gave an order that none of the ranks should advance more than ten feet from the standards. As a result, the fighting slackened briefly as his men moved closer together, thickening their formation. Norfolk's men were puzzled by Oxford's move and suspected a trick, so they too halted until Oxford's forces were ready to resume their advance in a close, wedge-shape formation.

Richard was able to observe all this. Northumberland was at the rear with a well equipped force which could not take part in the fighting – indeed, it never did so, not necessarily because of any treasonable intent but possibly because of the topography of the battlefield. Richard was informed by his scouts that Henry, who was also standing aloof from the fighting, had only a small company

Portrait of King Richard III (1452–85), by an unknown artist at the end of the fifteenth or early in the sixteenth century. This portrait comes closest to a likeness of the king; it once belonged to the Paston family of Norfolk.

with him, and eventually Richard was able to identify where he was by his standard. The king then took a most remarkable and courageous initiative to end the battle quickly by slaying Henry Tudor; that would undoubtedly have brought the fighting to a sudden halt. He spurred his horse, rode out from the flank – presumably the northern flank, though we do not know for certain – skirted the vanguards facing each other, and made straight for his adversary. Henry stood his ground as he saw the king of England descending towards him at full gallop. The force of the charge enabled Richard, 'making way with weapon on every side', to slay several of those around the pretender, to overthrow Henry's standard of the red dragon, to kill the standard-bearer, William Brandon, and to force the mighty John Cheyne to the ground. According to the Denbighshire poet, Tudur Aled, Rhys Fawr ap Maredudd held Henry's standard aloft during the battle, and it may be that he retrieved it as it fell from Brandon's hands. (Rhys's mutilated effigy can still be seen in Ysbyty Ifan Church, where he was buried years later.) King Richard's onslaught was a fearsome sight and an astonishing feat. Henry fought longer than some thought possible for a youngish man with no real experience of the toils of battle. It was only when he was close to despair that help came. On such a slender thread hung the decision of that day and the future of England's monarchy.

From whatever position he occupied, Sir William Stanley could see the king's onslaught and in the nick of time took his 3,000 men to Henry's rescue. He scattered most of Richard's troops, leaving the king alone 'fighting manfully in the thickest press of his enemies'. Though wounded many times, Richard disdained the offer of a horse and the advice of his companions to flee. Several contemporaries writing independently stressed his bravery and heroism. The Spaniards were told that he declared he would 'die like a king or win victory in this field'. Polydore Vergil heard the same, that 'that day he would make end either of war or life'. He fell, says the Croyland Chronicler, like a brave and valiant prince. According to 'The Song of the Lady Bessy', his crown was knocked off, his helmet smashed into his skull, and his body beaten lifeless. The Burgundian writer, Jean Molinet, maintains that the death-blow was struck by a Welshman's halberd, but this may simply be a tribute to Henry's Welsh blood. The deed was done at a ford, Sandeford, over one of the streams running beside the battlefield. Around the king lay his bodyguard: Sir Richard Ratcliffe, Sir William Conyers, Sir Robert Brackenbury, Sir Richard Charlton, and the royal standard-bearer, Sir Percivall Thriball, who still clung to the standard when his legs were hewn off.

Meanwhile, in the main engagement, the earl of Oxford had forced the front line of his opponents to break (and this may have been what prompted Richard's charge). We do not know the directions they took, but many were killed in the chase. Molinet recorded that Lord Stanley attacked them in flight; if so, it was his first and only active intervention in the battle and not a creditable one. The duke of Norfolk was caught by John Savage and (says Molinet) handed over to the earl of Oxford who had him killed. It was probably this enforced flight of Norfolk's which caused the observer sent to the battlefield by the city of York to report that the king's defeat and death were caused by the desertion of the duke and many others.

Like all battles, Bosworth offered an opportunity to settle personal scores between adversaries. Sir James Blount sought out and slew the Nottinghamshire gentleman, John Babington, thinking he was his cousin, Sir John Babington. Sir James hoped thereby to get the Babington lands for his wife, who was Sir John's niece; he must have been bitterly disappointed to discover that he had killed the wrong man. Polydore Vergil says that all told about 1,000 of Richard's men were slain that day, though there is no way of verifying this and Molinet is inclined to put the total casualties on both sides at only 400. Large numbers, including Northumberland, Surrey and William Catesby, were captured for, as Richard had foreseen when he made his charge, the death of one of the principals led most of his men to throw down their weapons and surrender. Few of the captives appear to have been executed for choosing the losing side, but there are three known exceptions to this. A few days after the battle, when Henry was still at Leicester, two members of the Somerset family of Bracher, who were connected with King Richard's household, were put to death. The third was William Catesby, one of Richard's most intimate counsellors. Appeals to his wife's uncle, Lord Stanley, did not save him: 'my lords Stanley, Strange and all that blood, help and pray for my soul, for ye have not for my body, as I trusted in you', he begged movingly in his will drawn up on 25 August before he went to the block. Others escaped, among them the earl of Lincoln, Lord Lovell, Lord Dacre, Humphrey and Thomas Stafford, and Richard's secretary, John Kendale.

Polydore Vergil put Henry's casualties at only 100, but there is even less reason for accepting this figure. They included those who fell protecting Henry, including William Brandon, his standard-bearer, who had been a good friend since Breton days.

The Battle of Bosworth had lasted more than two hours. It was known to those alive in 1485 – and ever since – as the battle at Bosworth, the largest village in the vicinity of Redmoor Plain and a mile or so to the north. After it was over, Henry, who had regarded himself as king long before, gave thanks for the victory and rode to a nearby hill, which tradition identifies as Crown Hill to the south of Ambien Hill. There he ordered his men to tend to the wounded and bury the dead (though no mass grave has ever been found near Redmoor Plain). He thanked his nobles and the gentry-leaders of retinues; the soldiery cried 'God save King Henry, God save King Henry'. All that was needed was a symbolic crowning to accompany what amounted to the acclamation, in time-honoured fashion, of King Henry VII. Among the spoil was Richard's crown which, according to Polydore Vergil and 'Bosworth Field', Lord Stanley took and placed on his step-son's head. A persistent tradition full of irony says that the crown was discovered under a thornbush. Despite the scepticism of modern historians, it is undeniably curious that within a generation a crown in a thornbush had become a Tudor symbol. It was now evening and after assembling their baggage, the victors moved off towards Leicester, Henry proudly wearing King Richard's crown all the way.

The treatment of Richard III's body was shameful. Polydore Vergil recorded that it was slung, naked, across the saddle of a horse, the arms and legs hanging on either side. The Croyland Chronicler did not shrink from saying that it was abused and insulted, and that a halter was thrown round the dead king's neck to symbolise his humiliation in death. 'The Song of the Lady Bessy' adds that his long hair was tied beneath his chin. Trussed in this way, the body was taken to the Franciscan Friary in Leicester, where it was put on public view for two days, naked from the waist down, save for a covering of poor black cloth. The burial took place in the friary with little ceremony. Nothing now remains of the friary church or its precinct, and at the Dissolution of the Monasteries in Henry VIII's reign, the grave was rifled and the body thrown out. The coffin was later used as a horse-trough and then part of cellar steps, but that too has now disappeared. Richard III is the only English king since the Norman Conquest to have no known grave.

Richard's defeat and death were in many ways a surprising outcome of the Battle of Bosworth. The day had begun with a great show of kingly pomp; and though worried by desertions, Richard had reason to believe that Henry was more apprehensive than he about how the Stanleys would behave. Before Sir William Stanley intervened, it was far from clear that Henry's forces were gaining the upper hand. If Sir William had delayed a little longer, it might have been Henry who fell beside his standard-bearer rather than the valiant king. On such chances, on rare occasions, the course of history depends.

12 The Obligations of Youth

Of all the Tudor monarchs, the first is the most obscure to us today. An awareness of Henry's past and his antecedents – an awareness which the king himself cultivated – can relieve some of the obscurity surrounding him and his reign.

Henry was twenty-eight years old when he won the Battle of Bosworth. His decisive victory and the death of the childless Richard III were his two greatest assets when he seized King Richard's crown. After all, despite his years, he was one of the least experienced of English kings since the Norman Conquest. His extraordinary early life and upbringing meant that he knew little about his realm and even less about the life of a king and the responsibilities of kingship. These were unpromising qualifications in a new king, as a number of contemporaries acknowledged immediately after Bosworth. Moreover, his flimsy claim to the crown was probably matched by negligible training in the arts of ruling. In such circumstances, it is not surprising that Henry relied heavily on the friendships and associations of his youth and was preoccupied with the details of his ancestry. These factors were of great importance for some while after the Battle of Bosworth and helped to determine Henry's approach to kingship. The prudent king – and Henry was nothing if not prudent – would turn these few, admittedly slender, assets to best advantage.

The New King

Henry's personality in 1485 had been moulded by his experiences over the past two decades and more. It is not easy to demonstrate this with any confidence because the king left no diary of his inner thoughts and detailed actions, and few of his friends recorded their precise impressions of him. We cannot do much more than make reasonable deductions about his personality from his actions and interpret the effect which those early experiences might have had upon his character. There is no reason to doubt the statement of the Burgundian writer, Molinet, that Henry cut an attractive and personable figure at the Breton court. And in 1485 the Spanish merchants were able to take home with them an impression of a man who was still 'of pleasing countenance and physique'. They were the good looks of an alert and bright-eyed individual. Although Polydore Vergil was describing from personal knowledge a king who was all of fifty years

of age, some of the physical qualities he noted then were those of the young
Henry too:

> His body was slender but well built and strong; his height above the
> average. His appearance was remarkably attractive and his face cheerful
> especially when speaking; his eyes were small and blue ...

The only blemish of an otherwise imposing presence may have been a wart!
'The Song of the Lady Bessy', in recording Humphrey Brereton's secret
mission to Henry in Brittany, describes how Brereton would be able to identify
the prince:

> I shall tell, said the porter then,
> The Prince of England know shall ye,
> How where he sitteth at the butts certain,
> With other lords two or three;
> He weareth a gown of velvet black
> And it is cutted above the knee,
> With a long visage and pale and black –
> Thereby know that prince may ye;
> A wart he hath, the porter said,
> A little also above the chin,
> His face is white, his wart is red,
> No more than the head of a small pin;
> You may know the prince certain,
> As soon as you look upon him truly.

His experiences left their mark on him. As a young man in captivity, in exile or
on the run, he developed qualities of persistence and determination, astuteness
and resourcefulness, which made him unabashed and unafraid when faced with
adversity. He was capable of swift and decisive reactions, and yet he also learned
the value of careful and detailed planning in order to avoid needless risks. He
appreciated the vital importance of adequate resources to avoid the dangers of
dependence on others. Henry showed himself capable of attracting men to his
side and retaining their loyalty, and according to the Spanish merchants, it was
he who inspired his apprehensive followers on the eve of Bosworth. All these
were lessons learned in the harsh school of penury and exile.

Some such qualities were recognised by those who got to know Henry or
heard about him in the months after Bosworth. With not a little flattery, it is true,
the University of Oxford in 1485 put his renown down to a piety equal to that of
his sainted uncle, Henry VI, and a military prowess comparable to that of his
grandfather (more accurately, his step-grandfather), Henry V. The Spanish
merchants in England concluded that he was a wise, prudent and courageous
man. John Fisher, who was Lady Margaret Beaufort's confessor, recalled at
Henry's lying in state in 1509 that he was a master of several languages – and
one fruit of his long exile was that he liked to speak French and had a perfect
command of the language – and was 'cold and sober with great hardiness' when
faced with danger. He noted, too, his wisdom, agility of mind, good memory and

Portrait of King Henry VII by Michiel Sittow, the Bruges-trained artist. Commissioned in 1505 by the Emperor Maximilian's agent for Maximilian's daughter Margaret, whom Henry was thinking of marrying, it shows the king holding the red rose of Lancaster.

becoming nature. And part of Polydore Vergil's assessment suits the younger as well as the older monarch:

> His spirit was distinguished, wise and prudent; his mind was brave and resolute and never, even at moments of greatest danger, deserted him. He had a most pertinacious memory. Withal he was not devoid of scholarship . . . He was gracious and kind and was as attentive to his visitors as he was easy of access.

These qualities quickly gave the lie to those who, in 1485, supposed that his inexperience was matched by a shallow mind. Equally his experiences took their toll on his physique, and visiting diplomats were soon whispering that the new king of England was not robust and seemed older than his years.

The Former Exile

Having been brought up in Brittany and France during the most formative years of his life, Henry had an unusually open mind when it came to absorbing the prejudices and attitudes of Englishmen towards other peoples – or so it seemed to some of the foreigners who knew him after 1485. In particular, it was noted that he did not hate the Scots, as most self-respecting contemporary Englishmen did; and not only did he like to speak French and employ foreign servants, but he was inclined to prefer the habits and methods of government which he had observed at the Breton and French courts. It may be true that English kings had long employed at court a number of knights and esquires for the body, but the small military company of yeomen-archers of the king's guard which Henry formed immediately after Bosworth – most of them were veterans of the campaign of 1485 – had more in common with the professional guards of Duke Francis and King Charles than with the largely honorific *corps* attached to the households of late-medieval English kings. Henry's interest in religion and education was different from that shown by his Lancastrian and Yorkist predecessors. The canonisation of King Henry VI, the crusade against the Moors in Spain, and the reform of certain religious Orders in England were projects more akin to those favoured at the French and Breton courts. Even the first design for his own tomb bore striking resemblance to that adopted for Charles VIII's tomb at St. Denis. 'Henry's Franco-Breton background led him to envisage his mission [as king] as being closely bound up with the renewal of the religious authority of kingship' (Anthony Goodman). The victory at Bosworth vindicated it most graphically.

With this somewhat Francophile frame of mind, Henry's relations with the kingdom of France and the duchy of Brittany after 1485 presented him with a dilemma. On the one hand, the French government had provided the resources, the ships and most of the men for the invasion of England in August 1485. Henry naturally felt deeply indebted to Anne of Beaujeu and the Regency Council of King Charles VIII. On the other hand, Francis II of Brittany had protected him when he had few friends. Henry felt considerable personal affection for the old duke and his duchy, and appreciated what Polydore Vergil called the 'fatherly kindness' which Francis had shown to the fatherless exile at his court. So long as the traditionally tense and volatile relationship between France and Brittany did not degenerate into violence or war, Henry might hope for stable and amicable relations with both. Circumstances at the outset of his reign allowed him to reach a placid understanding with his former patrons, but it did not last.

Anne of Beaujeu and the Council of Regency were preoccupied with the ambitions of the duke of Orléans and other factious noblemen. But when Charles VIII took up the reins of government himself, France would probably adopt a more active foreign policy that might well threaten her ancient enemy, England. In Brittany, too, times were moving out of joint. Duke Francis was ailing in his old age, and the prospect that would face his duchy when he died was an alarming one. He had no son, only two daughters; the accession of the eldest of these, Anne, who was about nine in 1485, would inevitably cause widespread political instability in Brittany, and it would encourage the French to resume their efforts to absorb the duchy in their realm.

Whatever Henry's personal inclinations were, long-standing English interests, the expectations of his subjects and the need to justify his own kingship by embracing traditional values had a powerful effect on English policy during his reign. France was the old enemy, and Henry VII could not afford to behave too supinely towards a monarchy that had seized the English lands in Normandy as recently as 1450 and, much worse, those in Gascony in 1453. It simply would not do to lie down too quickly or too readily with the wolf. This would be especially true if the French king marched into Brittany. It had long been English policy to fortify the independence of the Breton dukes, and English aid was likely to be urgently needed when Francis II died. Henry's personal inclinations were no sure foundation for an acceptable foreign policy in the longer term. Yet for the moment, he was able to follow his own preferences in relations with both France and Brittany, doubtless recalling the debt he owed to both of them; and he was fully conscious that at the start of his reign he needed friends, not enemies, and that he did not have the resources to indulge in expensive or risky adventures overseas.

Moreover, for some little time after Bosworth a number of the Frenchmen who helped him win his crown stayed in England. Contemporaries noticed how much he liked to have foreigners – presumably French-speakers – about him. Philibert de Chandée, the French commander in 1485, was rewarded with the earldom of Bath in January 1486; he was still in England in the summer of 1487 and acted as France's envoy at Henry's court. As a result, for two years Henry VII was able to marry public policy and personal preference, and to preserve friendly relations with France and Brittany. In October 1485, he announced a truce with France for a year, and in due time this was extended to January 1489. In July 1486 he concluded a commercial treaty with Brittany. But towards the end of 1487, when Francis's death seemed imminent, the French began to make military preparations against Brittany, partly with the aim of destroying the dissident French nobles who had taken refuge there. As the year 1488 began, it became clear that a lasting peace was an illusion, and that Henry would soon be faced with difficult political and personal choices.

Henry clung to his course as long as possible. When Maximilian of Austria and Burgundy, and Ferdinand of Spain promised to help Duke Francis in his extremity, Henry was reluctant to join them, and he seems to have disapproved of Sir Edward Wydeville's private expedition to Brittany. Rather did Henry offer to mediate between France and Brittany in May 1488, when he sent Christopher Urswick, his trusty agent who had travelled in Brittany on Henry's business before 1485, to persuade Francis to come to terms with the French. This mission failed, but even then Henry did not decisively adopt a traditional English policy: he preferred to extend the truce with France in July 1488 and he assured the French ambassador that Wydeville's expedition was not authorised by him. The collapse of Brittany, militarily and politically, in the course of 1488 forced Henry to review his position, disagreeable though that was. Despite assistance, the Bretons were crushed in the Battle of St. Aubin du Cormier on 28 July 1488 and Sir Edward Wydeville was killed. Francis II was forced to capitulate a month later, and in the middle of September he died.

These events precipitated the kind of decision which Henry had striven to avoid since his accession: should he intervene with an army to aid stricken Brittany or should he allow the French monarchy to dominate the entire Atlantic seaboard? Duke Francis's daughters – the eldest, Anne, was only twelve – were placed under French control in accordance with the terms of the recent capitulation, and a French conquest of all Brittany was in prospect. Even for Henry this was most unwelcome: a faithful ally would be betrayed, the Breton coast opposite England would be in French hands, and long-standing friends would be deserted. Yet Henry (along with Maximilian and King Ferdinand) continued to pin his hopes on diplomacy to extricate him from his painful dilemma; at the same time, he felt he had no option but to promise 6,000 men to help the desperate Bretons. Sir Robert Willoughby, who had been with Henry in Brittany and at Bosworth, commanded the English invasion force in 1489. It was too late. In December 1491 the Duchess Anne married Charles VIII and the absorption of France's last and largest independent principality was achieved. About the same time, Charles VIII began to show interest in the cause of Perkin Warbeck, a Yorkist pretender to Henry's throne. Henry's belated announcement some months earlier that he intended to assert his own claim to the French crown, in the tradition of Edward III, could not prevent the Breton marriage or French support for the pretender. The despatch to France of a large English army, 12,700 strong, in the autumn of 1492 signalled the complete failure of Henry's policy and the dashing of his hope that he would be able to retain the friendship of his two former protectors. The best he could do in the circumstances was to copy Edward IV's actions in 1475 and bargain for the profitable withdrawal of his army. The pension which the treaty of Etaples promised him in November 1492 was small compensation for a personal disappointment and a political and diplomatic defeat.

Henry VII never lost his affection for Brittany, and his memories of his treatment there did not sour or grow dim. Vannes, in particular, stirred pleasant memories for him. After occupying the English throne for a decade and a half, he could still recall the years spent in the town and the cathedral where he prayed. In January 1502 he sent to the cathedral chapter at Vannes a new chasuble of crimson velvet, richly decorated with gold leaf, the royal arms of

Terracotta Bust of King Henry VII by the Italian sculptor Pietro Torrigiano. It was made c. 1508–9 and is the best portrait of the king towards the end of his life. The original colours have been restored: black for the cloak and cap, brown for the hair.

England and the legend *Regis Henrici Septimi* on the back, and the sign of the Cross on the front. He also gave two altar frontals of crimson velvet, each woven in gold leaf and with a gold fringe, and they were specifically intended for the altar of St. Vincent Ferrier, whose shrine had been erected in the cathedral earlier in the fifteenth century. They were taken to Vannes by a Breton nobleman, the lord of Caymerch, whom Henry used as his envoy. When the king's magnificent tomb was built in Westminster Abbey, according to Henry's own design, one of the copper-gilt medallions that adorned it was reserved for Edward the Confessor and St. Vincent, the one the venerable forebear of English monarchs and the other the patron saint of the town that had once sheltered Henry Tudor.

Old soldiers and loyal friends

Henry Tudor felt a profound sense of gratitude towards the Frenchmen and

Bretons who helped him in 1485 – as well he might. A number of them were rewarded in the months following his accession, though most, as we might expect of a mercenary army, did not stay in the country very long. The king was most generous to the French commander, Philibert de Chandée, who, as we have seen, was granted an annuity of £40 which he continued to draw until he returned to France. He received, too, the novel title of earl of Bath. Why this title was chosen is still a mystery. Henry VII had not yet visited the old Roman city when de Chandée was created an earl in January 1486, though it is possible that Philibert himself had seen or heard of the famous baths. Nor had there been any earlier earls of Bath whose title was now in abeyance. Whatever the reason, Philibert played no discernible part in English public life before he left England for good about 1487.

The commander of the French fleet in 1485 was only a whit less crucial to the successs of the Bosworth campaign, but he did not stay long enough to be rewarded on the same scale as de Chandée; in fact, he put to sea almost as soon as he landed his passengers and cargo in Mill Bay. Admiral Coulon's ships spent a few weeks sailing south to Portuguese waters, where they behaved like privateers, capturing Venetian galleys carrying Spanish merchandise to the markets of Flanders. They put in at an English port to divide the spoils, possibly because Coulon could expect a friendlier welcome in Henry's realm than almost anywhere else.

The leader of the Scottish contingent at Bosworth, Alexander Bruce of Earshall, joined Henry's household in 1485 and became a valet of the royal Chamber. The overall commander of Charles VIII's Scots guard, Bernard Stuart, lord of Aubigny, had probably remained in France, but when eventually he did visit England, many years later, Henry was able to express his gratitude to him in person. In 1508 Stuart set out on a pilgrimage to his ancestors' home in Scotland. He travelled *via* England, and Henry extended a right royal welcome to him when he passed through London. He entertained him at Greenwich and (a great courtesy this) when Stuart arrived by barge at the king's manor, Henry went down to the landing stage to greet him.

The more lowly foreign soldiers who settled in early Tudor England are much more elusive, but one attracted the king's special favour and has been the subject of an intriguing myth ever since. Roland de Veleville was in Henry's company in 1485 and by 1488 had received modest recognition of his service. After helping to disperse the rebels gathered on Blackheath in 1497, he was knighted and given a position in the king's household. Later still, not long before the king's death, Henry made him constable of Beaumaris Castle on the island of Anglesey, and in 1512 Henry VIII conferred on him all the rights and privileges of an Englishman – in effect, naturalization. De Veleville married a Welsh girl to whom he left his property in Beaumaris. In his will of 1535, he also expressed a wish to be buried in Llanfaes Friary, where some of the earliest Tudors were interred. He was so well regarded by Henry Tudor (or his son) that he was even given part of the ancestral lands of the Tudors of Penmynydd and this grant was to be a germ of the tradition that de Veleville was none other than Henry Tudor's bastard son, born in Brittany. Supported by the fame of his grand-daughter, the much-married Katherine of Berain, who was lionized by Welsh poets during Elizabeth I's reign and became a figure of romance, this tradition is nothing more than a myth inspired by Henry Tudor's early life.

Several contemporaries commented on Henry's generosity to the foreigners whose company he enjoyed. What is especially striking about most of the people to whom he gave gifts and rewards in the months following his accession is less that they were old friends or loyal supporters (as they undoubtedly were) than that they were frequently of little public importance or social significance. This reflects the king's consciousness of the debt he owed to them – regardless of who they were – for their company during his exile and their support in 1485.

It is true that among them were a number of knights and esquires who had been attainted after the risings of October 1483. A few others, like William Collingbourne, Sir James Blount, John Fortescue and John Riseley, had offended Richard III in 1484 and had also been attainted. Henry VII's first Parliament, which met in November 1485, reversed the attainders of all these people who were still living. However, they were greatly outnumbered by the others who had a claim on Henry's gratitude. Some had served the king and his mother in the past, probably when Henry was a boy and still living in England or Wales. They included Philip ab Hywel and his wife Jane, who had been his nurse before 1461. Another had been in the service of the king's father, Edmund Tudor.

He rewarded, too, the loyalty of several servants of his revered uncle, Henry VI, whose crown he claimed to inherit. These were now able to repair their fortunes after two decades of disgrace, obscurity or poverty.

Among more recent supporters were those who had played a role in the conspiracies of 1483. Dr. Lewis Caerleon was well rewarded by Henry for his medical and other services, and among the latter we may include his secret missions between Margaret Beaufort and Queen Elizabeth Wydeville. His life annuity of forty marks, granted in February 1486, was increased by half in the following November. To ease his old age, in 1488 he became a so-called 'poor knight' of Windsor, which meant that he had free residence in the outer ward of the castle. He lived on until at least 1495; and if he can be identified with the Master Lewis who was a physician at court, he was still living in 1510. Hugh Conway, one of Margaret Beaufort's messengers to Brittany, enjoyed the king's trust throughout his reign. Henry appointed him keeper of the Great Wardrobe for life within a month of Bosworth; and Conway made his way upwards in the king's financial service thereafter, becoming treasurer of Ireland and of Calais; eventually he secured a knighthood. Discrete ability was evidently Conway's prime characteristic.

Close to the centre of the conspiracies of 1483–5 had been the king's step-father. Although Lord Stanley's actions in the days before Bosworth fell short of expectations, it is clear that Stanley fully backed the efforts to bring Henry to England. The king had no doubt about the debt he owed to Stanley. Apart from creating him earl of Derby in October 1485, he openly acknowledged that his 'entirely beloved father' had fought for his interests strenuously and at great cost and in various ways and on many occasions before the final victory. Even if they did not know one another well (and Stanley later admitted that they did not become *closely* acquainted until after Bosworth), the affection which Henry felt for him is reflected unmistakably in his treatment of him. Other Stanleys did well too. Lord Strange, who escaped execution in the heat of battle on 22 August 1485, became a royal councillor, and Sir William Stanley became chamberlain of King Henry's household. Henry recognised, also, how important had been Sir James Blount's role in helping the earl of Oxford to escape from Hammes Castle, thereby giving a boost to the exiles' cause just when Richard III was doing his level best to undermine their unity.

Henry was no less appreciative of those in England who had stood by him at great personal risk. He had in mind people like Piers Curteys who, despite being keeper of the Great Wardrobe under Edward IV and, for a time, Richard III, came to sympathise with Henry's cause and spent the year or so before Bosworth in sanctuary in Westminster Abbey, fearing for his life. Henry appreciated and rewarded such devotion.

Yet others had done personal acts of kindness to Henry, including Denis Beton of Harfleur, a merchant who helped to fit out the expedition in the Seine Estuary in July 1485.

Henry was most grateful – most generous – to the companions of his exile, whom he remembered in large numbers. He recalled with compassion those who had suffered in the bad old days, and he recalled with pride those who fought beside him in what he constantly referred to as his 'victorious journey', his 'victorious march', his 'victorious battle', his 'victorious field', his 'royal triumph', his 'triumphant war'. Roger Machado, Leicester Herald during the early part of Richard III's reign, and probably in Edward IV's too, had joined the marquess of Dorset on the continent; Henry appointed him 'Richmond Herald'. After Bosworth his status was raised to that of a King of Arms and, reflecting Henry's abiding sense of family history, he became the first Richmond King of Arms in English history.

Henry VII had an unusual range of personal obligations to discharge at his accession. His memory extended far into the Lancastrian past and across the Channel to the places that gave him refuge. He rewarded where reward was due, and although the same element of calculation that marked his later reputation for parsimony can be detected early on, he manifestly did not stint in being generous to those who deserved it in 1485. Most of those whom he patronised were minor figures; their rewards were not such as to prejudice the king's freedom of action later or to deprive him of valuable resources of finance or office. Henry's strong sense of obligation was matched by a shrewd sense of what was appropriate, possible and wise.

The new government

In assembling a team of ministers and officials to govern the country and organise his household, Henry relied heavily on the small circle of capable men who were known to him – and that meant mostly those who had shared his exile. On the other hand, it was essential to engage at least a few with recent experience of public affairs in England. In the first weeks of the reign, he installed in the two major offices of state two elderly clergymen who had served Edward IV but who had become disenchanted with Richard III. The sixty-two-

CLARVS WJNTONIÆ PRÆSVL COONOÏE FOXVS
QVI PIVS HOC OLIM NOBILE STRVXIT OPVS
TALIS ERAT FORMA TALIS DVM VIXIT AMICTV
QVALEM SPECTANTI PICTA TABELLA REFERT

Portrait of Richard Fox (d. 1528), whom Henry VII appointed bishop of Exeter (1487). Johannes
Corvus painted his portrait c. 1518; this copy of c. 1575 is in Corpus Christi College, Oxford,
which Fox founded. Fox joined Henry Tudor in Paris in 1485 and seems to have been his secretary, a
position he also occupied after Bosworth.

year-old archbishop of York, Thomas Rotheram, was reappointed chancellor of
England less than a month after the Battle of Bosworth. He was the most
knowledgeable minister alive, having been chancellor from 1474 until he was
removed by King Richard. What also commended him to Henry was his
connection with the Wydevilles, especially with Queen Elizabeth Wydeville
when she was in sanctuary. But Rotheram was very much a stop-gap to tide the
new régime over a particularly difficult period. After about a month and for the
same reasons, he was transferred to the Exchequer, to act as temporary treasurer
of England. In his place at the Chancery the king installed John Alcock, bishop
of Worcester, who had been tutor to Edward IV's eldest son and had worked
closely with Rotheram during Edward's reign.

Once Henry had taken stock of his kingdom and its organs of government, he
turned to John Morton, bishop of Ely, as his chief adviser. Morton became
chancellor in March 1486 and he stayed in office until his death in 1500; by then
he was archbishop of Canterbury and a cardinal. An astute, experienced and
resourceful man who had been one of the chief architects of the victory over
Richard III, he was Henry's most trusted adviser. Such continuity of service was

also provided at the Exchequer, where John, Lord Dynham was treasurer from February 1486 to his death in 1501. On the surface, Dynham's appointment seems a curious one, since he had been a staunch Yorkist since before 1461 and was not a particularly skilled administrator. But in Richard's reign he was captain of Calais and may have played a part in the escape of the earl of Oxford from Hammes Castle in 1484. Henry placed great trust in him and made him a knight of the Garter.

All the others whom Henry installed in high position were his friends. The small group of able clerics who had been in exile during Richard's reign – though not always in Henry's company in Brittany – included Richard Fox, Robert Morton (the new chancellor's nephew), Bishop Peter Courtenay and Oliver King. To a man they played a crucial role in the new régime. Bishop Courtenay was appointed keeper of the Privy Seal within two weeks of Bosworth, and was evidently the man charged with ensuring continuity of administration during the reign's first uncertain days. Fox was Henry's secretary, a position he seems to have occupied in France and England without a break; Oliver King succeeded him in 1487.

The royal household was naturally recast, so personal was it to each sovereign. Sir William Stanley became its chamberlain, and most other senior posts went to men who had shared Henry's exile: Sir Robert Willoughby, Sir Richard Edgecombe and Sir Thomas Lovell. Only the new steward of the household seems to us an unexpected choice: John, Lord Fitzwalter. But then he was the step-son of the new treasurer of England, Lord Dynham, and as a Calais landowner he may, like Dynham, have been involved behind the scenes in the flight of the earl of Oxford in 1484. Fitzwalter, too, was an East Anglian landowner who later was closely involved with Oxford, though he proved a harsher and more vindictive member of the victorious Tudor circle than did the earl himself.

These officials were joined in the king's Council by several others of the same ilk, loyal intimates of the king who had shown their devotion to him in 1483–5: Reginald Bray, Giles Daubeney, Richard Guildford and John Riseley. These were the people whom contemporaries regarded as the most influential in the kingdom after 1485, aside from Henry's mother, his uncle Jasper, his step-father Stanley and the earl of Oxford. To judge by the responsibilities given to him as a notable soldier (if not always a conspicuously successful one), Oxford was placed in overall charge of the security of the realm – as chamberlain of England, constable of the Tower of London and admiral of England.

13 The Blessings of Ancestry

Family and Lineage

Few kings have had so few relatives at their accession as Henry VII. He was the only child of a father who predeceased him. Edmund Tudor had two brothers, but one became a monk and the other, Jasper, was still unmarried in August 1485. Henry's mother was also an only child. To be without a well-stocked family could be a disadvantage for a king: it meant that he had no intimates within the English establishment. On the other hand, the absence of a substantial, ready-made family meant that there was less likelihood of a rival emerging for the king's crown or a focus of resentment against his régime. On this score, both Richard II and Edward IV might well have wished that they had had fewer relatives.

Henry Tudor seems to have appreciated the value, rather than the disadvantages, of his isolation at the pinnacle of English society. He took no significant steps to include more distant relatives within the royal family or to allow his wife's kinsmen much power in the realm. Her son, the marquess of Dorset, whom Henry summoned back from France where he had stayed as security for Charles VIII's loan, never acquired much influence at Henry's court. However, Henry did create four peers in October 1485. His uncle Jasper Tudor became duke of Bedford – the only new duke of the reign apart from the king's children – and soon afterwards he was restored to his earldom of Pembroke. The cautious Henry may have been prepared to raise his only uncle to a dukedom because he was about fifty-five years of age when he married in 1485 (Buckingham's widow, no less) and probably too old to start a family – which he never did. Henry's step-father, Lord Stanley, also in his fifties, was created earl of Derby; but then he and his wife had no children and Margaret Beaufort seems to have taken a vow of chastity. Henry's step-uncle, his mother's half-brother John Welles, was created a viscount early in 1486 and as yet he was unmarried. Edward Courtenay was the only other senior peer to be created by Henry VII at the outset of his reign. He had been one of his companions during 1483–5 and by making him earl of Devon, Henry in effect was restoring the earldom of Devon to a family which had held it for a long time in the past. The only baron to be created, Giles Daubeney in March 1486, was another of those friends from across the water on whom Henry continued to rely after 1485.

Great Seal of Jasper Tudor, earl of Pembroke and duke of Bedford, as lord of Abergavenny after 1485. Almost 4 inches in diameter, the obverse displays a shield of arms surmounted by a cap of estate and coronet; the supporters are a dragon and a wolf. The reverse shows a mounted figure with a coat of arms.

Henry's reliance on this tiny family and this small group of faithful friends from France was graphically illustrated at the coronation on 30 October 1485. The customary supporters at the king's side during a coronation were – and still are – the bishops of Durham and of Bath and Wells. But in 1485 these bishops were former cronies of Richard III and were therefore excluded from the ceremony. Their place was taken by Bishop Courtenay of Exeter and Bishop Morton of Ely, both key figures in Henry's victorious enterprise. During the coronation itself, Jasper Tudor bore the crown of England, Stanley held the sword of state, and the earl of Oxford carried the king's train. The seventy-five-year-old archbishop of Canterbury, Thomas Bourgchier, who had shown some sympathy for Queen Elizabeth Wydeville and her children during Richard's reign, performed the annointing and crowning despite his years. Following these solemnities, Bishop Courtenay sought the will of the people and received their acclamation of Henry as their king. Mass was then celebrated by the bishop of London, Thomas Kemp, who was well over seventy and had known better than to play a part in politics during the previous decade and more.

On the eve of coronation day, Henry created six new knights of the Bath. They were not his relatives, but once again show how his mind and emotions were affected by his experiences in 1483–5. The new knights were headed by the eight-year-old Edward Stafford, duke of Buckingham, and apart from Lord Fitzwalter, who was soon to be steward of Henry's household, the rest were men like Reginald Bray who had been closely connected with the Stafford family. Their knighting may have been a mark of respect for the memory of the duke who had led the first rebellion against King Richard in 1483. But it may also have been designed to eliminate the possibility that in the future the Stafford interest would publicise the Plantagenet blood of the young Duke Edward in opposition to Henry himself.

In the provinces of the realm, Henry looked to the same circle of relatives and friends to establish his authority: to his uncle Jasper in Wales and the March, where he dominated Pembroke, Glamorgan and, after he married Buckingham's widow, the Stafford lordships; to Stanley in the north-west; and to Oxford, who controlled East Anglia. Only in the far north of England, where Henry had to rely on the earl of Northumberland, whose behaviour at Bosworth puzzled contemporaries and later generations, was there an uncertain link in this chain of regional control.

If Henry had few living relatives and seemed content with that, he made the most of those who were dead. Writing a generation after Henry VII's death, the Welsh chronicler, Elis Gruffydd, thought that in 1485 many prominent people in the kingdom doubted whether the victor of Bosworth was equal to the task of kingship. He offered two justifications for their doubts: that Henry was not half

West Front of Llandaff Cathedral, near Cardiff. The Jasper Tower (left) *was probably commissioned by Jasper Tudor as lord of Glamorgan after 1485. The late-fifteenth-century pinnacles resemble those of other churches in South-East Wales and the West Country.*

Gold Medallion commemorating the marriage of King Henry VII and Elizabeth of York, 1486. The obverse shows the king and queen, the reverse the Tudor rose symbolising the unity of Lancaster and York. The marriage took place on 18 January 1486, soon after the arrival of a dispensation from the Pope.

the gentleman required of a king, and that he had an inexperienced and light-weight mind. From the moment of his accession Henry did his best to show that the first charge was not true; and his actions as king proved that, for all his inexperience, his was no second-rate intelligence.

Some may have been persuaded by Yorkist slurs on his lineage, or by King Richard's denigration of his ancestors; and such slights continued to circulate after Bosworth. Even the failure of the rebellions led by Lambert Simnel in 1487 and Perkin Warbeck in the 1490s did not silence such scurrilous attacks. Towards the end of the king's reign, pedigrees were still being produced in support of minor figures of the house of York. They reiterated how the house of Lancaster had seized the crown in 1399 against all right and custom; how Owen Tudor's father was a mere inn-keeper of Conway and his mother an obscure maid; how their son had committed adultery with Queen Katherine; and how Henry VII himself, as well as his father and his uncle Jasper, were bastards. One pedigree even claimed that the royal house of York had been all but extinguished by Henry himself, who allegedly imprisoned Edward V's younger brother, the duke of York, and then hanged him. These tales were encouraged by Henry's foreign enemies, notably the dowager-duchess of Burgundy, Margaret of York, and her son-in-law, Maximilian of Austria and Burgundy, King Richard's former ally. They were damaging charges for a new king whose lineage was certainly unusual and marred by more than one questionable liaison.

Henry was determined to refute what was slanderous and untrue and to emphasise what was unimpeachable. He did so by stressing the royal connections of the family of his mother, Margaret Beaufort, the ancient British blood of his father's Welsh ancestors, and, of course, the French royal descent of his grandmother, Katherine of Valois. The symbolism he employed and the pedigrees he inspired show Henry to have had a deep interest in his family and to have spared no opportunity to laud its royal and ancient qualities.

The use of the red rose to symbolise the house of Lancaster, whose legitimate representative Henry regarded himself in 1485, had a popularity after Bosworth which it does not seem to have had before. This is understandable since it could now be popularised as an emblem to counter-balance the white rose of York. While the red rose appeared in the iconography of public ceremonies and decoration, the double rose, combining white and red, the best known element in the visual, literary and music propaganda of the Tudors, reflects Henry's view of himself as the reconciler of the warring houses of Lancaster and York.

Henry was able to present himself as the heir of Lancaster because his mother's Beaufort family descended directly from John of Gaunt, duke of Lancaster, the father of England's first Lancastrian king. To strengthen this dynastic link, in 1485 Henry's first Parliament re-enacted the act of 1397 that had declared the Beaufort family legitimate and officially removed the stigma of bastardy. It did not re-enact the statute of 1407 which had added the caveat that the Beauforts should never succeed to the English throne. Henry thus provided himself with some kind of dynastic claim. Margaret Beaufort was the senior surviving Beaufort heir, and in strict dynastic terms her own claim was superior to her son's. But there had been no reigning queen in England since the turbulent twelfth century and the civil war that had then raged around Queen Matilda did not encourage anyone – not even Lady Margaret Beaufort – to think in terms of repeating the experience in the later fifteenth century. As it was, the Yorkists had maintained that an heiress could at least transmit a royal claim, and Henry therefore made much of his mother's descent from John of Gaunt, the third surviving son of Edward III.

The Beaufort emblem, the portcullis, which may represent Beaufort Castle in Champagne, where Margaret's grandfather had been born to John of Gaunt and his mistress, was adopted by Henry as a Tudor emblem. A clutch of portcullises adorn Henry VII's Chapel in Westminster Abbey and they appear elsewhere in profusion to commemorate the Tudor dynasty. The important niche which the Beauforts occupied in Henry's mind when he thought of his ancestors was appreciated by Archbishop Rotheram when he founded a new chantry in York Minster in 1489. The purpose of the chantry was to organise prayers for the souls of the king, the queen, Prince Arthur and the archbishop himself; but he also included in the list of beneficiaries the souls of the king's mother and of her parents, John Beaufort, duke of Somerset and Margaret Beauchamp.

Margaret Beaufort herself was treated with exceptional honour at her son's court, and not simply because of the deep affection which the king evidently felt for his mother. Her birthday, 31 May, was celebrated at Westminster during her lifetime, and at court she was known as the 'Full noble Princess Margaret, countess of Richmond and mother of our sovereign lord the king'. Her estates, which King Richard had confiscated and given to her husband, Lord Stanley, were restored to her, and as a reward for her practical support before Bosworth,

Bronze Gates of King Henry VII's Chapel, in Westminster Abbey. They were made between 1503 and 1519 by Thomas Ducheman and incorporate Tudor royal badges: the Beaufort portcullis, the lilies of France, the leopards of England, and the crown and thornbush.

King Henry put the sons of the late duke of Buckingham in her care, with an annual income of £1,000 from their estates. The depth of her feelings for her only son are revealed in a remarkable letter which she wrote to him in July 1501:

> My dearest, and only desired joy in this world. With my most hearty loving blessings and humble commendation . . . (she began).
> At Calais town, this day of St. Anne's that I did bring into this world my good and gracious Prince, King and only beloved son . . . (she concluded).
>
> Margaret R

Henry was hardly less affectionate when he penned a letter to his mother in July 1503 when his own sight was beginning to fail:

> . . . I shall be as glad to please you as your heart can desire it, and I know well that I am as much bounden so to do as any creature living, for the great and singular motherly love and affection that it hath pleased you at all times to bear towards me. Wherefore, my own most loving mother, in my most hearty manner I thank you, beseeching you of your good continuance in the same . . .

Margaret Beaufort died in 1509, two months after her son's death. She had been a tower of strength to the king throughout his reign, just as she had looked after his interests before 1485. She remained close to Henry, as was symbolised by her role in the endowment of his new chapel at Westminster, where Margaret too is buried. Her black marble tomb was constructed by the same master craftsman, Pietro Torrigiano, who worked on King Henry's tomb, and the effigy of Margaret in gilt bronze is widely regarded as his masterpiece.

Eulogies are not usually reliable material for a dispassionate biography, but Bishop John Fisher's eulogy, delivered at Margaret Beaufort's funeral, carries a certain conviction. Fisher, who had been her chaplain, described an elderly lady in her late sixties, studious by nature, capable of translating religious works from French into English (though Margaret always regretted that she had not learnt Latin properly in her youth), and of strong religious convictions. Her daily devotions caused her back pain! 'All England for her death had cause of weeping', concluded the bishop, and the great Dutch humanist and theologian who knew her, Erasmus, composed the epitaph for her tomb.

Henry VII demonstrated his fervent Lancastrianism by the reverence he showed for the last Lancastrian monarch, Henry VI, who was deposed in 1461 and died in 1471 a prisoner of the Yorkists. The citizens of Worcester chose the symbolic figure of Henry VI to deliver their welcome to Henry Tudor on his visit to their city in 1486. This was an inspired choice and may indicate that the king was already known to hold his dead uncle in special regard. Thereafter, Henry offered every respect, both privately and publicly, to his uncle's memory. Henry VI's martyrdom at the Yorkists' hands was well publicised and so was the story that he had foretold his nephew's accession to the throne. Henry Tudor sought to harness the veneration of his name and his tomb which had been growing since his death in 1471, and this culminated in a campaign to persuade a successsion of Popes to canonise the dead monarch.

Gilt-Bronze Effigy of Lady Margaret Beaufort (1443–1509), countess of Richmond and Derby, in the south aisle chapel of King Henry VII's Chapel in Westminster Abbey. It is Pietro Torrigiano's masterpiece.

In August 1484 Richard III had already transferred Henry VI's body from Chertsey Abbey (Surrey) to St. George's Chapel, Windsor, probably as a symbolic act of reconciliation with the past. But Henry VII planned to move it again, to the new Lady Chapel he began to build at Westminster Abbey in 1503. For Henry VI to rest finally in the most venerable mausoleum of medieval English kings, where Henry V and Queen Katherine lay buried, seemed much more appropriate than to leave him in Edward IV's Chapel at Windsor. Henry Tudor accordingly came to prefer Westminster to Windsor as his own resting place, and even though his uncle's body was never in fact moved from St. George's Chapel, Henry VII, his wife and his mother were interred in what became known as King Henry VII's Chapel in Westminster Abbey.

The king's subjects took their cue from the royal campaign. Miracles by the score were attributed to Henry VI, his tomb became a popular place of pilgrimage, and pictures of him as a saint were painted on the screens of English parish churches and appeared in stained glass. A book of his miracles was compiled, probably to advance the cause of canonisation in Rome. Henry VI's saintly reputation had been growing well before 1485, but during Henry VII's reign it received vigorous royal encouragement. Within a year of the king's death the eulogy of Henry VI, written about 1485 by his old chaplain John Blacman, was printed for wider circulation. Only Henry VIII's break with Rome in the 1530s prevented the last Lancastrian from becoming England's first officially canonised royal saint. The sanctification of this king, even though his reign had been politically disastrous, could not fail to enhance the respectability and reputation of his nephew and act as a valuable support to his régime.

Henry's Welsh blood gave him no kind of claim to the crown of England. His father, Edmund Tudor, was Henry VI's half-brother, but Edmund's own father was a minor Welsh squire and his mother a princess of France. But Welsh ancestry did enable Henry to claim a descent that went back to those ancient British kings who had fought against heathen Saxon invaders in the Dark Ages. Edward IV had been aware of, and had laid emphasis on, the Welsh lineage of his Mortimer ancestors back to the thirteenth-century princes of North Wales, and Henry's wife, Elizabeth of York, inherited these claims. But Henry could not personally claim so much; indeed, the medieval Welsh princes had been overlords and employers of his own forebears. However, this did not stop him and his publicists from stressing the ancient British heritage of his Welsh ancestors. In particular, the Welsh elements in the British descent of England's kings were valuable propaganda for a man with a slender claim to his throne. At Bosworth Field, one of Henry's banners featured a red dragon, in British tradition the symbol of victory over the Saxons (represented by a white dragon). This banner, with its traditional Welsh green and white backcloth, fluttered over King Henry as Richard's crown was placed on his head. Together with the banner of St. George and the Beaufort emblem, it was carried in state to London after the battle and offered at the north door of St. Paul's Cathedral to be laid up. Henceforward, the red dragon became one of the two supporters of the royal arms of the Tudor monarchs. It figures in the commemorative stained glass of King's College Chapel, Cambridge, which Henry completed in honour of his sainted uncle who had founded it; it figures on Henry's tomb which

King Henry VI as a Saint, c. 1500, on the wooden screen of Ludham Church, Norfolk. Henry Tudor's uncle appears (right) *with St. Edmund. Such depictions of the dead king coincide with the attempt to secure his canonisation.*

Arms of King Henry VII, supported by the dragon of Cadwaladr and the greyhound of Elizabeth of York. This example is in the fan vault of the Holy Trinity Chapel constructed behind the high altar of St. David's Cathedral by Bishop Edward Vaughan (1509–22).

Torrigiano finished in 1513; and a new pursuivant of arms called Rouge Dragon was created by the king.

Henry's Welsh descent and its propaganda possibilities appealed to both Englishmen and Welshmen. It was given precision by attempts to trace Henry's lineage back to ancient Welsh kings, and especially to Cadwaladr, the last and most revered of them. When the king's champion rode into the coronation banquet to challenge, according to custom, any who would question Henry's right to the crown, his horse's trapper was richly embroidered with what were believed to be Cadwaladr's arms. Henry's subjects adopted the same motifs. In the preparations made to receive the king at Worcester in 1486, Henry's descent from Cadwaladr was included in the speech intended as the centre-piece of the citizens' welcome:

> Cadwalader's blood lineally descending,
> Long hath be told of such a Prince coming,
> Wherefore Friends, if that I shall not lie,
> This same is the Fulfiller of the Prophecy.

Descent from Cadwaladr was a central element of English royal propaganda during the reign, and the court historian, Bernard André, gave it prominence in his Memoir of the king. It warmed the hearts of Welshmen and it helped to persuade others that Henry had venerable dynastic right on his side.

King Arthur, too, was a worthwhile figure from the British past to include among the pantheon of Tudor ancestors. Edward IV had named his bastard son Arthur and Henry VII was to do the same with his eldest son who, moreover, was born in Winchester, a city with Arthurian associations. Yet neither Edward nor Henry seems to have placed Arthur precisely among his forebears. The red dragon was thus associated with the British descent of England's kings and with Arthur, the legendary protector of the British. But the early death of Prince Arthur in 1501 seems to have stunted the growth of the cult of Arthur in early Tudor England.

Henry's claim to part-Welsh ancestry stemmed from his father, Edmund Tudor. But Henry's attachment to Edmund's memory was naturally far less strong than that to his mother – for both personal and dynastic reasons. Henry had never known his father; indeed, he may not have visited his tomb in the Greyfriars Church in Carmarthen more than once or twice, certainly not after he went into exile in 1471. Moreover, the only royal blood that flowed in Edmund's veins was French – from his mother, Katherine of Valois. Nevertheless, Henry remembered his father on more private occasions. He marked the anniversary of his death on 1 November 1456, and the tourney accompanying the celebrations to mark the creation of Henry's second son as duke of York in 1494 were interrupted for almost a week because of the anniversary of the death of 'the full noble the king's father'.

Edmund's earldom of Richmond, granted to him by Henry VI, meant much to his son. Henry Tudor inherited it at birth, for he was born almost three months after his father died; and he was not formally deprived of the earldom until 1484. Richard III may have referred scathingly to him as 'Henry Tudder', but for twenty-eight years Henry regarded himself as Henry of Richmond and so signed his name until shortly before Bosworth. His mother, too, though married to Stanley since 1473, always referred to herself as countess of Richmond. The title was so much a part of Henry that he gave the name of Richmond to the new palace which he built on the banks of the Thames in the 1490s. The old royal manor house at Sheen had been largely demolished by Richard II and rebuilt by Henry V. But in December 1497, when Henry and his court were there for the Christmas holiday, a disastrous fire occurred. Henry set about rebuilding the house almost immediately, and some fragments of his work are still standing today. When it was finished in 1501 he called the residence Richmond. Among the great sculptured statues which adorned the hall were some that harked back to the British past – Brutus, Hengist the Saxon, and Arthur the Briton. Henry showed less direct interest in his paternal grandparents, Katherine of Valois and Owen Tudor. However, when the Lady Chapel at Westminster Abbey was demolished to make way for its magnificent replacement, Henry made sure that Queen Katherine's coffin was moved and placed beside the tomb of her first husband, Henry V. It was not Henry's fault that it could still be easily opened in 1668, when Samuel Pepys went to the abbey and 'kissed a Queen' to celebrate his birthday!

Henry apparently felt no shame at the relatively remote and humble origins of Owen Tudor, though he was embarrassed and affronted by suggestions that his birth was meaner than it was. To judge by Henry's treatment of his Tudor

Alabaster Effigy of Sir David Owen (1459–c.1542), in Easeborne Church, West Sussex. A collar of Lancastrian SS and Tudor roses is about his neck. The illegitimate son of Owen Tudor, he married Mary Bohun of Midhurst: two of their sons were called Henry and a third Jasper. Alone of the later Tudors, he incorporated Ednyfed Fychan's arms in his own, and instructed that a tomb be built for his father's body in the Greyfriars Church, Hereford.

kinsmen, he had some affection for them, but not a great deal. Owen Tudor and Queen Katherine had had three sons and one daughter. Apart from Henry's father, Edmund, and his devoted uncle, Jasper, the third son, Owen, became a monk of Westminster Abbey and was still a member of the community there in 1485. Henry gave him money and when Owen died in 1502 bells rang out at St. Margaret's, Westminster, and Henry paid for the funeral.

At the time of Queen Katherine's death in 1437, Owen Tudor was still a fairly young man. He was taken into the household of his step-son Henry VI, and he had at least one liaison thereafter which produced an illegitimate son. Who the mother was, how she and Owen met, how long they stayed together, and what personal connection the bastard boy had with the young Henry Tudor, his nephew, is unknown. After 1485 the boy, David Owen, prospered. He later confided that he had been born in Pembroke Castle in 1459, presumably when his father and his half-brother, Jasper Tudor, were rallying Wales in the Lancastrian cause. Whether David crossed to Brittany with his nephew, Henry Tudor, is not known, but when Henry landed in Mill Bay on 7 August 1485 David was one of the first to be knighted. He was made welcome at Henry's court, and when the queen was crowned in 1486, he carried the canopy for part of the procession through the streets of London. He also married a well-to-do wife, Mary, the daughter and heiress of John Bohun of Midhurst in Sussex, and it is in Easeborne Priory Church nearby that Sir David Owen's fine tomb can still be seen.

Henry VII acknowledged his Welsh relatives, but on the whole modestly and privately. He showed no interest in the ancestral Tudor estates in North Wales. The patrimony at Penmynydd in Anglesey was granted away, part to the abbey of Conway and part to Sir Roland de Veleville, Henry's Breton servant who settled in Wales after 1485. The descendants of Gwilym ap Gruffydd, the man who had replaced the earliest Tudors at Penmynydd after they had rebelled with Glyndŵr, made little of their kinship with the new royal house. Several of them served in humble positions in the households of Henry VII and Henry VIII, and another, named Jasper, recalled his great namesake. But these Anglesey Tudors (or Theodores as they preferred to be known) were far less prominent in local society than their ancestors had been in the thirteenth and fourteenth centuries: they occupied no offices on the island and Welsh poets ignored them.

Nevertheless, Henry VII went to considerable lengths to discover the details of his own pedigree – or so it was claimed by the Denbighshire historian, David Powel, in his *History of Cambria* which, though published in 1584, partly depended on the writings of his fellow Denbighshireman and antiquary, Humphrey Lhwyd (who died in 1568). According to Powel, Henry appointed a commission to chronicle his descent from Welsh princes and British kings. Scholars have been sceptical – unduly so – about whether such a commission was ever set up, though several pedigrees exist today which claim to be its outcome. The circumstantial evidence for it is strong. According to Powel, the commissioners whom Henry VII appointed included the abbot of Valle Crucis in Denbighshire, Dr. Owen Pole, a distinguished cleric attached to the dioceses of St. David's and Hereford, Gutun Owain, a notable poet and genealogist from the Oswestry area, Robert ab Hywel ap Thomas, a man from Denbighshire who married a daughter of the Cheshire squire, William Brereton, Gruffydd ap Llywelyn Fychan from Flintshire, and three others. Most of these men are indeed known to have been living in Henry's day and several of them had links with that area of North-East Wales which Lhwyd and Powel knew. These Elizabethan writers could therefore easily have learned about an important commission on which men from their own area served. Moreover, long before Lhwyd and Powel wrote, the chronicler Elis Gruffydd, who came from the same area, was aware that Robert ab Hywel ap Thomas had in fact delivered a genealogy of the king to Henry some time after his coronation.

If, as seems likely, Henry VII did order an investigation of his pedigree, his motives may have been mixed: partly personal – arising from a natural curiosity about the ancestors of his paternal grandfather, Owen Tudor – and partly dynastic, to combat hostile propaganda that was casting aspersions on his forebears and on Owen Tudor's in particular.

The Lancaster-Beaufort-British-Welsh associations which Henry's pedigree claimed were perpetuated in his own family. The names he chose for his three sons and four daughters, born between 1486 and 1499, are revealing. His first-born was called Arthur. If he had succeeded to the throne instead of dying in 1501, the poets, propagandists and pageant-makers who already regarded him as the fulfiller of ancient British prophecies would have risen to even greater

Gilt-Bronze Tomb Effigies of King Henry VII and Elizabeth of York, in King Henry VII's Chapel in Westminster Abbey. They were made by Pietro Torrigiano between 1512 and 1519. Guardian saints, including St. Vincent, are depicted on the sides of the tomb.

heights of flattery than they did during his short lifetime. At an early stage the ancient British descent and its place in Henry's dynastic scheme of things were brought to the fore in support of the dynasty. The second son, born in 1491, was christened Henry. There can be little doubt that his name commemorated the last Lancastrian king whom Henry VII claimed to succeed and whose cult was at the height of its popularity and was actively encouraged by the king. For his third son, born in 1499 but dead within a year, Henry chose the name of his own father, Edmund.

Dynastic and family motives also dictated the choice of names for the king's four daughters. The eldest, born in 1489, received the name of Henry's mother, Margaret, a tribute to the woman who had kept his cause alive and for whom Henry rediscovered real affection after years of separation. The second daughter, who did not live long, was called Elizabeth after her mother. But the third, born in 1496, was named Mary. The Virgin herself may have inspired this choice, yet it is worth recalling that the wife of the first Lancastrian king was Mary Bohun. And the fourth daughter, who also died young, bore the Christian name of Katherine Swynford, the mother of John of Gaunt's illegitimate Beaufort children. What is equally striking is that none of Henry's children was given a name favoured by the Yorkist kings: there was no Edward, no Richard and no George.

The Welsh connection

There is a very common belief that Henry VII had a special relationship with Wales and Welshmen, and his landing in Pembrokeshire in 1485 is usually regarded as confirming it. There is some foundation for this belief. Just as it

Detail of the Tomb Effigy of King Henry VII in Westminster Abbey. The original design by Guido Mazzoni, itself based on King Charles VIII's tomb at St. Denis, seems to have been rejected by Henry. A modified design was executed by Pietro Torrigiano after the king's death.

distorts reality to state that Wales waited with growing impatience for Henry to come to claim his royal inheritance and that he was the first Welshman to sit on the throne of England, so it is inaccurate to say that his Welsh blood meant little or nothing to him.

As with most of his actions, Henry's attitude to Wales and Welshmen combined the personal and the political: a personal attachment to the land of his ancestors and a shrewd awareness of the political, propagandist and dynastic value of the British element in his descent from Welsh stock. Contemporary Wales and its people were not such an influential political force – certainly not such a threat – that he had to pander to Welshmen's ambitions and Welsh traditions. Rather did Henry appreciate the help he had received from the landowners of Wales during his march from Pembrokeshire to Shrewsbury, and their services at Bosworth Field. When he became king, his Welsh blood and his strong sense of obligation left their mark.

It is unlikely that Henry could count Welsh among the languages he spoke in 1485. Even if he had picked up some fragments of it at Raglan in the 1460s, most of these had probably slipped from his grasp during the following decade and a half. Nevertheless, unlike English kings of the past, he joined the Welshmen at his court to celebrate St. David's Day (1 March). Right up until his death, he gave gifts to the Welsh yeomen of his household to mark the feast-day of Wales's premier saint. Henry also encouraged some of the cultural pastimes of his Welsh servants. On several occasions he offered special rewards to Welsh rhymsters at court; perhaps, indeed, Henry shared his fellow-countrymen's passion for poetry and prophecy on other than a propagandist level. If his patronage of harpists continued a custom followed by earlier fifteenth-century kings, he welcomed Welsh harpists in particular to his court, and in 1501 helped to pay for the burial of one of them.

This was no affectation or public pose; it seems to have reflected genuine sentiment. That this was so is indicated by certain of the king's acts of no political significance. When his second son, Henry, was born in 1491, the king sent for his old Welsh nurse, Jane, the wife of Philip ab Hywel, to take care of the baby in the royal nursery. He employed a number of Welsh servants in his household, men who had perhaps joined him before Bosworth and were retained thereafter as esquires for the body and the like. And who was the 'great Welsh child' whom Henry supported for several years, and the woman from Milford Haven who, in May 1498, received £2 from the king for services unspecified?

The attitude of Wales and Welshmen to Henry VII is very difficult to gauge. Some Welshmen were doubtless wary of a new king in an age of dynastic revolution, and some were cautious about declaring their sympathies. The Vaughans of Tretower, with a tradition of Yorkist loyalty and personal animosity towards Jasper Tudor behind them, even raised rebellion at Brecon in April 1486. But many were enthusiastic. We do not know much at all about the audience and patrons for whom Welsh poets wrote in the late fifteenth century, but it is significant that the hopes they placed in both Henry and Jasper Tudor before 1485 turned into a flood of praise after news of the victory at Bosworth reached Wales. Dafydd Llwyd of Mathafarn, who may have met Henry and

Detail of the Tomb Effigy of Elizabeth of York in Westminster Abbey. Made more than a decade after the queen's death (1503), the face seems less realistic than Henry's.

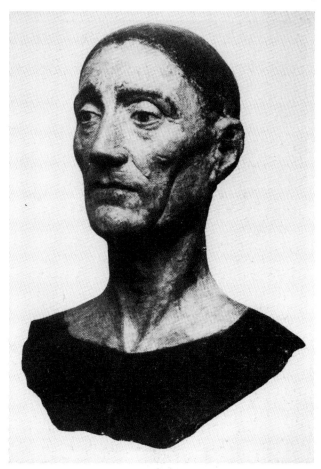

The Wax Death-Mask of King Henry VII, restored after the second world war. The nose is a recent addition and the ears seem crude; otherwise it is likely to be a faithful depiction of Henry in death (1509).

Jasper on their journey through Wales in August 1485, greeted the news of Richard III's death with undisguised satisfaction. He had heard rumours of the murder of the princes in the Tower and stories that Richard himself had put Henry VI to death. For Henry Tudor, he now had nothing but praise and, echoing the new king, he identified Henry with his step-uncle, 'the sainted one'. 'Harri was, Harri will be, Harri is, long may he live.' Dafydd Llwyd was to compose a number of other poems lauding Henry VII, referring to his descent from Owen Tudor and his lineage from ancient Welsh princes. He associated Henry's success with St. David, whose popularity in Wales and in the Christian calendar was greater in the fifteenth century than it had been before, and, as we have seen, Henry encouraged devotion to this special Welsh saint at his court.

Dafydd Llwyd was no hack poet obediently mouthing the sentiments that a wealthy patron wanted to hear. He came from a prominent family long settled in the Dyfi Valley in Western Powys and he therefore could afford to express his own opinions in his verse. His attitude to Henry and his victory may well have been shared by many other Welshmen, influential and humble alike. In the south, the poet Rhys Nanmor, who spent most of his adult life near St. David's, was patronised by the most influential Welshman of the region, Sir Rhys ap Thomas. The latter's support for Henry in August 1485 encouraged Rhys Nanmor to write enthusiastically about the new king. So did Lewis Glyn Cothi, perhaps the most prolific of all fifteenth-century Welsh poets. He too was a South Walian, with patrons among the landowners of Carmarthenshire, Cardiganshire and Radnorshire. For a few years after 1485 (Lewis was probably dead by 1490), he exulted in Henry Tudor's success and in one poem wished him a long and happy reign. Lewis Glyn Cothi also acclaimed Jasper Tudor and made much of the ancient British ancestry of Henry's family. For him, the British Isles were now entrusted to men of British blood whose future lay glorious before them. When the king died, the poet-cleric Dafydd Trefor of Caernarfonshire produced a moving elegy that recalled the mythical links between Henry's family, ancient Welsh princes and Arthurian romance; but it also stressed the distinction of his father Edmund and the Beaufort ancestry of his mother.

The birth of Prince Arthur in 1486 roused these poets to even greater efforts. Both Dafydd Llwyd and Rhys Nanmor once more recalled the Arthurian past, the ancient British blood of the Tudors and the distinguished members of their lineage – Katherine of Valois, Owen and Edmund Tudor, and the Beauforts.

Such enthusiasm was lavished on Henry and his family as on few other kings of England. The elements that were used and popularised were the elements which fascinated Henry himself and which his own propagandists deployed. The pedigrees spring from the same stock of prophecy and genealogy which the poets and, perhaps, their patrons had at their finger-tips. In this sense, if not in more practical matters of politics and government, there was a rapport between Henry and his Welsh subjects. They rejoiced in his victory at Bosworth, and many who joined him on his march or at his court sustained his awareness of the expectations of many of his Welsh subjects.

FURTHER READING

Prologue

The only attempt to chronicle the early history of the Tudor family is in the first part of Godfrey Turton's *The Dragon's Breed: The Story of the Tudors, from the Earliest Times to 1603* (1970). But the choice of sources on which this relies is rather eccentric. Those captivated by historical romance might find the following absorbing: Hilda Lewis, *Wife to Henry V* (1954); Jean Stubbs, *An Unknown Welshman* (1972); Gwynedd Sudworth, *Dragon's Whelp* (1973); Iris Davies, *Tudor Tapestry* (1974); and Rosemary Hawley Jarman, *Crown in Candlelight* (1978). But the best of the genre are Rosemary Anne Sisson's *The Queen and the Welshman – a play* (1958), subsequently published in 1979 as a novel; and her play, *The Dark Horse* (1980), which alone among these titillating works deals with Jasper Tudor. These novels stem from the Victorian tradition represented by two tedious books: E. Robinson, *Owen Tudor: an historical romance*, published in three volumes (!) in 1849; and W. Pritchard, *Owen Tudur – rhamant hanesyddol* (1913). Glanmor Williams's delightful booklet, *Harri Tudur a Chymru: Henry Tudor and Wales* (Cardiff, 1985), includes some pages on Henry VII's reputation at the hands of Welsh historians.

1   Servants of Welsh Princes

Two new books provide the context in which Ednyfed Fychan and his sons are properly studied: A.D. Carr, *Medieval Anglesey* (Llangefni, 1982), and David Stephenson, *The Governance of Gwynedd* (Cardiff, 1984). The origins of the Tudors were first revealed by J. Williams, 'Penmynydd and the Tudors', *Archaeologia Cambrensis*, 3rd series, XV (1869), and especially by Glyn Roberts, '"Wyrion Eden": the Anglesey descendants of Ednyfed Fychan in the 14th century', *Transactions of the Anglesey Antiquarian Society and Field Club*, 1951, pp. 34–72, reprinted in his *Aspects of Welsh History* (Cardiff, 1969), pp. 179–214; and in his article on Ednyfed Fychan in *The Dictionary of Welsh Biography down to 1940* (London, 1959), pp. 180–1. For the family's role in Welsh society, see Glyn Roberts, 'The Dominican Friary of Bangor', in E.W. Jones and J. Haworth (eds.), *The Dominican* (Friars School 4th Centenary Number, 1957), pp. 5–25, reprinted in his *Aspects of Welsh History*, pp. 215–39. The family's relations with contemporary Welsh poets is best approached *via* D.M. Lloyd, 'The Poets of the Princes', in A.O.H. Jarman and G.R. Hughes (eds.), *A Guide to Welsh Literature*, vol. I (Swansea, 1976), pp. 157–88, and then pursued (for example) in J. Vendryes, 'Poèmes de Bleddyn Vardd', *Revue Celtique*, XLIX (1932), 189–264, and in J. Morris-Jones and T.H. Parry-Williams (eds.), *Llawysgrif Hendregadredd* (Cardiff, 1933), for Bleddyn Fardd. The chronicle obituary of Goronwy ab Ednyfed is in T. Jones (ed.), *Brut Y Tywysogyon, or The Chronicle of the Princes: Peniarth MS. 20 Version* (Cardiff, 1952), p. 115.

2 A Question of Allegiance

Stephenson, *The Governance of Gwynedd*, provides the essential background to the reaction of Ednyfed Fychan's family to the Edwardian conquest of North Wales; it should be supplemented by J.B. Smith, 'Welsh Dominicans and the Crisis of 1277', *Bulletin of the Board of Celtic Studies*, XXII (1968), 353–7. Carr, *Medieval Anglesey*, covers the late middle ages more generally. In addition, J.E. Lloyd, *Owen Glendower* (Oxford, 1931), is the classic study of the rebellion, and K. Williams-Jones, 'The Taking of Conway Castle, 1401', *Transactions of the Caernarvonshire Historical Society*, XXXIX (1978), 7–43, concentrates on the most famous incident involving the Tudors. Glyn Roberts's articles (listed above) continue to provide details of the family's history in this period; his 'Teulu Penmynydd', *Transactions of the Honourable Society of Cymmrodorion*, 1959, pp. 9–37, reprinted in his *Aspects of Welsh History*, pp. 240–74, should be added to them. Goronwy ap Tudur's tomb now in Penmynydd Church is described in *Royal Commission on Ancient and Historical Monuments, Anglesey* (London, 1937), pp. 129–30 (with illustrations). The rise of Gwilym ap Gruffydd of Penrhyn is chronicled in J.R. Jones, 'The development of the Penrhyn Estate up to 1431' (University of Wales, Bangor, M.A. thesis, 1955), and in *Dictionary of Welsh Biography*, pp. 1123–4 (by Glyn Roberts). For a discussion of the poets' relations with these early Tudors, see D.M. Lloyd, 'The Later Gogynfeirdd', in Jarman and Hughes, *A Guide to Welsh Literature*, vol. II (Swansea, 1979), pp. 36–57, and in R. Bromwich, 'The Earlier Cywyddwyr: Poets contemporary with Dafydd ap Gwilym', *ibid.*, pp. 144–68. A selection of the poetry may be found in O. Jones, E. Williams and W. Owen (eds.), *The Myvyrian Archaiology of Wales* (Denbigh, 1870); H. Lewis, T. Roberts and I. Williams (eds.), *Cywyddau Iolo Goch ac Eraill, 1350–1450* (2nd ed., Cardiff, 1937); for Gruffydd Gryg's lament for Rhys ap Tudur, see J.P. Clancy, *Medieval Welsh Lyrics* (London, 1965), pp. 124–6.

3 From the Country to the Court

There is no biography of Queen Katherine, but see *Dictionary of National Biography*, IX, 189 (by Sidney Lee). The two chapters in Agnes Strickland's *Lives of the Queens of England*, vol. II (new ed., London, 1857), pp. 106–61, are a compendium of fascinating information interspersed with unwarranted conjecture. The background to her first marriage is best provided by J.H. Wylie and W.T. Waugh, *The Reign of Henry V* (3 vols., London, 1914–29). The existence of the statute governing the remarriage of dowager-queens, and the consequences for Owen Tudor, are now best examined in R.A. Griffiths, 'Queen Katherine of Valois and a missing statute of the realm', *Law Quarterly Review*, XCIII (1977), 248–58. The political context of the marriage is fully given in R.A. Griffiths, *The Reign of King Henry VI* (London, 1981). H.T. Evans, *Wales and the Wars of the Roses* (Cambridge, 1915), is still worth reading for the early years of Edmund and Jasper Tudor, and John Blacman's statement about Henry VI's role in their upbringing is in J. Blacman, *Henry the Sixth*, ed. M.R. James (Cambridge, 1919). But this whole subject, and the Tudors' ennoblement and endowment, has been authoritatively investigated by R.S. Thomas, 'The political career, estates and "connection" of Jasper Tudor, earl of Pembroke and duke of Bedford (d. 1495)' (University of Wales, Swansea, Ph.D. thesis, 1971). The early Beauforts have been studied by M. Jones, 'The Beaufort family and the war in France, 1421–1450' (University of Bristol Ph.D. thesis, 1982). Margaret Beaufort has no modern biography, but C.H. Cooper's *Memoir of Margaret, countess of Richmond and Derby* (Cambridge, 1874), is still useful. S.B. Chrimes's *Henry VII* (London, 1972), has some valuable early pages on Henry's parents, and the context in which their elevation to the peerage took place is fully analysed in Griffiths, *The Reign of King Henry VI*.

4 The King's Brothers and the Civil War, 1452–61

H.T. Evans, *Wales and the Wars of the Roses*, is still useful for the political activities of the Tudors, and three newer books, each entitled *The Wars of the Roses*, provide up-to-date accounts of the civil war more generally; they are by Charles Ross (1976), A.E. Goodman (1981) and John Gillingham (1981). R.S. Thomas's Ph.D. thesis (noted above) is a thorough study of the Tudors' movements in these years; and R.A. Griffiths, 'The Sense of Dynasty in the Reign of Henry VI', in Charles Ross (ed.), *Patronage, Pedigree and Power in Late Medieval England* (Gloucester, 1979), pp. 13–36, and *The Reign of King Henry VI* place them in context. Relations with Gruffydd ap Nicholas in South Wales are examined by R.A. Griffiths, 'Gruffydd ap Nicholas and the Rise of the House of Dinefwr', *National Library of Wales Journal*, XIII (1964), 256–68, and 'Gruffydd ap Nicholas and the Fall of the House of Lancaster', *Welsh History Review*, II (1965), 213–31. And for relations with the duke of Buckingham, see T.B. Pugh, *The Marcher Lordships of South Wales, 1415–1536* (Cardiff, 1963), and Carole Rawcliffe, *The Staffords, Earls of Stafford and Dukes of Buckingham, 1394–1521* (Cambridge, 1978). Edmund's death and Henry's birth are described in John Fisher's address to Henry VII at Cambridge in 1503: J. Gairdner (ed.), *Letters and Papers illustrative of the Reigns of Richard III and Henry VII*, vol. I (Rolls Series, 1861), pp. 422–3. Henry Tudor's birth is alluded to in *Leland's Itinerary in Wales*, ed. L.T. Smith (London, 1906), and in National Library of Wales, Mostyn MS. 158 (Elis Gruffydd's Chronicle). Tenby's fortifications are described by E. Lewis, 'Notes on the fortifications of medieval Tenby', *Archaeologia Cambrensis*, 5th series, XIII (1896), 177–92, and R.F. Walker, 'Jasper Tudor and the town of Tenby', *National Library of Wales Journal*, XVI (1969), 1–22. The latest account of the Battle of Mortimer's Cross is by G. Hodges, 'The civil war of 1459 to 1461 in the Welsh Marches, 2. The campaign and battle of Mortimer's Cross – St. Blaise's Day, 3 February 1461', *The Ricardian*, VI, no. 85 (June 1984), 330–45; the contemporary description of the battle is taken from J. Gairdner (ed.), *Three Fifteenth-century Chronicles* (Camden Society, 3rd series, XXVIII, 1880). For Edmund Tudor's tomb, see E. Allen, 'The tomb of the earl of Richmond in St. David's Cathedral', *Archaeologia Cambrensis*, XIII (1896), 315–20. The growing poetic interest in the new generation of Tudors can be gauged from G. Williams, *An Introduction to Welsh Poetry* (London, 1953), as well as, more particularly, from T. Roberts and I. Williams (eds.), *The Poetical Works of Dafydd Nanmor* (Cardiff, 1923); H. Lewis, T. Roberts and I. Williams, *Cywyddau Iolo Goch ac Eraill*; W.J. Gruffydd (ed.), *Y Flodeugerdd Newydd* (Cardiff, 1909); O. Jones (ed.), *Ceinion Llenyddiaeth Gymreig* (London, 1876), and E.D. Jones (ed.), *Lewis Glyn Cothi (Detholiad)* (Cardiff, 1984). Most recently, E.D. Jones has analysed the political poetry of the century in *Beirdd y Bymthegfed Ganrif a'u Cefndir* (Aberystwyth, 1984).

5 Jasper Tudor: The Lancastrian Champion

Charles Ross, *Edward IV* (London, 1974), is now the standard biography of the king, but C.L. Scofield's classic study, *The Life and Reign of Edward the Fourth* (London, 1923), retains value for its details on the reign. On Wales, H.T. Evans, *Wales and the Wars of the Roses*, is complemented by the more recent Ph.D. thesis of R.S. Thomas, and by R.A. Griffiths, 'The Southern Counties of the Principality of Wales, 1422–1485' (University of Bristol Ph.D. thesis, 1962). The Herbert family has been studied in depth by D.H. Thomas, 'The Herberts of Raglan as supporters of the House of York in the second half of the fifteenth century' (University of Wales, Cardiff, M.A. thesis, 1968), and G.H.R. Kent, 'The Estates of the Herbert family in the mid-fifteenth century' (University of Keele Ph.D. thesis, 1973). On Henry Tudor's upbringing, see Bernard André, *Vita Henrici VII*, ed. J. Gairdner (Rolls Series, 1858); H. Owen and J.B. Blakeway, *A History of Shrewsbury* (2 vols., London, 1825); and A.B. Emden, *A Biographical Register of the University of Oxford to A.D. 1500* (3 vols., Oxford, 1956–9). Jasper Tudor's adventures are noted in Lord Mostyn and T.A. Glenn, *History of the Family of Mostyn of Mostyn* (London, 1925); W.W.E. Wynne, 'Historical Papers (Puleston)', *Archaeologia Cambrensis*, I (1846), 145–6; and 'Jasper Tudor, earl of Pembroke, at Barmouth', *Archaeologia Cambrensis*, 4th Series, IX (1878). Michael Jones's 'Richard III and Lady Margaret Beaufort – a re-assessment', *The Ricardian*, forthcoming, has new information about Margaret Beaufort and her son in these years. Welsh opinion, as expressed in poetry, can be assessed in T. Roberts and I. Williams, *The Poetical Works of Dafydd Nanmor;* T. Roberts (ed.), *Gwaith Tudor Penllyn ac Ieuan ap Tudur Penllyn* (Cardiff, 1958); and G. Mechain and I. Tegid (eds.), *Gwaith Lewis Glyn Cothi: The Poetical Works of Lewis Glyn Cothi* (Oxford, 1837). A suggestive analysis of the political poetry of this period is E. Roberts, *Dafydd Llwyd o Fathafarn* (Caernarfon, 1981), though it does not substantiate all it claims.

6 A False Dawn, 1470–1

There is a dearth of contemporary and later writing on the Restoration of Henry VI, but an important assessment is in Michael Hicks, *False, Fleeting, Perjur'd Clarence* (Gloucester, 1980). On Wales in this brief period, see H.T. Evans, *Wales and the Wars of the Roses*, and R.S. Thomas's Ph.D. thesis. And for Margaret Beaufort's attitude to Edward IV and her son, see Michael Jones's forthcoming article (noted above); this supplements the old biography which is still worth reading, C.H. Cooper's *Margaret, countess of Richmond and Derby*. The alleged meeting between Henry VI and Henry Tudor is recorded in Bernard André's *Vita* and in Polydore Vergil, *Three books of English history*, ed. H. Ellis (Camden Society, Old Series, XXIX, 1844).

7 The Years of Exile

Polydore Vergil's *English History* provides the fullest and most reliable narrative of the Tudors' adventures in Brittany and of the diplomatic exchanges in which they figured. The English background is described in the studies of Edward IV's reign by Charles Ross and C.L. Scofield (see above). The Breton situation is fully explored in B.A. Pocquet du Haut-Jussé, *François II, duc de Bretagne et l'Angleterre* (Paris, 1929); whilst French concern at the fate of the Tudors is noted in J.L.A. Calmette and G. Périnelle, *Louis XI et l'Angleterre* (Paris, 1930). Important re-evaluations of the Tudors' significance in these years are made in R.S. Thomas's Ph.D. thesis and Michael Jones's article (both noted earlier). Three local Breton studies have interesting sidelights: J. Allanic, *Le Prisonnier de la Tour d'Elven, ou la Jeunesse du Roy Henri VII d'Angleterre* (Vannes, 1909); H. Marsille, *Vannes au Moyen Age* (Vannes, 1982); and H.G. Gaignard, 'A propos du droit d'asile malouin: tentative d'enlèvement d'Henri Tudor, comte de Richmond', *Annales de la Société d'Histoire et d'Archéologie de Saint-Malo*, 1981, pp. 97–106.

8 Claimant to a Throne

This brief but hectic period has not been especially illuminated by the various books on Richard III that have tumbled from publishers in expectation of the anniversary of the king's accession – with the singular exception of Charles Ross's major biography (1981). The Stafford family of the dukes of Buckingham has been well studied by Carole Rawcliffe, *The Staffords, earls of Stafford and dukes of Buckingham* (see above). The rebellion of 1483 lacks an authoritative study, but Rosemary Horrox, 'The patronage of

Richard III' (University of Cambridge Ph.D. thesis, 1975), contains much of interest and so does P.B. Farrer and A.F. Sutton, 'The duke of Buckingham's sons, October 1483–August 1485', *The Ricardian*, VI, no. 78 (September 1982), 87–92. There are good accounts of the Stanley family in J.M. Williams, 'The Stanley family of Lathom and Knowsley, *c.* 1450–1504: a political study' (University of Manchester M.A. thesis, 1979), and in B. Coward, *The Stanleys, Lords Stanley and earls of Derby, 1385–1672* (Manchester, 1983). For Lewis Caerleon, see P. Kibre, 'Lewis of Caerleon, Doctor of Medicine, Astronomer and Mathematician (d. 1494)', *Isis*, XLIII, part 1 (1952), 100–8; and for Hugh Conway, N. Tucker, 'Bodrhyddan and the families of Conwy, Shipley-Conwy and Rowley-Conwy', *Flintshire Historical Society Publications*, XIX (1961), 61–85. Bishop Morton lacks a full biographical study; in the meantime, see C. Harper-Bill, 'The *familia*, administrators and patronage of Archbishop John Morton', *Journal of Religious History*, X(1979), 236–52, and R.I. Woodhouse, *The Life of John Morton, archbishop of Canterbury* (London, 1895), is still of some use. In addition to the works noted earlier, the attitude of the French government to the Tudors' predicament can be followed in P. Pélicier, *Essai sur le gouvernement de la Dame de Beaujeu, 1483–1491* (Chartres, 1882). But when all is said and done, there is no substitute for browsing through some of the original sources for this exceptionally obscure period, especially Philippe de Commynes, *Memoirs*, ed. M.E.C. Jones (London, 1972); Rosemary Horrox and Peter Hammond (eds.), *British Library, Harleian Manuscript 433* (4 vols., Gloucester, 1979–83), which is an unique record of Edward V's and Richard III's government; and Polydore Vergil's *English History*.

9 The Die is Cast

The reading noted in the two previous sections is relevant here also. Additional works help us to understand – but do not entirely clarify – what is a particularly fascinating few months of Henry Tudor's exile. The Herbert family has been studied in depth in the theses of D.H. Thomas and G.H.R. Kent (noted earlier). French support for the expedition of 1485 can be traced also in A. Spont, 'La Marine Française sous le règne de Charles VIII', *Revue des Questions Historiques*, nouvelle série, XI (1894), 387–454; Y. Labande-Mailfert, *Charles VIII et son milieu* (Paris, 1975). The question of Scottish involvement is examined in N. MacDougall, *James III* (Edinburgh, 1982). C.S. Scofield, 'The early life of John de Vere, thirteenth earl of Oxford', *English Historical Review*, XXIX (1914), 228–45, recounts the earl's escape from Hammes. Among the little used original sources for the period is J.A. Buchon (ed.), *Chroniques de Jean Molinet*, vol. 2 (Paris, 1828), a Burgundian observer.

10 The March through Wales

Accounts of Henry Tudor's landing and march through Wales are legion, though far from being authoritative. S.B. Chrimes's biography of the king (noted above) and his 'The landing place of Henry of Richmond, 1485', *Welsh History Review*, II (1964–5), 173–80, are the best. D. Williams, 'The Welsh Tudors', *History Today*, IV (1954), 77–84, and A. Makinson, 'The road to Bosworth Field, August 1485', *ibid.*, XIII (1963), 239–49, still have some interest (including conjectured route-marches). But an important (and neglected) piece of evidence for the march and Henry's appeal for aid in Wales is in G. Grazebrook, 'An unpublished letter by Henry, earl of Richmond', *Miscellanea Genealogica et Heraldica*, 4th series, V (1914), 30–9. Henry's relations with Welsh landowners at this time can also be glimpsed in J. Ballinger (ed.), *The History of the Gwydir Family written by Sir J. Wynn of Gwydir* (Cardiff, 1927), and in Rosemary Horrox,

'Henry Tudor's letters to England during Richard III's reign', *The Ricardian*, VI, no. 80 (March 1983), 155–8. For the role of Rhys ap Thomas, see J.M. Lloyd, 'The rise and fall of the House of Dinefwr (The Rhys Family), 1430–1530' (University of Wales, Cardiff, M.A. thesis, 1963); and the misleading eulogy in *Cambrian Register*, I (1796). See also H.T. Evans, *Wales and the Wars of the Roses* (noted earlier), and, for Welsh poets, E. Roberts, *Dafydd Llwyd o Fathafarn* (also above). The attempt by E.W. Jones, *Bosworth Field . . . A. Welsh Retrospect* (Liverpool, 1984), to emphasise the Welsh character of Henry's enterprise in 1485 is not always well founded, but it contains some useful material on poetic opinion. Richard III's reaction to news of the landing is noted in O.D. Harris, 'The transmission of the news of the Tudor landing', *The Ricardian*, IV, no. 55 (December 1976), 5–12.

11   Bosworth Field

Published accounts of the English section of Henry's march and of the Battle of Bosworth leave much to be desired. Henry's reception in Shrewsbury is described in H. Owen and J.B. Blakeway, *A History of Shrewsbury* (2 vols., London, 1825), and for some valuable background material, see D.R. Walker, 'An Urban Community in the Welsh Borderland: Shrewsbury in the fifteenth century' (University of Wales, Swansea, Ph.D. thesis, 1981). The participation of the Stanleys is carefully considered in J.M. Williams's M.A. thesis (noted earlier), and she includes a valuable critique of the two ballads, 'Bosworth Field' and 'The Song of the Lady Bessy', which are published in *Percy Society Publications*, XX (1847). The accounts of the battle itself are legion. S.B. Chrimes's *Henry VII*, Charles Ross's *Richard III*, and D.T. Williams, *The Battle of Bosworth* (Leicester, 1973), are as good as any but inevitably rely on varying amounts of conjecture. A recent history of Market Bosworth is P.J. Foss, *The History of Market Bosworth* (Wymondham, 1983). A few artefacts supposedly found at the site of the battle are in the excellent Jewry Wall Museum, Leicester, but their authenticity remains doubtful. As to contemporary accounts of the battle, the most detailed is in Polydore Vergil's *English History*, but this can be supplemented by H.T. Riley (ed.), *Ingulph's Chronicle of the Abbey of Croyland* (London, 1854), and by 'A Spanish account of the Battle of Bosworth, 1485', *Bulletin of Spanish Studies*, IV (1927), 34–7, which has been re-examined by A.E. Goodman and A. MacKay, 'A Castilian report on English affairs, 1486', *English Historical Review*, LXXXVIII (1973), 92–9. York's reaction to the battle can be gauged from A. Raine (ed.), *York Civic Records*, I (Wakefield, 1939).

12   The Obligations of Youth

Of the available studies of Henry VII and his reign, that by S.B. Chrimes is the most dependable. Further details of how Henry discharged his obligations to his earlier supporters appear in S.B. Chrimes, 'Sir Roland de Veleville', *Welsh History Review*, III (1967), 287–9; E. Cust, *Some account of the Stuarts of Aubigny in France* (London, 1891); and R.B. Merriman, 'Edward Woodville – knight-errant', *Proceedings of the American Antiquarian Society*, new series, XVI (1903–4), 127–44. But an analysis of his grants, gifts and appointments must be made from the records of his government, e.g. in *Calendar of the Patent Rolls, 1485–1509*; J. Gairdner (ed.), *Letters and Papers illustrative of the reigns of Richard III and Henry VII* (2 vols., Rolls Series, 1861–3); and W. Campbell (ed.), *Materials for a history of the reign of Henry VII* (2 vols., Rolls Series, 1873–7). Apart from the works of S.B. Chrimes, B.A. Pocquet du Haut-Jussé, A. Spont and Y. Labande-Mailfert (all noted earlier), Henry's relations with France and Brittany can be studied most easily in R.B. Wernham, *Before the Armada* (London, 1966), and, on the cultural level, in A.E. Goodman's suggestive article, 'Henry VII and Christian Renewal', *Studies in Church History*, XVII (1981), 115–25. The personnel and methods of his government have recently been explored by M. Condon, 'Ruling Elites in the Reign of Henry VII', in Charles Ross (ed.), *Patronage, Pedigree and Power in Later Medieval England* (Gloucester, 1979), pp. 109–42.

13 The Blessings of Ancestry

Henry's family has been little studied. The best available biography of his mother, Margaret Beaufort, is still that of C.H. Cooper (see earlier), but Michael Jones's article in *The Ricardian* (noted above) breaks new ground. The funeral orations on Henry and his mother in *The English Works of John Fisher*, part 1 (Early English Text Society, extra series, XXVII, 1876), make moving reading. On Henry VI's posthumous reputation, see J.W. McKenna, 'Piety and Propaganda: the Cult of King Henry VI', in B. Rowland (ed.), *Chaucer and Middle English Studies in Honour of R.H. Robbins* (London, 1974), pp. 72–88, supplemented by R. Lovatt, 'A Collector of Apocryphal Anecdotes: John Blacman Revisited', in A.J. Pollard (ed.), *Property and Politics: Essays in Later Medieval English History* (Gloucester and New York, 1984), pp. 172–97. Henry's uncle Jasper is fully treated in R.S. Thomas's Ph.D. thesis (noted earlier), and for Henry's rebuilding of Richmond Palace, see H.M. Colvin and others (eds.), *The History of the King's Works: The Middle Ages* (2 vols., London, 1963); and for Tudor *motifs* in his religious buildings, *ibid.*, vol. III (1485–1660) (London, 1975). Henry's links with Wales and Welshmen immediately after 1485 have attracted a fair amount of Welsh attention, e.g. in D. Williams's article, 'The Welsh Tudors' (noted earlier), and in C.A.J. Skeel, 'Wales under Henry VII', in R.W. Seton-Watson (ed.), *Tudor Studies* (London, 1924). His interest in the myth of *British History* has been coolly explored by Sydney Anglo, 'The *British History* in Early Tudor propaganda', *Bulletin of the John Rylands Library*, XLIV (1961–2), 17–48, and in his *Spectacle, Pageantry and Early Tudor Policy* (London, 1969). Aside from these works, P.C. Bartrum, 'Bonedd Henri Saithved', *National Library of Wales Journal*, XIV (1965–6), 330–4, examines Henry's supposed interest in his pedigree, and Elis Gruffydd's chronicle (noted earlier) has significant comment on Henry and Wales. Welsh euphoria at his accession may be sampled in A.O.H. Jarman and G.R. Hughes, *A Guide to Welsh Literature*, vol. 1 (see above).

INDEX